Canadian Gardening

teplants

expert advice
on choosing and growing
the best plants
from CANADIAN GARDENING
MAGAZINE

edited by LIZ PRIMEAU
foreword by ALDONA SATTERTHWAITE

McArthur & Company
Toronto

First published in 2005 by
McArthur & Company
322 King St. West. Suite 402
Toronto, Ontario
M4V 1J2
www.mcarthur-co.com

Editor: Liz Primeau
Design: Gordon Sibley
Cover photo: Tracy Cox

Library and Archives Canada Cataloguing in Publication

Favourite plants / Liz Primeau, editor.

Includes index.
ISBN 1-55278-487-8

1. Gardening—Canada. I. Primeau, Liz

SB453.3.C2F39 2005 635'.0971 C2004-907024-X

The publisher would like to acknowledge the financial support of the Government of Canada through the Book Publishing Industry Development Program and the Canada Council for our publishing activities. The publisher further wishes to acknowledge the financial support of the Ontario Arts Council and the Government of Ontario through the Ontario Media Development Corporation's Ontario Book Initiative.

Printed in Canada by Transcontinental Printing Inc.

10 9 8 7 6 5 4 3 2 1

This book is dedicated to all our fellow gardeners who spend Saturday mornings staring at plants in the nursery, wondering what on earth to buy. In this book we hope they find what they need—both the information and the inspiration to help them choose just the right genus, species and cultivar.

Contents

favourite perennials

favourite roses

favourite trees & shrubs

Foreword

As kids, my friends and I used to know all sorts of little games and rhymes. One had to do with misunderstanding, and part of it went: "When God said noses, I thought he said roses so I asked him for a big red one." It made me giggle, but the joke's on me. Although my nose is not big and red (at least, not most of the time), I've been led around by it all my life.

When I was 2 or so, my grandmother picked a deep purple petunia and gave it to me to smell. As I took a really good, long sniff, its soft, velvety petals clamped firmly over my nostrils. Though it was a terrifying experience, the petunia smelled sweet and it was the beginning of my love affair with plants.

Over the years, my nose has had many other adventures, coming away covered in orange pollen from sniffing fragrant lilies (which permanently marked my best shirt, too) and abruptly pulling out of a deep plunge into an old, perfumed, dew-kissed rose with a throbbing bee sting on its end. It's inhaled the odd ant (that got sneezed out) and some even tinier bugs (which didn't).

But oh, the pleasure it's had, joyfully investigating the fragrance of certain daphnes, viburnums, daffodils, honeysuckles, lindens, clematis, peonies, mock orange, catalpas, scented geraniums, magnolias, lavenders, lilies of the valley, lilacs, wisteria—the list goes on and on.

However, it's not just about the nose, it's about the eyes, too. For me, examining the beauty of plants (fragrant and otherwise) and how they work in the garden—both outdoors and through the pages of a really gorgeous book such as this one—brings equal enjoyment. So whether you're an armchair gardener or a hands-in-the-dirt type, you'll be inspired and encouraged by the expertise and enthusiasm of the gardeners, writers and photographers who have imbued the stories in this book with their own magic. Use it to help you plan and plant your own garden, or just laze away the hours in a comfortable chair, preferably with a soothing drink and a pretty vase of flowers at your elbow. Skilfully edited by my friend and colleague Liz Primeau, with a handsome design by Gordon Sibley, *Favourite Plants* is a fitting companion to our previous best-selling books, *The Cook's Garden* and *City Gardens*. Happy reading—and don't forget to smell the roses every chance you get.

Aldona Satterthwaite

Aldona Satterthwaite
Editor, *Canadian Gardening*

Introduction

I am told that there are more than 75,000 species and varieties of hardy garden plants available to gardeners—some are rare and obscure, while others as readily found as milk at the corner store. So it's no wonder I was daunted by the task of purchasing plants for my first garden.

Although I'd had the advantage of being taught to garden by my wonderfully talented mother, there was so much to choose from and so many decisions to make. What should be planted in sun? What needed the shade? And what kind of soil did they like? How tall would they grow? Were they fragrant? After purchasing my plants and gently positioning them in their new surroundings, it occurred to me that a gardener is very much like the conductor of an orchestra. It's not the sound of one particular instrument that creates the symphony, it's the harmony of all those instruments working together. And so it was with the plants in my garden.

Through my coaching (yes, I talk to my plants), training (watering, pruning, deadheading) and trial and error experiments (lots of plants got moved around), in time I created a pleasing composition. There have been some false notes and casualties along the way, and some seasons have seen my plant "orchestra" performing better than in others. And just like an orchestra conductor, I've had to change my repertoire more than once, too.

During 15 years of publishing *Canadian Gardening* magazine, I have learned from so many of the gardeners we've featured in its pages. Their plant selections have been well researched, creative and sometimes just plain serendipitous. At the same time, I've been inspired and encouraged to try new varieties by the plant profiles written by horticulturists and other garden experts. Backed by this cumulative garden wisdom, and along with our book publishing partner, McArthur & Company, we are pleased to share *Favourite Plants* with you. I hope it helps you along the way to confidently create your own personal garden symphony.

Jacqueline Howe
Publisher, *Canadian Gardening*

favourite perennials

↑ *A. stelleriana* 'Silver Brocade'

↑ *A. schmidtiana* 'Silver Mound'

favourite perennials

Artemisias

Subtle, silvery and luminous, they are the perfect foil in a bright garden

BY JO ANN GARDNER

↓ *A. ludoviciana* 'Silver King'

I love the elegance and versatility of artemisias. For almost 30 years, their intricately cut leaves of pure silver, near white, silvery green and soft grey have created a striking contrast and an aura of calm in my colourful garden in Orangedale, Nova Scotia. I grow them for the foliage rather than for their flowers; they're lovely accents in the border, from low, shimmering cushions at the edge to tall, handsome shrubby growth at the back. Because they're supremely indifferent to long periods of hot, dry, windy weather, they're also ideal for hanging baskets.

Artemisias have downy leaves that protect them from the burning

Artemisia was named for Artemis, the Greek goddess of the hunt, and in former times its camphor-scented leaves were strewn on floors to repel bugs.

↑ *A. lactiflora* or white mugwort

Hardiness

Zones 3 to 5, depending on variety

Growing conditions

Exposed, sunny sites; ordinary soil, preferably dry

Colour range

Valued for its silvery foliage, not the flowers

Growing season

All summer

Size

20 to 180 centimetres

winds and intense heat of their dry, native habitats. On trips to Israel's Negev Desert I've seen white wormwood (*Artemisia siberi*) growing over vast stretches of barren, rock-strewn land; in wet years its greyish white, shrubby presence is enhanced by thousands of sunrose (*Helianthemum* spp.) in varying shades of pink. This wild landscape always impressed me with its perfect combination of colour and texture and greatly influenced me when I began to seriously regard artemisias as landscaping plants.

Pairing artemisias with complementary partners can create luminous highlights and soothing oases of light on sunny and cloudy days. Artemisia's silvery foliage deepens adjacent colours and smoothes the transition from bright or dark flowers, such as purple veronicas or blue delphiniums, to the soft yellows of daylilies and yarrow. Alternatively, a silver-on-silver effect can be breathtaking: try grouping artemisias with woolly foliage plants, such as lamb's-

Artemisia's silvery grey foliage is a good foil for brightly coloured flowers and also provides continuity in muted gardens of whites and soft blues.

↑ *A. ludoviciana* 'Silver King'

↑ White echinacea with 'Powis Castle', a hybrid of *A. absinthium* and *A. arborescens*

ears (*Stachys byzantina*), rose campion (*Lychnis coronaria*), Russian sage (*Perovskia atriplicifolia*) and horehound (*Marrubium vulgare*).

History

Artemisias have long been grown in herb gardens for their herbal properties. As well, their silvery accents add brightness to crafts such as wreaths and swags. Except for southernwood (*A. abrotanum*), which becomes brittle, artemisias dry well. 'Silver King' is especially popular for wreaths because it provides a soft, neutral background for more colourful dried flowers.

Members of the *Asteraceae* family, artemisias were named for the Greek goddess Artemis, goddess of the hunt, and are native to Asia, the Mediterranean, Europe and North America. In ancient households, the bracing, camphor-scented leaves were strewn on floors to repel bugs; today—used alone or mixed with the foliage of other herbs—they act as a moth repellent. Thujone, a bitter chemical in the plant's makeup, has been used in healing for thousands of years; however, although it may be beneficial in small quantities, it's fatal in large ones. The leaves of a few species have been used in liquors as well, most famously in absinthe, which is now banned in North America because of its lethal properties. No variety of artemisia should be eaten, except for *A. dracunculus* var. *sativa*, better known as French tarragon.

Growing

Most artemisias are sub-shrubs—woody-based perennials—that flourish in exposed, sunny sites and in dry, lean soil; but they also grow well in ordinary garden soil. They're immune to pests and disease and, with few exceptions, are winter-hardy in most of Canada. They're also vigorous growers; a few, like Roman wormwood (*A. pontica*) and 'Silver King' (*A. ludoviciana*), are even invasive, but these can be controlled by chopping out extra growth in spring and cutting back plants in fall. All types are easy to propagate by division, layering or stem cuttings. See each variety for specific advice.

Recommended varieties

Artemisia species include low mounds and groundcovers, as well as medium to tall shrubby types. Here's a selection to suit every garden.

Short varieties

A. schmidtiana 'Silver Mound' grows into a satisfyingly perfect mound 20 to 25 centimetres) tall and 45 centimetres wide. I grow it at the corners of my timber-lined raised beds.

↓ *A. stelleriana* 'Silver Brocade' showing greyish white blooms

The silky, shimmering foliage on soft grey stems covers the sharp corners, creating a kind of low hedge against the bluish foliage of pink dianthus, purple *Allium senescens,* blue fescue and rose campion—a combination that carries on from spring through fall. I've also admired a classic silver-on-silver mix of 'Silver Mound' and *Salvia argentea*, a magnificent plant with huge, silvery blue leaves.

Divide well-established plants in spring after the soil has warmed or else by midsummer the mounds will collapse in the middle from the weight of their stems. In my normally cool garden 'Silver Mound' occasionally flowers in a hot growing season. The flowers are small, silvery balls nearly covered by surrounding foliage. I shear plants back almost to the ground by midsummer.

A grouping of artemisias in various tones of green and grey makes a splendid, subtle display. At left: common wormwood (*A. absinthium*), once an ingredient in absinthe; feathery southernwood (*A. abrotanum*); beach wormwood (*A. stelleriana*), a favourite of Gertrude Jekyll; and western mugwort (*A. ludoviciana*).

Roman wormwood (*A. pontica*), also called old woman, is an ingredient in vermouth. It grows to a 30-centimetre loose mound of frothy, soft grey, lacy foliage—the richer the soil, the looser and more sprawling the growth. Because it's amenable to clipping, it's effective in knot gardens—intricately designed formal gardens—where its intricately cut grey leaves contrast well with green-leafed plants. I use Roman wormwood as a groundcover at the base of roses, especially a purplish rugosa. In a perennial border its colour and form contrast with the dark purple spires of salvia 'East Friesland', rosy lupines and brassy yellow *Allium moly*.

Beach wormwood (*A. stelleriana*) grows in great sprawling white patches on beaches throughout North America's northeast. Its virtues as an ornamental aren't widely appreciated here, although it has long been cultivated in England. Given light soil and a sunny exposure, beach wormwood, which grows to 15 centimetres, keeps grass at bay along paths and at the garden's edge by luxuriantly spreading its thick, white, deeply cut leaves shaped like white oak. Garden designer Gertrude Jekyll praised beach wormwood and advised growing it as a substitute for dusty miller (*Cineraria maritima*), a tender perennial. A master of the painterly garden in England during the early 1900s, Jekyll used frosty white beach wormwood to great effect with the blues, purples

Artemisas thrive in hot, sunny conditions and range from low and shrubby to tall and airy. The group at right contains common wormwood (*A. absinthium*); Russian tarragon (*A. dracunculus*); beach wormwood (*A. stelleriana*); western mugwort (*A. ludoviciana*); and southernwood (*A. abrotanum*).

and pinks of larkspur, delphinium, salvia and dianthus.

Beach wormwood also works well in hanging baskets. When licorice plant succumbed to intense, dry heat one summer, I replaced it with a barely rooted piece of beach wormwood. In a short time (and with minimal attention), it had comfortably settled in and spread out its beautiful felty white leaves, demonstrating in dramatic fashion that artemisias possess a fierce will to survive.

'Silver Brocade', an elegant cultivar of *A. stelleriana*, was introduced by the University of British Columbia Botanical Garden several years ago. More wide-spreading, it's used as a groundcover and in hanging baskets. To keep both the species and the cultivar tidy, shear plants back close to the ground when the small yellow flowers appear.

Medium varieties

Tree wormwood (*A. arborescens*), a frost-tender upright shrub, has fringy silver-grey foliage and grows naturally to 90 centimetres. I grow it in tall tubs and clip it to 30 centimetres, moving it indoors before the first frost. During the summer I take cuttings (a 10- to 15-centimetre lateral stem with a woody "heel") and these root in four to six weeks. I place the tubs of tree wormwood deep in my borders among purple-flowered perennials such as veronicas and salvias. When the wormwood shows its first signs of flowers (small yellow panicles), I trim them off to refresh the foliage. More compact, the 60-centimetre, dwarf non-flowering 'Powis Castle', probably a cross between tree wormwood and common wormwood, is also frost-tender and grows well in containers.

If left untrimmed, southernwood (*A. abrotanum*) grows into a wide, sprawling, never-fail shrub about 90 centimetres in diameter, hardy to Zone 5. A favourite of the English cottage garden, it has feathery, grey-green foliage with a strong scent of lemon and camphor. Its various folk names, from old man to maiden's ruin, refer to its use in ointments to promote beards and prevent baldness.

In addition to providing an attractive shrubby foil for roses in my garden, southernwood has proved invaluable in an exposed, sunny site with hard soil, where little else grows. To confine its height to a 30-centimetre mound, I clip stems back to 15 centimetres in spring and again in early summer. To propagate, cut a 15-centimetre piece of stem near the plant's base and place it in well-drained soil about 8 centimetres deep—it will grow to bush size in two seasons. A taller, citrus-scented cultivar named 'Tangerine' (sometimes called tree southernwood) is a striking, more upright columnar plant that grows to 180 centimetres. It's well worth looking for in specialty herb nurseries.

The native western mugwort (*A. ludoviciana*), hardy to Zone 3, is rarely grown. More commonly seen is 'Silver King', its best-known cultivar, which is a bit taller (to 90 centimetres) than the species; it has an abundance of narrow leaves growing in tufts on grey stems. The foliage is silvery green on one side and pure silver on the other, and because the

↑ 'Powis Castle', a hybrid of *A. arborescens* and *A. absinthium*

Most artemisias are sub-shrubs, which means they are woody-based perennials that flourish in exposed, sunny sites and in dry, lean soil. They're generally immune to pests and diseases.

leaves grow upward, the whole plant has a light grey ghostly cast (another common name is ghost plant).

In late summer the plant produces panicles of yellowish flowers good for wreath-making. I grow my 'Silver King' in a bed of abundant flowers and herbs, where it's a cool foil for purple clary sage (*Salvia viridis*) and a contrast in colour and form for blue-green mounds of rue (*Ruta graveolens*).

'Silver Queen' and 'Valerie Finnis' (both to 60 centimetres) are more compact variations of western mugwort. At Royal Botanical Gardens in Burlington, Ontario, 'Valerie Finnis' is beautiful backed by dark orange sneezeweed (*Helenium* 'Bruno') and faced with low-growing silvery *Veronica spicata* var. *incana* and 'Blue Clips' campanula. Western mugwort cultivars vary in leaf form and habit, but since the types are often confused in the trade, gardeners sometimes complain they see no differences among them. 'Silver King' and 'Silver Queen' are similar except for height and habit; 'Valerie Finnis' is shorter and has pure silvery grey leaves.

The last of the medium-tall artemisias is common wormwood (*A. absinthium*), hardy to Zone 4, famed as a vermifuge (which means it expels intestinal worms) and as an ingredient in absinthe. Its aroma is pleasantly medicinal in small doses, but it can also cause a headache. In my garden, it makes a 90-centimetre loose hedge of velvety grey leaves, similar in shape to chrysanthemum leaves, behind *Echinacea purpurea* 'Magnus'. It's amenable to clipping—good if you want to keep it low and neat.

As common wormwood ages, it becomes woody and gnarled, but it's easy to propagate in the spring by digging up and replanting some of the new growth that has roots. 'Lambrook Silver', an attractive, compact variety 45 to 80 centimetres tall, has luxuriant silvery foliage and greyish flowers.

Tall varieties

The tallest artemisias, which grow to 150 to 180 centimetres, are white mugwort and the annual sweet wormwood (*A. annua*), or sweet Annie, a Chinese medicinal plant. Both are admired more for their flowers than for the foliage.

White mugwort (*A. lactiflora*), Zone 5, is the only artemisia that tolerates damp soil and partial shade. It reaches about 150 centimetres in height. Its mid-green, deeply divided leaves are a good background for the mass of much-admired creamy white, scented flower sprays that bloom in mid to late summer. When in flower, it makes a light, feathery backdrop for bright scarlet monardas, purple coneflowers and lilac cleome. The cream-white flowers show up particularly well on 'Guizhou', a purple-stemmed cultivar. I cut white mugwort back by a third in July to produce a bushier, 120-centimetre form that doesn't need staking. It spreads slowly, gradually forming a larger clump that's easily divided in early spring. A plant with no vices I can detect, unfortunately white mugwort is greatly ignored.

Sweet wormwood (*A. annua*), also known as sweet Annie, is an annual that can reach 180 centimetres by late summer. It's wide at the base and tapers to a point at the top. It's striking by a fence, and grows well in full sun or partial shade. The soft, filmy branches of much-divided bright green foliage and tiny gold flowers in late summer are dramatic in the fall landscape. The plant has a warmly citrus aroma with a note of camphor that is bothersome to some people and irresistible to others. (It's commonly used to make scented, dried wreaths.) I like to grow sweet wormwood close to white-flowering pole beans and scarlet runner beans, which entwine themselves around it and rise with it to the top of a tall fence. In favourable conditions (a long, hot growing season) sweet wormwood self-sows.

Culinary Artemisia

If you like the flavour of tarragon in your cooking, choose the right variety. Russian tarragon (*A. dracunculus*), named for its place of origin, is easy to grow but flavourless. French tarragon (*A. dracunculus* var. *sativa*), on the other hand, is revered for its tangy, anise flavour. It's a staple in French cuisine.

↑ French tarragon *(A. dracunculus* var. *sativa)*

Propagate French tarragon from a root or by plant division—it doesn't set seed. (Tarragon seeds offered for sale invariably produce Russian tarragon, with leaves that, though similar in appearance, don't produce the characteristic tarragon flavour.) Hardy to Zone 5, the plant grows 45 to 90 centimetres tall and thrives in sun or partial shade and loose, quickly draining soil. Soil conditions, more than winter temperatures, determine its survival; mulch for added protection. Plants tend to die out in the centre after three years. Divide the mother plant in the spring or take cuttings in summer.

The narrow, green leaves have a unique flavour and are used fresh or dried, alone or combined with neutral-flavoured herbs such as parsley. Tarragon shines in fish and poultry dishes, cheese and mushroom quiches, in sauces (chiefly Béarnaise) and as a flavouring for vinegar. Use leaves from well-established plants; taking leaves from a young plant may affect its survival.

Aster spp. ↑

Hardiness

Zones 2 to 5, depending on variety

Growing conditions

Rich, moisture-retentive soil; good air circulation

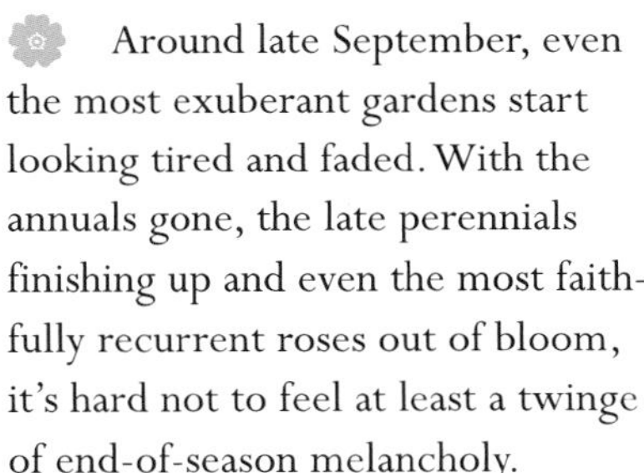

Colour range

White; glowing reds and magenta; many shades of blue; purples; pinks

Bloom time

Early to late fall, depending on variety

Size

30 to 120 centimetres

favourite perennials

Asters

Extend the season with these dependable fall beauties BY CAROL HALL

Around late September, even the most exuberant gardens start looking tired and faded. With the annuals gone, the late perennials finishing up and even the most faithfully recurrent roses out of bloom, it's hard not to feel at least a twinge of end-of-season melancholy.

But wait. Aster season is just beginning. These bright, starry flowers ("aster" is derived from the Greek word for "star") positively shine in the early-fall garden. Most begin blooming in August—some start as early as July—and they extend the season by as much as six weeks. Although some of the later blooms are lost to early frosts in the coldest zones (early-blooming types suitable for short-season areas are available), asters are tough, reliable perennials hardy just about anywhere in Canada.

As if that were not enough, the copious flowers, in shades of blue, pink, red or white, are renowned for attracting butterflies. Asters make superb, long-lasting cut flowers, too.

And although their nickname, Michaelmas daisies, makes them sound quaintly English, the ancestors of almost all cultivated asters are native to Canada from Newfoundland to B.C., and to the northern half of the U.S., encompassing Zones 2 to 5. Aster species grow almost anywhere: prairies, mountain slopes, seashores, damp meadows, woodland edges, scrublands and even along roadways—these plants are survivors.

History

Very early in the 1700s, seeds of two species of North American asters were taken to England, where their hybridized progeny quickly became popular in formal borders and cottage gardens. One was *Aster novae-angliae* (literally "New England aster"), a tall (120 centimetres) species hardy to Zone 2 that was native from Quebec to Alberta and as far south as North Carolina to Colorado. The other was *A. novi-belgii* ("New Belgium aster," an early name for New York), a slightly shorter, Zone 3 species native from Newfoundland, Quebec and Nova Scotia south to Georgia. Because of their unusually late blooming time—around Michaelmas, an English church holiday celebrated on September 29—the new daisy-

Cultivated asters now come in short, medium and tall varieties, and many shapes and colours. Best of all their tendency to ranginess and their susceptibility to powdery mildew have been nearly bred out of them.

A. dumosus 'Professor Anton Kippenberg' ↓

← *A. x frikartii* 'Mönch'

← *A. dumosus* 'Jenny'

Mildew Prevention

Powdery mildew is the common cold of the plant world. A disease of opportunity rather than an indication of a sickly plant, it shows up when external conditions favour its development. Dry soil, moist air, overcrowding, shade and stagnant air all contribute to mildew. When all five conditions occur together—as commonly happens in early fall—mildew is almost guaranteed. To keep your fall asters mildew-free, take these preventive steps:

- Plant in moisture-retentive soil and do not allow it to dry out.
- Water at ground level to avoid wetting foliage.
- Plant in full sun, making sure clumps won't be shaded later by taller perennials.
- Allow plenty of space between clumps for good air circulation. Avoid planting asters close to buildings or fences that can block air flow.
- Replace older, mildew-prone plants with resistant varieties. Mildew tends to be more prevalent on cultivars of *A. novae-angliae, A. novi-belgii* and the Dumosus hybrids than on other species. Asters have fewer problems with powdery mildews if they are grown in moist, rich soil.
- Clean up garden debris and deadhead spent perennials to deny mildew a starting place.
- If mildew does show up, spray with wettable sulfur, a natural fungicide that can be purchased in either powdered or pre-mixed, liquid suspension form. Like the common cold, powdery mildew is highly contagious, and although it's rarely fatal, repeated or severe cases can seriously weaken plants. Sulfur can also be used as a mildew preventive; spray every 7 to 10 days.

petalled, yellow-centred hybrids became known as Michaelmas daisies. The name now refers to any cultivated aster that blooms in the fall.

Whatever you call them, these stars of the fall garden now come in tall, medium and dwarf forms; with single, double or semi-double flowers; in upright, rounded or mounding shapes; and in tones of pink, white, purple, violet, rose-red, magenta, mauve and every conceivable shade of blue. Best of all, in modern hybrids the two drawbacks of the earliest hybrids—ranginess and a susceptibility to powdery mildew—have been all but eradicated.

Growing

All asters really ask for is sun, a steady supply of water and a little compost (or a balanced fertilizer such as 10-10-10) once or twice early in the season. Withhold fertilizer once flower buds form or you'll get rank growth at the expense of flower production. Be sure to plant them before July 1 to allow them time to get established.

Although a few varieties are tolerant of drier soils, most asters (including modern hybrids) definitely need rich, moisture-retentive soil that does not dry out in late summer or early fall. Full sun and good air circulation are also

↓ White heath aster *(A. ericoides)* with goldenrod

↓ *A. sedifolius* 'Nanus'

↑ *A. pringlei* 'Monte Cassino'

↑ *A. novae-angliae* 'September Ruby'

The starry shapes and brilliant colours of asters brighten the garden from late summer well into fall. They thrive almost everywhere in Canada, probably because the parents of nearly all of today's cultivars were the native species that grew from Newfoundland to British Columbia and south into the northern half of the United States.

important; asters evolved in wide-open, exposed sites and are not happy in shady or crowded conditions.

To keep taller types more manageable and encourage even more flowers, pinch plants back as they grow, ideally at about 20 centimetres and again at about 30 centimetres. Pruning clumps to half their height in mid-June works just fine. Cut each stem just above a leaf for best results.

Ideally, asters should be lifted and divided every two or three years. But if you don't mind your clumps migrating a bit here and there, quickly survey the site every spring just as new growth is beginning. Pull out older, exhausted clumps, thin out congested ones and space any seedlings you want to keep. With an appropriate planting site and this modicum of attention, fall asters will produce their multitudes of starry flowers for many years to come.

Recommended varieties

Dumosus hybrids (*A. dumosus* x *A. novi-belgii*), Zone 4, are vigorous, disease-resistant dwarf mounds blanketed with flowers in September and October. Some of the finest cultivars are:

'Audrey', mauve-blue single, 30 by 45 centimetres: one of the best blues

'Jenny', double rose-red, 40 by 60 centimetres: bright and cheerful

'Little Pink Beauty', semi-double bright pink, 40 by 50 centimetres: reputed to be the best semi-double pink

'Lady-in-Blue', semi-double blue, 25 by 45 centimetres: compact, early-blooming and free-flowering

'Professor Anton Kippenberg', semi-double bright purple-blue, 30 by 45 centimetres: a reliable favourite

Heath aster (*A. ericoides*), Zone 3, is a North American species native from Maine to B.C. and as far south as Georgia to Arizona. Plants form upright, bushy clumps of tiny leaves topped with even tinier white flowers. Pastel blue and pink cultivars are available. All grow 90 centimetres tall and about 60 centimetres wide and bloom from August to October. Heath asters tolerate drier soils and are mildew-resistant.

A. x *frikartii* 'Mönch', Zone 5, is an outstanding perennial. Its large, clear lavender-blue single flowers bloom profusely from July to October. Sturdy clumps grow 75 by 60 centimetres, and it tolerates drier soils without developing mildew. Height can vary significantly (from 35 to 75 centimetres) according to growing conditions, with rich, moist soil producing taller plants.

In the group commonly known as Michaelmas daisies (*A. novae-angliae*), 'September Ruby', Zone 2, shows blooms in a deep, glowing raspberry red. Plants grow 120 by 45 centimetres and need staking. The lower leaves wither early (use at the back of the border) and the plant is subject to mildew, but the colour is spectacular. They bloom from August to October and tolerate wet soils.

A. pringlei 'Monte Cassino', Zone 4, shows masses of tiny, starry, multi-petalled pure white flowers on clumps of delicate, lacy foliage that is disease-resistant. The plant is about 90 by 60 centimetres and blooms late-September to November. This is a European species cultivated since the 16th century, and its baby's breath–like flowers are highly valued in the cut-flower trade.

Rhone aster (*A. sedifolius*) 'Nanus', Zone 2, has small, spidery, single lilac-blue flowers on widely branched, bushy foliage during August and September. Plants grow to about 45 by 45 centimetres and are somewhat inclined to flop over; but they're reputed to be reliable bloomers on the prairies and a good choice for very cold climates. They are not fussy about soil type and are mildew-resistant.

↑ *E. pinnatum*

Hardiness

Zone 4

Growing conditions

Loose, moist, woodland-type soil; light to dappled shade

Colour range

White; bright to pale yellow; pink to scarlet and purple; some blooms bicoloured

Bloom time

April and May; pleasing summer foliage

Size

30 to 40 centimetres; clumping and creeping varieties

favourite perennials

Barrenwort

Plants that shine in the shade BY JUDITH ADAM

↓ *Epimedium* spp. (small plant at lower left)

↓ *E.* x *versicolor*

In medieval times barrenwort (*Epimedium* spp.) was used to prevent conception; in other eras it was considered a sexual stimulant and used in folk medicines. One species is still known as horny goat weed (*E. sagittatum*). It's also commonly known as bishop's hat.

↑ *E.* 'Niveum'

No matter how long a gardener has been putting trowel to earth, there's always interest in perennials that excel in shade. And therein lies an important distinction, for although many plants can tolerate shade or can be coaxed into a half-hearted shadow display, few actually relish the low light.

A list of plants requiring shade to demonstrate their best attributes would be short indeed, but barrenwort (*Epimedium* spp.) would certainly be front and centre in the shade parade. Naturalized colonies of barrenwort grow best in moist woodlands under the dappled shade of deciduous trees, where the soil is undisturbed and enriched with leaf mould. The carpet abruptly halts where shade gives way to brighter light. (If you grow them in full-day sunlight, a martyring regimen of daily irrigation is necessary to keep them happy.)

History

Before the 19th century, barrenwort proliferated only in China (which escaped the huge glacial flows that obliterated the plant from most of the European and American continents) in shady valleys and on north-facing mountain slopes, breeding through centuries of seclusion. (The shy *Vancouveria* is its only North American cousin and represents a prehistoric relationship to *Epimedium*.) Some specimens were sent back to Europe by adventurer-botanists in the early 1800s, when plant travel from Asia to Europe took six months by boat (shipments of 1,200 plants leaving China were reduced to 260 live specimens on arrival in England). Victorian gardeners filled their dark corners with the obliging barrenwort—Gertrude Jekyll grew *E. pinnatum*, with its orchid-like spikes of pale yellow bloom, which she found "very useful for combining with greenhouse flowers of delicate texture." It wasn't until after 1979, when the Chinese Cultural Revolution ended, that new species and hybrids began to appear in the West. Of the recognized 44 species, 36 were discovered and documented after 1975.

↓ *E. pubigerum*

Except for *E. pubigerum* and *E.* x *rubrum*, most barrenwort don't adapt well to dry soil. Make sure to water them frequently if you plant them under maple trees or other trees that absorb a lot of moisture from the soil.

Barrenwort, the plant's common name, refers to its pharmaceutical properties and association with human fertility. In medieval times it was thought to prevent conception and suppress the breasts of virgins, whereas in other centuries the plant was considered a stimulant to the libido, hence the species known as horny goat weed (*E. sagittatum*), which explains its use in herbal medicine—and leaves little to the imagination. But gardeners are more likely to know *Epimedium* as bishop's hat (*E. grandiflorum*), which describes the racemes of charming, mitre-like flowers that dangle and dance about in early-spring breezes. Like other perennials with thin, wiry stems

↑ Red barrenwort (*E.* x *rubrum*)

Even after they stop blooming, barrenwort graces the garden all summer with a tidy clump of shield-shaped leaves. Some take on a scarlet flush in fall.

(coral bells, columbines, Siberian bugloss), bishop's hats seem to hover, ethereally suspended in flight over their clumps of arrow- or heart-shaped leaves.

Growing

Epidemium species are either clump-forming or carpet-forming, both ideal growth patterns for groundcover. Clumping varieties expand their girth and extend their leaves over the soil,

↓ *E. perralchicum* 'Fröhnleiten' with white leujocum

Soil for Shade

Trees and large shrubs take up the majority of water and nutrients in shade gardens. To make up for these deficiencies, soil for perennial plants must be rich in organic matter and provide plenty of moisture and oxygen. Here's a good mix for perennial beds under trees:

- 2 parts organic material (compost, peat moss, leaves, pine and spruce needles, small particles of tree bark)
- 1 part sharp builder's sand
- 1 part loamy soil

Bright Lights

↑ *E.* x *versicolor* 'Sulfureum'

Here are some Zone 4 varieties of barrenwort to brighten shady spots in your garden. All are clump-forming (unless otherwise stated) and range in height from 20 to 30 centimetres. Compact varieties have a spread of 20 to 30 centimetres, while others have a spread of 30 to 45 centimetres:

- *E.* x *cantabrigiense*, orange-brown blooms splashed with red, dark green foliage
- *E. grandiflorum* 'Lilafee' ('Lilac Fairy'), compact, vigorous, deep violet-purple flowers, leaves tinged purple in spring
- *E. perralchicum* 'Fröhnleiten', compact, bright yellow flowers, bronze-marbled foliage, spreading habit
- *E.* x *rubrum*, small, scarlet red flowers, light green leaves edged red in spring, spreading habit, vigorous
- *E.* x *versicolor* 'Sulfureum', light primrose yellow flowers
- *E. warleyense* 'Orangekönigin' ('Orange Queen'), pale orange flowers
- *E.* x *youngianum* 'Niveum', compact, pure white flowers
- *E.* x *youngianum* 'Roseum', compact, lilac-rose flowers

Different varieties of barrenwort creep into low carpets or grow in slightly taller clumps. They accept some morning sun, but strong sunlight stresses the plant; moist, rich soil is important.

while carpeting species slowly spread from shallow black rhizomes. The leaves rise from the soil in April and May and are often flushed or rimmed in vivid colours of copper or red. Loose clusters of orchid-like flowers ascend with the leaves (or sometimes slightly in advance), and carry their dancing blossoms for three to four weeks. Even when no longer in bloom, the tidy clumps with shield-shaped leaves are pleasing all summer, and some take on flushes of scarlet in late autumn.

Barrenwort is attractive company for other denizens of the shade bed—and an interesting foil for the broad leaves of hostas and the spotted foliage of lungwort (*Pulmonaria* spp.).

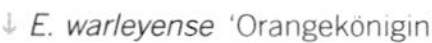

↓ *E. warleyense* 'Orangekönigin'

Barrenwort requires little special care, wanting only a loose, moist woodland soil enriched with leaf mould, pine or spruce needles, and a once-a-year feeding with compost or rotted manure. Sufficient organic content in the soil is key to success; barrenwort expands and only when satisfied with the meal at their feet. Plants are evergreen in mild regions above Zone 6, but winter winds in colder climates desiccate the foliage (which you should remove entirely before the handsome new leaves appear in spring).

Barrenwort is generally pest-free, tolerant of alkaline conditions and will accept some morning sun, but stronger sunlight causes stress. Flower production is decreased in dark shade, so it's best to site them in light to dappled shade. With few exceptions, such as *E.* x *rubrum* and *E. pubigerum*, most won't adapt to chronically dry soil; more frequent irrigation is necessary when grown close to maple and other thirsty trees.

Seed is produced in a thin-walled capsule (although hybrids may not produce any because some are sterile) and the low-flying bumblebees of May and June ably assist pollination. It's a rare form of entertainment to see a nectar-seeking bumblebee's cumbersome bulk embrace a tiny flower as the whole raceme bobs wildly up and down. The barrenwort in my garden are such workhorses that I always want more. Each autumn I split clumps or separate the carpet-forming rhizomes and set them where I need to fill space. (They can also be divided in spring after the blossoms are finished.)

Recommended varieties

Clump-formers such as red barrenwort (*E.* x *rubrum*) can be used to fill one small space or be planted in colonies to follow a path or edge a bed. Red barrenwort performs well in dry shade alongside a garage or on a slope and is dramatic in early spring, with its fresh green, spiny-edged leaves margined and veined with copper red, and its dainty flowers with crimson inner sepals and white spurs.

Longspur barrenwort (*E. grandiflorum*) 'Rose Queen' is another drought-tolerant plant with large, long-spurred, rose-pink flowers and it grows to a height of 30 centimetres. 'Rose Queen' is a technicolour match for *E.* x *perralchicum* 'Fröhnleiten', with its brown-flushed leaves and bright yellow flowers that are particularly striking at the feet of white birch trees.

Persian barrenwort *(E. pinnatum)* has delicate, orchid-like spikes of pale yellow bloom. *E. youngianum* 'Niveum' has pure white flowers in dainty inflorescences above the foliage, and is the last of the genus to bloom.

Bleeding Hearts

↑ *D. spectabilis,* white form

An old-fashioned favourite brings new beauty to the garden

BY LORRAINE HUNTER

Hardiness

Zone 3

Growing conditions

Humus-rich moist soil; cool, semi-shade

Colour range

White; pink to deep rose

Bloom time

Mid to late spring, depending on variety

Size

30 to 90 centimetres

Yes, they're old-fashioned and grown so frequently some people consider them common, but bleeding hearts (*Dicentra* spp.) are definite assets in any garden, formal or natural: they add elegance and grace to beds and borders, they're dead easy to grow in sun or shade, and they're hardy to most parts of Canada. Gardeners who appreciate bleeding hearts love the quick-growing, clump-forming, classic perennial (also known as lady's locket and lady in a boat) for its spring blooms and ability to thrive under myriad conditions.

Dicentra (from the Greek words *dis*, meaning "two," and *kentros*, meaning "spurs," referring to the flower's unusual shape) are spring-blooming, but some varieties flower longer than others. Generally, the cooler the location, the longer the blooming period lasts. Most species come from the forest floors of deep woods and moist canyons and are thus well acclimatized to shade gardens.

There are more than 150 species of *Dicentra* growing from 30 centimetres to as much as 90 centimetres in height. The varieties that follow are most often grown in Canada. All except some hybrids are hardy to Zone 3.

Growing

Bleeding hearts need a well-drained, humus-rich soil and won't survive in soil that remains wet. They appreciate some shade during the day, particularly in hot areas, and may be short-lived in climates with mild winters.

Before you plant, dig a couple of pails full of good compost or well-rotted manure into the planting

Pluck a single blossom, turn it upside down and gently open its pink wings. Inside you'll see a white lady in her bath. Bleeding hearts are also known rather colourfully as lady in a boat and lady's locket, as well as valentine flower.

↑ Common red bleeding heart *(D. spectabilis)*

hole—starting plants off in rich soil ensures stronger growth and better bloom in future. Each spring, mulch with organic material to maintain soil moisture and fertility.

Plants grow from a pronged root similar to a rhizome; some have a tuberous root. Roots can be brittle, so handle them gently. Fall is the best time to plant bleeding heart roots, for this is their dormant time. Alternatively, buy potted plants to set out in spring or fall and avoid snapping off precious roots. Space a group of larger varieties at least 90 centimetres apart so they can show off their natural arching form—even more space for a lone specimen set among other plants in a mixed border. Dwarf varieties look good massed 45 centimetres apart.

Because the foliage of bleeding hearts dies back in summer, it can leave an awkward gap in the border.

↑ Fringed bleeding heart *(D. eximia)*

Fringed bleeding heart is native to the Appalachian Mountains and prefers to grow in rocky woods. Plant it in shady places; keep it moist in summer and dry in winter. Frequent deadheading will keep it blooming into fall.

↑ *D. spectabilis* 'Gold Heart'

Conceal the space with plants that develop later in the season, such as hostas, astilbes and ferns.

Bleeding hearts are notorious self-seeders, especially the dwarfer forms, but plants take time to mature. Established plants can be propagated by root division in spring or fall, but be sure to treat the roots with care. You can also propagate by taking cuttings from plants after flowering, or by separating young side shoots once they've started to grow in spring.

Recommended varieties

Common bleeding heart (*D. spectabilis*), old-fashioned bleeding heart, or valentine flower (take your pick of its garden-variety name), is the one most familiar to many gardeners, and it's definitely worthy of notice—which is, in fact, what *spectabilis* means. Native to northern China, Korea and Japan, it was introduced to English gardens in 1857, where it still thrives. It grows in leafy clumps from 60 to 90 centimetres tall and features nodding, rose-pink, heart-shaped flowers 2.5 centimetres long, with protruding white inner petals that hang in rows from graceful stems. The entire plant goes dormant in summer.

D. s. forma alba is the white-flowered form of common bleeding heart. Its heart-shaped blooms (also 2.5 centimetres long) hang one side of arching racemes above the foliage mound. It has soft green, fernlike leaves. Good soil drainage is essential for all forms of *D. spectabilis*. Foliage goes dormant in summer.

Although it's hardy only to Zone 5, a recent hybrid from England, *D. spectabilis* 'Gold Heart', adds a bright touch to a shady spot with shining sprays of golden foliage and pink blooms.

Fringed bleeding heart (*D. eximia*) is native to rocky woods in the Appalachian Mountains. It forms a mound about 45 centimetres tall and has fine-textured, blue-green leaves. The chief blooming period is late spring, but with good moisture and deadheading it will bloom into the fall; the plant also maintains its attractive foliage, making it a good choice for small, shady gardens. Wet soils during winter and dry soils in summer, however, can lead to plant loss.

Western bleeding heart (*D. formosa*), also known as fernleaf or Pacific bleeding heart, thrives in rich, moist woods along the Pacific northwest coast, and prefers similar conditions in the garden. Its fernlike, greyish green foliage, which persists throughout the growing season, is a highlight. Flower buds open in late spring to display pale or deep rose-pink flowers with a slightly elongated heart shape on long, leafless, arching stems that rise slightly above the foliage.

D. formosa 'King of Hearts', hardy to Zone 4, is a dwarf hybrid from the U.S. that features rosy flowers all summer.

Quicktips

- Plant *Dicentra* in spring, preferably in humus-rich, moist soil enriched with compost or leaf mould, in full sun or partial shade.
- Do not plant in hot or windy areas of the garden.
- Plants can grow very large; be sure to leave ample space around each bleeding heart—at least 90 centimetres for *D. spectabilis* and 45 centimetres for *D. formosa.*
- Apply mulch in May.
- Plants can be potted up and forced into bloom inside.
- Deer don't usually eat *Dicentra*, with the exception of *D. eximia*.
- Sprigs of flowers and foliage look lovely in mixed bouquets.

Hardiness

Zones 3 to 5, depending on variety

Growing conditions

Full sun; partial shade where summers are intensely hot; ordinary garden soil

Colour range

Pink, white, purple, blue

Bloom time

Early to midsummer and beyond, depending on variety

Size

8 to 90 centimetres, depending on variety

favourite perennials

Campanulas

There's a bellflower for every corner of the garden BY ALAIN CHAREST

← *C. punctata* 'Cherry Bells'

Pink, white, purple or blue, *Campanula* spp. are tried-and-true plants you can always depend on, which explains their enduring popularity. The genus contains more than 300 biennials, perennials and a few annual varieties, and they're commonly known as bellflowers, harebells or bluebells.

Campanulas come in a great variety of sizes, so whether you're looking for a tall, willowy type for your cottage garden, something more formal with upright stems, or a low-growing star for the rock garden, you'll find a variety to fit your purpose. Most bloom in early summer, and some might provide a second show if they're cut back before their flowers fade.

Campanulas come in many sizes and heights and suit nearly every style of garden. 'Chettle Charm' peach-leafed bellflower (*C. persicifolia*) on this page does well even in poor soil. It blooms on strong stems that grow from a rosette of leaves and looks good with plants with loose, horizontal forms, such as astilbes and hostas.

↑ *C. latifolia* 'Alba'

Milky bellflower (*C. lactiflora*), opposite, suits a casual cottage garden, but it needs to be staked. The flowers of *C. latifolia* 'Alba' at right are more tubular and less long-lived, but its stems are stronger. It's easy to confuse the botanical names of these two varieties.

Growing

Bellflowers thrive in full sun, but where summers are intensely hot, they will be happier in partial shade. They grow well in average, neutral to alkaline soil and are, for the most part, not susceptible to pests or disease (slugs and snails are their only serious enemies). Species are simple to start from seed, but for named varieties, buy young plants—seeds taken from cultivars are likely to revert to the species. Both perennials and annuals grow readily from spring-sown seed, sown indoors under lights or outdoors where they are to stay. Keep in mind that sown seeds need light to germinate, so don't cover the bed or seed tray.

If you can't find a cultivar or named variety you have growing in your garden and you want more, try reproducing them from divisions or rooted cuttings. Mature plants can be divided in spring: either dig up the plant and separate some of the roots, or trowel up a section of root. Plant the divisions in prepared holes, water well and apply some water-soluble root fertilizer.

Cuttings should be dipped in a rooting hormone and put in small containers with vermiculite; once cuttings have taken root and look sturdy and healthy, transplant to pots of planting medium. Cuttings can be taken in late summer and the seedlings nurtured for next summer's garden.

Some varieties, such as peach-leafed bellflower (*C. persicifolia*), seed themselves gracefully throughout the garden, and since they tend to be reticent about their appearances should be allowed to have their way, unless they interfere with another plant. In fact, it's a good idea to frequently separate clumps that form, to keep them growing vigorously.

One species to avoid is creeping bellflower (*C. rapunculoides*). This bell from hell is very attractive but it spreads rapidly and is hard to eradicate.

Most campanulas are hardy to Zone 3.

Recommended varieties

Extensive breeding and selection of *Campanula* species have resulted in hundreds of cultivars to choose from. Here are some favourites to make welcome in your garden borders.

↑ Milky bellflower (*C. lactiflora*) with rose astilbe

Short varieties

The rock garden is where bellflowers really shine. Here are a few favourite shorter types.

Fairies' thimbles (*C. cochleariifolia*), Zone 5 with reliable snow cover, are jewels that grow in dense mats of small rosettes; in early summer, 8- to 15-centimetre-tall stems hold one or more nodding, 2-centimetre bells in colours ranging from pure white to deep purple. They thrive in cracks between rocks but also grow well in any spot with well-drained soil.

For Shady Spots

Although bellflowers typically prefer full sun, some are happy in partial shade—especially where summers are intensely hot. An advantage of shade is that the blooms last longer and their colour fades less than it would in full sun. Here are a few to try:

- *C. punctata* (likely the most shade-tolerant)
- *C. carpatica*
- *C. cochleariifolia*
- *C. garganica*
- *C. medium*
- *C. persicifolia*
- *C. poscharskyana*

↑ *C. carpatica* 'White Clips' and 'Blue Clips'

C. poscharskyana, Zone 3, and its sister Dalmatian bellflower (*C. portenschlagiana*), Zone 5, both reach about 15 centimetres tall and produce spreading mats without being invasive. The former has light blue or pale lavender star-shaped flowers with pointed petals; the latter has deep purple, upward-facing, funnel-shaped flowers that grow profusely, hiding the foliage. In a sunny site, both will bloom throughout the summer without the need for any deadheading.

Adriatic bellflower (*C. garganica*), Zone 5, produces lilac-blue stars, grows 5 centimetres high and is well adapted to container growing. 'Dickson's Gold' has gold foliage.

Carpathian harebell (*C. carpatica*), Zone 3, is perhaps the best known and easiest to grow of the rock garden bellflowers, but it also works well at the front of a border. This 15-centimetre-tall plant looks like a short peach-leafed bellflower, producing masses of upright-facing, white or blue open bells. The most popular cultivars are 'Blue Clips', 'Deep Blue Clips', 'White Clips' and 'Light Blue Clips'. Unlike most cultivars, these usually come true from seed.

C. raddeana, Zone 4, is my favourite among rock garden bellflowers. It's similar to fairies' thimbles, but the small bells seem to face whichever way they please. I started mine from seed 10 years ago and it still blooms profusely, occupying only about 5 square centimetres of gravel near my pond.

Tall varieties

Peach-leafed bellflower (*C. persicifolia*), Zone 3, is a long-lived perennial bloomer that can stand up to wind and rain and remain fresh-looking. It does well even in poor soil.

A mat of rosettes produces 60- to 90-centimetre-tall rigid stems, which in early summer are covered in white or blue cup-shaped flowers, each 2.5 to 4 centimetres across. The strong, upright stems contrast well with plants that have loose or horizontal forms, such as astilbes or hostas. These bellflowers also look good behind a drift of shorter maiden pinks. Divide and replant every two or three years. 'Moerheimii' has double, white flowers; 'Chettle Charm' has pale blue blooms.

Milky bellflower (*C. lactiflora*), Zone 5, is more casual in appearance. It produces billowing masses of tiny, open bells on arching, 1-metre-tall stems; unfortunately, it needs to be staked. The most popular cultivars are 'Loddon Anna' (pinkish white), 'Prichard's Variety' (violet-blue) and 'White Pouffe' (white).

C. latifolia, Zone 3, is one of the easiest perennial types to grow. I started some from seed about 15 years ago and, despite being neglected, they bloom faithfully every June, opening with the first flush of roses. They have sturdier stems than milky bellflower, and because the blooms are not as long-lived, they might be better suited to a wilder part of the garden. They grow 90 to 120 centimetres high and the tubular flowers, about 5 centimetres long, appear only in the upper half of the stems. 'Alba' is a white form; *C. l.* var. *macrantha* has dark purplish blue blooms.

Canterbury bells (*C. medium*), the biennial in this genus of mainly perennials, have been a popular cottage-garden plant since the Middle Ages. The first year plants form a low rosette of leaves; the next summer the 30- to 90-centimetre stems of spectacular flowers, which resemble frilled bells, rise. This type doesn't generally self-seed, so seeds should be started every spring for bloom every year. Flowers are about 4 centimetres across and come in a wide range of blues, pinks and whites. They do well in pots but look best in a drift in a flower bed.

Ivory bells (*C. alliariifolia*), Zone 3, has an intriguing texture and shape, but may not be as readily available as other bellflowers. Cream-coloured, tubular bells, 2 to 5 centimetres long, hang from 45-centimetre-long, arching stems with woolly leaves. Good for the front of a border.

C. punctata, Zone 5, is also not for the back of the border; from its 60-centimetre stems hang wide, white or pinkish, 5-centimetre tubular bells. This species requires sandy or well-drained soil; keep an eye on the plants because they have a tendency to spread. 'Cherry Bells' is a dark pink cultivar.

↓ Fairies' thimbles (*C. cochleariifolia*)

The tiny fairies' thimbles love small sunny spaces, such as the crevices between rocks. The Clips Series grows a little higher, forming a dense mound of larger, bell-shaped blooms, but it is also useful in small spaces.

↑ *C.* 'Nelly Moser'

Clematis

Clematis isn't difficult; it just wants to be happy

BY LAURA LANGSTON

Clematis, the queen of vines, festoons walls and fences, clambers up arbours and posts, and forms breathtaking partnerships with climbing roses, shrubs and trees. Most varieties are deciduous climbers, but there are a couple of herbaceous types suited to the perennial border, as well as several evergreen climbers that provide year-round foliage in warmer parts of Canada. Blooms vary from spectacularly large, showy and star-shaped to small, shy and bell-shaped. Some—such as *Clematis alpina* 'Odorata', *C. armandii* and the hybrid 'Fair Rosamund'—are faintly scented; most are not.

Still, despite its many great qualities, this perennial vine has a reputation for being difficult to grow. Not so. These plants aren't difficult, just exacting. Given the right location, a regular supply of water and good support, clematis will establish itself and thrive for decades.

Hardiness

Zones 2 to 7, depending on variety

Growing conditions

Well-drained slightly alkaline soil; sun; shaded roots; trellis or support

Colour range

White; pinks to reds; purple; blues

Bloom time

Spring to early fall, depending on variety

Size

1.8 to 10 metres, depending on variety

Give clematis the simple things in life—its head in the sun, its feet in cool soil and enough to drink—allow it three years to feel comfortable and it will thrive for decades.

← *C.* 'Ville de Lyon'

↓ *C. paniculata* (syn. *C. terniflora, C. maximowicziana*)

↑ *C. integrifolia* 'Alionuska'

↑ *C.* 'Henryi'

Growing

Clematis appreciates well-drained, average or slightly rich soil with a pH of 7. Choose a cool, weed-free spot, ideally one where clematis can have its feet in the shade and its head in the sun. A low-growing shrub nearby will create the shade the roots need, as will rocks, pebbles or groundcovers.

Morning sun is a bare minimum. Most varieties need at least four hours of full sun to flower properly, though pastel hybrids such as 'Henryi' and 'Nelly Moser' often produce more intense blooms in light shade.

In parts of Canada where winter temperatures drop below –20°C, plant clematis against the house for additional warmth, and mulch with compost or bark chips for protection against extreme cold and the freeze-thaw cycle. If you choose a sunny southern or western wall, protect clematis from sweltering summer sun by planting it behind a small shrub that will keep the first metre of the plant in shade.

Plant in spring as soon as the soil can be worked. First soak the plant, nursery container and all, in a bucket of cool water for 15 to 20 minutes to hydrate the roots. Dig a hole 45 centimetres deep and wide, or twice the diameter of the root ball, whichever is larger. Cover the bottom of the hole with well-rotted manure or compost mixed with a handful of bone meal, and add enough topsoil to cover the compost (don't let the manure contact the roots or crown). Gently slip the clematis and its stake from its container and place the root ball in the hole so that 10 to 15 centimetres of stem are below the soil line. Fill the hole with good-quality topsoil.

The exposed stem will scramble quite quickly up the existing stake to its new host, which can be a nearby shrub or tree, a taller bamboo stake, a trellis or a decorative piece of driftwood. The stem should be securely but carefully attached to the support with string or a twist-tie. After that, the original stake can be discarded if you wish.

Three new cultivars at right are worth looking for. 'Arabella' blooms June through September, grows to 1.8 metres and is hardy to Zone 4. Non-clinging, it can be left to ramble through shrubs. The free-flowering *C. viticella* 'Blue Angel' grows to 2 metres, blooms all summer and is hardy to Zone 3. 'Inspiration' shares 'Arabella's characteristics.

↑ *C.* 'Arabella'

↑ *C. viticella* 'Blue Angel'

↑ *C.* 'Inspiration'

Stem damage makes young plants susceptible to fungi, particularly clematis wilt (*Ascochyta clematidina*), which can cause the entire plant to collapse. It most commonly occurs as the buds open. At the first sign of trouble (a wilting plant that doesn't respond to watering), remove and destroy affected stems down to about 2.5 centimetres below the point of infection to make sure no fungus lingers.

Mildew can also be a problem late in the season, particularly if air circulation is poor. Minimize the risk by watering early in the morning and keeping the foliage as dry as possible. Fungicides sometimes work if applied early enough; prune out badly infected areas if the problem becomes acute.

Slugs consider young clematis shoots a delicious spring feast, and in summer, earwigs can turn blooms and leaves into lace overnight. Whatever your choice of pest control (organic or chemical), be vigilant and respond quickly.

Plants should be watered deeply and regularly—4.5 litres a day during hot, dry spells. If the bottom leaves of the plant start to deteriorate before the end of the season, you haven't been watering your clematis enough. Ensure good drainage, though—clematis doesn't like wet feet. Fertilize with several handfuls of bone meal in spring and fall.

Clematis plants generally take about three years to mature. But no

↓ Purple *C.* 'Jackmanii' and magenta-red *C.* 'Ernest Markham'

↑ *C. texensis* 'Duchess of Albany'

With so many varieties available, it's possible to have clematis blooming in your garden all season, from dainty bell-shaped spring cultivars to large, showy summer blooming ones and sweetly scented fall varieties.

↓ *C. montana* var. *rubens* 'Tetrarose'

↑ *C. macropetala 'Blue Bird'*

matter how vigorous or impressive a new plant looks when you get it home from the nursery, all varieties should be cut back after planting in the spring—or the following spring if planted in the fall—to encourage strong root development and a healthier, multi-stemmed plant. Prune when the plant breaks dormancy and leaf buds start to develop. Leave two sets of buds on each stem between the soil level and where you make your cut.

After the first year, prune clematis according to when it blooms. It's not as complicated as it sounds: if your variety is an early bloomer that flowers on last year's wood, prune minimally, cutting out any weak or dead stems as soon as you see buds swelling in spring. Depending on where you live, this can be as early as February or as late as April. Varieties that bloom on the current year's growth start producing flowers in early summer and continue to autumn. Cut back severely in early spring before they bloom—to about 30 centimetres from the ground. Varieties that flower twice—both on wood hardened by the previous season's growth and the current season's growth—should be lightly pruned to tidy the plant only after the first flush of bloom is finished, usually in late spring.

Recommended varieties

With so many new cultivars to choose from now, it's possible to have clematis blooming sequentially spring to fall even in Zone 2. The biggest challenge is making the choice of what to plant. Consider bloom time first, and then narrow the field according to your colour preference.

Late winter/early spring

- *C. armandii* 'Snowdrift' has highly scented, saucer-shaped white flowers in March and April. The foliage is evergreen; it's vigorous but needs a frost-free location. Grows 6 to 9 metres tall and is hardy to Zone 7.
- *C. armandii* 'Apple Blossom' also has highly scented saucer-shaped blooms, but in blush pink, in March and April. The foliage is evergreen; it needs a frost-free location, grows to 6 to 9 metres tall and is hardy to Zone 7.

Spring

- *C. alpina* 'Constance' has bright pink, bell-shaped blooms in April and May, followed by attractive seed heads. Grows 1.8 to 2.5 metres tall and is hardy to Zone 2.
- *C. alpina* 'Odorata' has medium to light blue, delicately scented, bell-shaped flowers in April and May, also followed by attractive seed heads. Height reaches 1.8 to 2.5 metres and it's hardy to Zone 2.
- *C. alpina* 'Jacqueline du Pré' is slightly more vigorous than other *alpinas*, with rose-mauve, bell-shaped flowers and good-looking seed heads. Grows 2.4 to 3 metres tall and is hardy to Zone 2.
- *C. macropetala* 'Blue Bird' was bred in Manitoba. Its lavender-blue, bell-shaped blooms appear in April and May. A vigorous and free-flowering plant, it reaches 2.5 to 3.5 metres and is hardy to Zone 3.
- *C. macropetala* 'Rosy O'Grady' is less vigorous than 'Blue Bird'. The large, light pink, bell-shaped flowers bloom in April and May, and they're followed by attractive seed heads. The plant grows 2.5 to 3.5 metres tall and is hardy to Zone 3.

Most of the top growth of the following *montanas* freezes out in Zone 6 or colder, resulting in few blooms:

- *C. montana* 'Rubens' is slightly hardier than other varieties and shows masses of large, deep pink flowers with golden stamens in May and June. It grows 9 metres or more tall and is hardy to Zone 6.
- *C. montana* var. *rubens* 'Elizabeth' is also hardy to Zone 6 and has pale pink, vanilla-scented blooms in May and June. Grows 7 to 10 metres tall.
- *C. montana* var. *rubens* 'Tetrarose' is a compact member of this group, reaching about 6 metres. Its unusually large, rose-pink, star-shaped flowers appear in May and June. Foliage is bronze-green; it's also hardy to Zone 6.

Early summer

- 'Nelly Moser' has huge, 17- to 23-centimetre, pale mauve-pink, star-shaped, crimson-striped blooms appearing in May or June and again in September. The plant reaches 2.5 to 3.5 metres, is shade-tolerant and hardy to Zone 4.
- 'Ville de Lyon' has crimson-edged, star-shaped red blooms that fade to silvery red, with large, yellow stamens. It blooms June through September, reaches 2.5 to 3.5 metres and is hardy to Zone 3.
- 'Henryi' has huge, creamy white, star-shaped flowers with dark stamens that appear from June to September. This variety grows to 2.5 to 4 metres tall and is hardy to Zone 3.
- 'The President' has deep purple-blue, star-shaped flowers and striking, red-tipped stamens. It blooms from June to September on plants 2.5 to 3.5 metres tall and is hardy to Zone 3.
- 'Proteus' Double has mauve-pink blooms that appear in May and June, followed by single blooms throughout the summer. The plant reaches 2.5 to 3.5 metres and is hardy to Zone 4.
- 'Miss Bateman' has large, creamy white, double, star-shaped flowers

with contrasting dark red stamens in early May and June. Grows 2 to 2.5 metres tall and is hardy to Zone 4.
- *C. vitalba* is also known as old man's beard or traveller's joy. It's a vigorous-species clematis that produces small, white pendant blooms with prominent stamens from mid-June to September. The conspicuous seed heads have a woolly look. Reaches 15 metres and is hardy to Zone 3.

Midsummer

- 'Comtesse de Bouchard' has pinkish mauve, star-shaped blooms from June to September. Grows 2.5 to 3.5 metres tall and is hardy to Zone 3.
- 'Jackmanii' has large, deep purple, star-shaped blooms that appear from mid-June through August on vines 3.5 to 6 metres tall and is hardy to Zone 3.
- 'Ernest Markham' has bright, magenta-red, star-shaped flowers from July to September on a vigorous vine about 3.5 metres tall and is hardy to Zone 3.
- *C. tangutica* 'Sheriffi' has nodding, yellow blooms from June through September, followed by furry-looking seed heads. It's extremely vigorous, reaches 4.5 to 6 metres and is hardy to Zone 2.

Late summer

- *C. viticella* 'Little Nell' shows masses of small, creamy white, star-shaped flowers with mauve edges and green stamens from June to September. Grows 3 to 3.5 metres tall and is hardy to Zone 2.
- 'Polish Spirit' blooms with deep purple, saucer-shaped flowers from June through September. A vigorous plant, it reaches 3 to 3.5 metres tall and is hardy to Zone 2.
- *C. texensis* 'Pagoda' has pale mauve-pink, pitcher-shaped flowers from July through September and smooth, almost round leaves. The plant requires good air circulation, grows 2.5 to 3.5 metres tall and is hardy to Zone 4.
- *C. texensis* 'Duchess of Albany' has clear pink, pitcher-shaped flowers with rose-pink bars that appear from July through September. Grows 2.5 to 3.5 metres tall and is hardy to Zone 4.
- *C. integrifolia* 'Durandii' has rich, indigo-blue, slightly nodding flowers with deeply furrowed midribs and white stamens that appear from June to September on plants 1 to 2 metres tall and is hardy to Zone 3.
- *C. integrifolia* 'Alionushka' is a herbaceous variety of clematis producing lilac-purple, slightly nodding flowers on strong stems from June to September. It grows 1.8 to 2 metres tall and is hardy to Zone 3.
- *C. paniculata* (syn. *C. terniflora* or *C. maximowicziana*) is also known as sweet autumn clematis. It bears masses of small, white, hawthorn-scented flowers in September and October. Although it's considered hardy to Zone 5, it should be protected over winter below Zone 6. The vine grows 6 to 9 metres tall.

↓*C. integrifolia* 'Durandii'

Pruning clematis is not as complicated it seems. The rule of thumb is to prune early bloomers minimally because they flower on last year's wood. Early summer varieties bloom on the present year's wood and should be cut back severely before growth begins.

↑ *C. integrifolia*

Clematis in Pots

Given the right conditions, clematis can be successfully grown in pots if you're short on space or want to try tender varieties. The latter can overwinter in a cool garage, but keep in mind that clematis can get pretty big, so consider compact varieties.

Choose a container made of wood or terra-cotta, rather than heat-conducting plastic or metal. Make sure the pot is at least 45 centimetres deep, wide and high. Bigger is even better.

Use a high-quality potting soil and add peat moss for good drainage. Centre the root ball in the pot, and then follow the same method used for planting clematis in the ground. A loose mulch helps retain moisture and discourage pests. If your container is large enough, interplant clematis with annuals or a groundcover.

Proper support is critical—use a well-constructed trellis if the pot is going to be set against a wall, or a sturdy tripod of bamboo or cedar stakes if it's free-standing.

Water often. Fertilize every few weeks with 15-30-15 diluted to half the recommended strength. Repot when flowers get small and plant growth slows.

C. 'The President' →

↑ A. McKana hybrid

favourite perennials

Columbines

Sprightly but elegant, and at home in any garden BY LORRAINE HUNTER

Hardiness	Growing conditions	Colour range	Bloom time	Size
Most varieties to Zone 3; some to Zone 2	Sun to semi-shade; humus-rich soil; water in dry weather	Solids and combinations of white, red, orange, yellow, pink, blue, purple	Late spring to early summer	20 to 90 centimetres, depending on variety

Columbines (*Aquilegia* spp.) grow all over the world and more than 70 species are native to North America. Many varieties have long, curving spurs that resemble an eagle's spread talons, suggesting the botanical name was derived from the Latin *aquila*, for eagle.

Freely sprouting in sidewalk cracks, along fencelines and at the edges of porches, columbines offer an endless array of delicate flowers in dazzling colours dancing above lacy bluish or bright green foliage. They attract ladybugs, bees, butterflies and hummingbirds and make excellent cut flowers.

The columbine's spurred petals resemble an eagle's spread talons, suggesting that its botanical name, *Aquilegia*, may be derived from *aquila*, the Latin word for "eagle." Its common name probably comes from *columba*, meaning "dove" in Latin, denoting that the blossoms en masse resemble doves in flight.

Columbines are members of the *Ranunculaceae* family and thus are related to the clematis, peony and buttercup. More than 70 species are native to open woodlands, meadows and mountainous regions in the northern hemisphere, but they're found in north temperate regions all over the world, including Siberia and Japan. They thrive in the Canadian Rockies and the forests of Alaska.

Most gardeners plant the long-spurred hybrids, but the smaller alpine species, such as the nodding red-and-yellow *Aquilegia canadensis,* have a subtle charm, as does the rather less showy *A. vulgaris*, which blooms in varying shades of purple and pink. Columbines are suited to almost every part of the garden: the perennial border, the cutting garden and the wild garden; the smaller varieties are ideal candidates for a rock garden. Most are hardy to Zone 3.

Growing

Columbines produce elegant single or double flowers in solid tones or combinations of white, purple, orange, yellow, red, pink and blue. They're easy to grow but are rampant self-seeders and will hybridize wantonly if different species are grown together, producing new colour combinations every year or so. Columbines are hardly invasive, however: undesirable seedlings that have sprung up in the middle of a path or in the wrong place in the perennial border can be easily pulled out. Since columbine is generally a short-lived perennial lasting sometimes no more than three years, it's not a bad idea to encourage or even transplant new seedlings as they spring up.

Columbine species and cultivars are readily available at nurseries, but they're easy to grow from seed, although seed can be slow to germinate. Seeds sprout more successfully when subjected to cold, moist conditions. For outdoor starting, sow seeds in damp sand, vermiculite or other sterile media in open flats and set outdoors in fall or very early spring. Cover seeds thinly or simply press them into the surface: the seeds need light to germinate, which should occur in about 28 days.

To start seeds indoors, use bulb pots (they're shallower than most pots) and the same planting medium and method as above; start in April and sow about a dozen seeds to each pot. Store pots in the refrigerator for six weeks. Once

Quicktips

- Water columbines daily in very hot weather, especially in drought-like conditions.
- Columbines prefer dappled sunlight but will tolerate full sun to partial shade.
- Plant in groups for best display.
- Cut off wilted flowers to prolong their bloom period and to eliminate self-seeding.
- Fertilizing is unnecessary, although columbines love humus-rich soil.
- Columbines bloom well near plants that offer some shade for part of the day.

↑ Fan columbine (*A. flabellata*)

Some columbines, such as the Japanese fan columbines, are spurless and shorter than other varieties, so that they resemble violets. They have many admirers.

germination occurs, put pots in a sunny window and make sure they stay moist but not waterlogged. Water pots from the bottom by setting them in a foil pan filled with an inch or so of water.

Once indoor seedlings have five or six true leaves, transplant them carefully to small, individual pots, give them a few days to settle in and gain some new growth, and then harden them off to outdoor weather by putting them in a sheltered, shady spot for increasing amounts of time each day. Plants started in flats outdoors should also be divided once they've grown to a manageable size, either to their permanent spot in the garden or to a transitional bed to allow them to fatten up over the summer.

Plant the seedlings in the garden about 30 centimetres apart; the crowns should be about 1 centimetre below soil surface. Columbines will grow in well-drained, average soil, but thrive best in soil that's moist and humus-rich. They prefer partial shade, and the young plants especially should be shaded and protected from wind. Keep them well watered—they suffer in dry weather.

Although pests and diseases rarely attack columbines, leaf miner can make foliage unsightly, producing light tan, wavy lines through leaves. If plants show these symptoms, cut them back to the ground; this allows a fresh mound of foliage to develop. Or remove the damaged leaves as soon as leaf miner trails appear.

Recommended varieties

Note: The following are all hardy to Zone 3 except where indicated.

Granny's bonnet (*A. vulgaris*) is a British native and is the most common European species. It grows 40 to 70 centimetres tall, has mid-length to short spurs, fernlike, blue-grey foliage and blue, pink or white flowers in May. 'Nora Barlow', an old favourite with green and pink double flowers (and named for Charles Darwin's granddaughter), reaches 90 centimetres. *A. v.* var. *stellata* 'Black Barlow' is a double, spurless purple-black variety, 60 to 75 centimetres tall, that was specifically bred for cut flowers; it blooms in May and June.

Alpine columbine (*A. alpina*) originated in mountainous regions throughout Europe. It's hardy to Zone 4 and grows to a height of about 45 centimetres, with rich blue, flared flowers in late spring.

Fan columbine (*A. flabellata*) is a Japanese alpine that has tiny, blue flowers with creamy white centres; it grows to 30 centimetres. *A. f.* var. *pumila forma alba* syn. 'Nana Alba' is more compact, reaching a height of 20 centimetres, with proportionally smaller, white flowers. Both are hardy to Zone 2 and bloom in May and June.

Canada columbine (*A. canadensis*) grows across North America on rocky ledges, in woods and ravines and along cliffs and bluffs. It can reach 90 centimetres in height. The delicate flowers, with scarlet sepals and yellow petals, taper into erect, red spurs and appear from April through July. Similar in colour and height but flowering from May through August, its cousin, *A. formosa*, is found west of the Rockies.

↑ Alpine columbine (*A. alpina*)

↑ *A.* x *hybrida* 'Nora Barlow'

The fully double 'Nora Barlow', an old favourite, was named for Charles Darwin's granddaughter, and has the same ancestry as granny's bonnet, a British native. Rich blue alpine columbine has flared flowers and short spurs.

Music Series is a popular variety of *A. caerulea*. This family of columbines grows to heights between 30 and 45 centimetres and has long-spurred flowers in May in combinations of blue/white, red/white and red/gold to solid white. Available hybrids are: McKana, 75 centimetres tall, with a range of bicolours in late spring and early summer that includes blue and yellow, salmon and white, and pink and lemon; and Mrs. Scott-Elliot, 90 centimetres tall, which blooms in contrasting bicolours of blue/white and red/yellow from May to June.

Cranesbills

Relaxed and charming, perennial geraniums are the backbone of many gardens

↑ *G. sanguineum* 'Max Frei'

Hardiness

Most to Zone 4; some to Zone 2

Growing conditions

Average soil with some humus; shade to sun, depending on variety

Colour range

White; pink, rose, magenta; blue and shades of purple

Bloom time

Mid-June through July

Size

10 to 120 centimetres tall, depending on variety

BY JUDITH ADAM

Ask me to name the most dependable, resilient and versatile plant in the garden and my answer is cranesbill, botanically known as *Geranium*. Some years are good for roses and others for delphiniums, but every growing season is successful for the cranesbill.

These hardy perennials, whose common name relates to their long, pointy seed capsules, are related to the South African annual geranium, properly called *Pelargonium*, often found stuffed into pots on sunny decks and patios. But the perennial geranium is a native of temperate regions, and a northern gardener's problem-solver and joy—generous with its bloom, free from pests and easily maintained. These relaxed and charming flowers, most of which are hardy to Zone 4, are the backbone of many happy gardens. Some even have leaves that turn red in autumn.

G. psilostemon 'Patricia' →

History

Known by country folk as old maid's nightcap or shameface, the *Geranium* has long been used for medicinal purposes and was well represented in the pages of Old World herbal apothecary books. For example, 17th-century physician and herbalist Nicholas Culpeper said they were astringent, good for healing wounds and curing ulcers. Herb Robert, a wild variety, was used in Elizabethan times to edge garden beds, and some modern hybrids are useful and attractive for that purpose as well.

Wild Herb Robert

Among nearly 800 species in the family *Geraniaceae*, the many cultivated cranesbills are close cousins of *Geranium robertianum*, the familiar herb Robert found carpeting forest floors with tiny pink flowers, pungent lacy leaves and hairy red stems. Herb Robert is thought by some to be named for Robert Goodfellow, best known as the outlaw cavalier Robin Hood. Another legend names this plant for St. Robert of Molesme, a 12th-century Catholic cleric whose festival falls at the same time the flowers appear in late April. Herb Robert and other geranium wildings, such as the dove's foot geranium (*G. molle*), are sometimes classified as weeds, yet they are attractive groundcovers and rockery plants in woodland landscapes—and in corners of my yard.

Growing

Geraniums are incredibly easy-care plants with a few basic requirements. They like average garden soil, although they prefer it amended with organic material such as compost or leaf mould, and they need a good drink each week, especially during hot, dry periods, to keep soil slightly moist.

Apply composted manure or garden compost around (but not over) the plant crowns in early spring or autumn for nourishment. Creeping rhizomes should be carefully lifted and divided every three years. Clump-forming geraniums can be propagated by division in early spring: lift the clump with a fork and divide into two or three pieces.

Propagation is also easily done by seed, or by taking small cuttings from the edge of a clump.

Most varieties benefit from having all the foliage cut back once blooming is finished. Although this can seem like a drastic measure, it prevents plants from becoming floppy, and if you water them well, they'll reward you with fresh new leaves that may turn red in autumn.

Recommended varieties

The dwarf alpine hybrids (10 to 15 centimetres tall) of *G. cinereum*—pale lilac-pink 'Ballerina', reddish plum 'Purple Pillow' and magenta 'Splendens'—are all suited to edge

↑ White bloody cranesbill (*G. sanguineum* 'Album')

↑ *G. psilostemon* 'Ann Folkard' with yellow yarrow

planting. For slightly taller plants, I like two *G.* x *cantabrigiense* hybrids (both 15 to 20 centimetres tall): milk white with a pink-flushed throat 'Biokovo' (a self-hybridizing Balkan cultivar, from *G. dalmaticum* and *G. macrorrhizum*); and pinkish mauve 'Cambridge', named for its English breeding site.

The first geranium to find a place in my garden was an impulse buy spied in another customer's basket in the nursery checkout line. The black-eyed, sizzling, magenta-purple flowers of *G. psilostemon* (90 to 120 centimetres tall) vibrate with intensity, and its leaves turn a brilliant flame red in autumn. This lanky plant needs a bit of discreet support, but its hybrid descendant 'Patricia' (60 to 75 centimetres tall), with black-eyed, magenta-pink flowers, stands up all by herself. 'Ann Folkard' adds chartreuse-yellow leaves and a clambering habit to the black-eyed, magenta-purple colour combinations and can weave herself through the lower regions of rose canes.

Long-lasting colour is always a bonus with cranesbill geraniums, and they usually remain in bloom for four to six weeks. My longest-blooming

Centuries ago the perennial geranium plant was valued for its astringent quality and used to heal wounds and cure ulcers.

↓ Bigroot geranium (*G. macrorrhizum*)

↑ '*G. phaeum* 'Lily Lovell'

↑ *G.* x *oxonianum* 'Claridge Druce'

plants are the magenta-purple-flowered bloody cranesbill (*G. sanguineum*) and its white-flowered sister, 'Album' (both 45 to 60 centimetres tall). They have passed along their staying power to their more compact offspring, such as carmine-rose 'Max Frei' (15 to 20 centimetres tall), reddish purple 'New Hampshire Purple' (20 to 30 centimetres tall) and *G. s.* var. *striatum* 'Lancastriense' (15 to 20 centimetres tall), which boasts pale, blush pink blooms with dark crimson veins. All open their first flowers in mid-May; if their soil is kept moist, they'll keep flowering into August, or even later.

I'm always looking for blossoming plants that will spread out in wide clumps and smother weeds. My most valuable groundcover in sunny areas is *G.* x *oxonianum* 'Claridge Druce' (60 centimetres tall). It's a clump-forming plant with shiny leaves and bright pink-purple flowers with darker veins that bloom for six weeks from mid-June through July. Its modestly self-seeding habit has supplied me with enough thick clumps to move around the garden where they are needed. 'Claridge Druce' has sufficient substance to combine with larger clumps of pale yellow 'Hyperion' daylilies and makes a dense collar of foliage around the feet of woody shrubs.

For the dry-shade areas under my garage eaves, nothing beats the coverage provided by the low, creeping mounds of fragrant-leafed bigroot geranium (*G. macrorrhizum*), which is 25 centimetres tall. In dappled or dense shade, it quickly spreads, producing generous masses of flowers from May to June, and its semi-evergreen foliage doesn't droop, even in the frigid temperatures of late November. Magenta-pink 'Bevan's Variety' (30 centimetres tall) is a good match with hostas, and I have it growing near blue-grey 'Halcyon' and chartreuse 'August Moon', with dark-leafed 'Plum Pudding' and 'Velvet Night' heucheras nearby. Bigroot geranium is easy to divide in early spring: lift the clump and separate its creeping underground rhizomes into dinner-plate-sized sections, and then replant them 45 centimetres apart.

I wouldn't be without that old standby dusky cranesbill (*G. phaeum*) in my garden (60 to 75 centimetres tall), also known as mourning widow (each leaf is marked with a small black spot to denote the poor woman's grief). It tolerates the dry shade canopy of woodland trees, putting out dark, nodding, maroon-purple flowers in May and June. My favourite cultivar of this species is 'Lily Lovell', which has a brighter and larger mauve-purple flower with a white eye, but she is hard to find.

Cranesbills for Full Shade

In shady spots try these geraniums:

- Spotted cranesbill (*G. maculatum*), 45 to 60 centimetres, Zone 4
- Dusky cranesbill or mourning widow (*G. phaeum*), 60 to 75 centimetres, Zone 4
- Wood cranesbill (*G. sylvaticum*), 60 to 75 centimetres, Zone 2
- Bigroot geranium, which can be grown in dry shade (*G. macrorrhizum*), 25 centimetres, Zone 4

Her place has been taken by a new *G. phaeum* introduction, 'Samobor' (60 centimetres tall), its leaves heavily marked with a rich, chocolate-maroon colour.

'Espresso' spotted cranesbill (*G. maculatum*) has even more dramatic, dark coffee brown foliage and soft pink flowers (30 to 40 centimetres tall), while two of the meadow cranesbills, *G. pratense* 'Midnight Reiter' (20 to 25 centimetres tall) and 'Victor Reiter Jr.' (45 to 60 centimetres tall), have plum purple leaves and violet-blue flowers and grow well in part shade to sun.

Although I'm loyal to old favourites, new cultivars catch my attention. The best of these might be a Canadian introduction, 'Luzie' (30 to 45 centimetres tall), Zone 3, with black-marked leaves and very large, lipstick-pink flowers with a white eye. She's in the same *G.* x *oxonianum* group as the hot pink 'Phoebe Noble' (40 to 45 centimetres tall), which is hardy to Zone 4. I also admire the tall and willowy 'Spinners' bloody cranesbill (*G. sanguineum*) for its violet-blue flowers with white eyes (75 to 90 centimetres tall), Zone 3, and the even bluer G. 'Rozanne' (40 to 50 centimetres tall), which has the largest flowers of any geranium I've seen. They're held on wiry, upright stems from May to September. My pot of 'Rozanne' bloomed by the front steps into early autumn before finding a place in the border. This acquisitive gardener's heart always has room for one more.

G. x *oxonianum* 'Claridge Druce'→

Most geraniums offer something for the senses during two seasons—flowers in early summer and mounds of lush, sometimes bi-coloured, foliage after the bloom is gone. The foliage of many varieties has fall colour or a tangy, citrus scent.

G. cinereum 'Ballerina'→

H. 'Black Prince' ↑

Hardiness

Zones 2, 3, 4, depending on variety

Growing conditions

Average soil; shade to sun, depending on variety; drought-resistant

Colour range

Creamy white to yellow and gold; melon to orange; red and burgundy

Bloom time

July and August, depending on variety

Size

30 to 90 centimetres, depending on variety

favourite perennials

Daylilies

Single blooms may be queens for a day, but a clump can flower all summer

BY EVA WEIDMAN

It's been called false lily, outhouse lily, and the Cinderella of herbaceous perennials. Janice Dehod knows all the nicknames—and a whole lot more—about daylilies (*Hemerocallis* spp.). Not just her favourite perennials, they are her passion, her hobby and almost her full-time preoccupation.

The original orange-coloured tawny daylily (*H. fulva*) and the yellow citron (*H. citrina*) were brought to this country by European settlers, and clumps of them can still be found around long-abandoned homesteads across Canada, providing living links with pioneer families of yesteryear. Janice's fascination with *Hemerocallis* (which means "beautiful for a day" in Greek) began many years ago in her grandmother's garden, but it was a patch of yellow daylilies flourishing in the shade of a huge oak tree in her own front yard in the River Heights neighbourhood of Winnipeg that started her crusade to find out more.

Thanks to extensive hybridizing, gardeners have daylilies in many flower and petal shapes to choose from—ruffled, recurved, spidery, trumpet and double. Colours range from pale melon to bronzy red. Only pure whites and true blues are missing.

H. 'Lake Norman Sunset' →

← *H. fulva*

Edible Daylilies

The common orange *H. fulva* was grown for its flowers and culinary usefulness. The dried buds, called *gum-tsoy* or *gum jum* (or "golden needles" in English recipes), were used to thicken soups, and the spring shoots were cooked and eaten as a green vegetable similar to asparagus. In China, *H. fulva* was known as "thousand gold coin vegetable" because only the emperor could afford to eat it. *H. fulva* is sterile and multiplies by sending out its fleshy roots.

Janice knew from her own experience that the plant did well in Manitoba, and she discovered that thousands of cultivars continue to be hybridized in North America. But the cultivars were virtually ignored in her home province. "I started to look for them in Winnipeg nurseries and garden centres, but besides the common orange I couldn't find many others," she says. It seemed strange, since daylilies are one of the easiest perennials to grow. Drought-resistant, almost disease- and pest-free, they grow well in most soils and many varieties survive to Zones 2 and 3.

Then Janice discovered that her passion for daylilies was shared by at least 27 others on the Prairies, who have formed the Canadian Prairie Daylily Society, with members as far north as Fort McMurray, Alberta. Communicating mainly through the Internet, members exchange information and tips on where to seek out new cultivars. They are also creating a database of cultivars that grow in Zones 2, 3 and 4 (for more information, contact Janice Dehod at jdehod@shaw.com).

Janice wanted more people in Manitoba to share her enthusiasm, so once she had persuaded friends and neighbours to plant daylilies, she turned to community gardens. In the summer of 2000 she got involved in a unique garden project at Montrose School, as well as an adopt-a-park project. In the park Janice and her neighbours adopted, which adjoins Montrose School, they plant and care for six small flower beds filled with daylilies as well as other Prairie-hardy perennials. When her proposal for a daylily garden at Assiniboine Park Conservatory, Winnipeg's premier park, was favourably received, Janice put out a call on the Internet asking daylily adherents for donations of plants. The response, she says, has been overwhelming.

Janice's project has captured the imagination of daylily gardeners across the continent; plants have come from as far away as Mechanicsville, Virginia, and Homestead, Florida.

Grandma wouldn't recognize the lemon and tawny daylilies (*H. citrina* and *H. fulva*) she once grew in her garden. They're been pretty well replaced by new cultivars that bloom in early, mid- or late summer.

↓ *H.* 'Irish Whim'

↑ *H.* 'Sound and Fury'

Some of these cultivars are unusual and include the latest on the market, which tend to be expensive. Janice and her daylily group chose 'Apple Tart', 'Little Missy', 'Black Prince', 'Java Sea', 'Lake Norman Sunset', 'Golden Prize', 'Sound and Fury', 'Kindly Light' and 'Irish Whim' to start the Assiniboine Park Conservatory gardens.

"It's a treat to have one species showcased like this for our visitors and to have such a dedicated group looking after the plants," says Linda Glowacki, who is the education co-ordinator for Assiniboine Park Conservatory.

Having tasted daylily success, there's no stopping Janice now. She's travelled from Niagara-on-the-Lake, Ontario, to the Florida Everglades seeking out daylilies and giving talks on growing them in Manitoba.

"When I gave a presentation in southern Ontario, and mentioned that we have to put our pipes almost two metres underground because of the cold winters, there was a stunned silence," she says. "I think that's partly why people have been so generous

↑ *H.* 'Prairie Blue Eyes'

↑ *H.* 'Java Sea'

with their donations. They're curious to see how their particular cultivar will do in our tough climate."

So far, under Janice Dehod's vigilant and enthusiastic care, all the donated daylilies are doing just fine.

Growing

Introduced to European gardens in 1576, the daylily became a particular favourite in British gardens, where it was valued for its toughness and ability to grow just about anywhere, under just about any condition. Most daylilies can withstand very cold winters—even temperatures as low as –40°C and frozen ground to 1.8 metres deep—without special care or protection. They adapt to sun or shade, to hot, dry gardens or cooler conditions, and a wide range of soils.

But of course, a deep, fertile loam that doesn't become a desert in summer is preferable. Try to give plants a thorough watering once a week in dry weather, and apply a mulch of straw, compost or chopped leaves to retain moisture and maintain soil quality.

A light application of a complete balanced fertilizer when growth begins in spring is usually enough to keep the plant healthy and blooming well; don't overfeed—too much nitrogen could result in excessive vegetative growth and fewer blooms. In small gardens, try to deadhead daily. Removing spent blooms isn't necessary in larger, more naturalized gardens.

Hybridizers have created colours ranging from the most delicate pale melon to shimmering bronze (the only colours not part of the daylily palette are true white, true green and true blue). Flowers can be circular, triangular or star-shaped, with ruffled, recurved, trumpet, spider or double forms, in heights ranging from short (15 centimetres) to tall (90 centimetres). And because these cultivars come in early-, mid- and late-blooming types, a well-planned daylily garden can have sequential blooms that last for most of the summer, even in areas where summers are short, such as the Prairies—look for varieties labelled E (early blooming); M (mid-season); or L (late blooming). Each flower may bloom for just one day, but there are many flower buds on each flower stem, called scapes, and many stalks in each clump of plants. As a result, the flowering period of a clump

↓ *H.* 'Golden Prize'

Daylilies have always been valued for their toughness, but now they're sought by collectors looking for more striking colours and unusual shapes. Many blooms are bi-coloured or have contrasting throats. Some have more than one flowering period, if faded blooms are removed.

usually lasts several weeks.

If the weather co-operates, a few varieties have more than one flowering period and may give a second flush of bloom if you prevent the plant from going to seed and cut the scapes to half their original height just after the first bloom.

Many named cultivars are available from nurseries and catalogues, and this is the easiest way to acquire a variety of colours and plants with successive bloom. But daylilies can be started from seed, or even hybridized in the home garden (see "Making Your Own Hybrids" below). Daylily clumps can also be divided for more plants, and should be divided if they start to overwhelm other plants or take up too much space. In early spring, just as the shoots begin to show, lift the clump with a fork, cut carefully between the shoots and down through the roots. Replant the roots firmly and water generously to help them survive transplant shock.

Even when they're not in bloom, daylilies are attractive plants. Their graceful strap-shaped, arching leaves look great next to ponds or streams, or massed along sidewalks. They contrast well with astilbes, hostas and ferns, and look good in natural gardens with tall verbascum and rudbeckia.

Making Your Own Hybrids

Not all daylilies are created equal. Daylilies that cannot accept pollen are called pod sterile, while those that cannot fertilize another daylily are pollen sterile. Daylilies that can be cross-pollinated are not sterile and do produce seeds (the only way to tell if a daylily is sterile is through research, or trial and error).

To make your own hybrids:

1. Plan to make your crosses on a clear day, about mid-morning when the pollen is dry and fluffy. Select two different plants with pretty flowers. Every daylily flower has six male stamens and one female pistil standing above the stamens. With small scissors, remove one of the stamens from the flower you've selected to be the male parent, and use it as a wand to dab its pollen on the sticky tip of the mother plant's pistil.

2. Be sure to label your crosses, indicating which plants are the mother and father of the forming seeds. Don't remove the mother flower; allow it to age and drop naturally. A seed case will form and the seeds are ready for harvest when the case splits open or cracks with gentle pressure.

3. Air-dry the seeds overnight and then put them and their labels in sealable plastic bags in the refrigerator for six weeks. (Do not freeze!) Plant the seeds in potting mix and keep them under lights until they can be transplanted to the garden. With luck, the new daylily hybrids will flower in their second year, combining the best attributes of their parents.

–Judith Adam

favourite perennials

Delphiniums always stand out in borders—their stately stems are smothered in flowers that range from blue, white and purple through to violet, pink and rose, often with contrasting centres (called eyes or bees). And because delphiniums are one of the few perennials available in shades of clear blue—from sky to midnight—they're especially prized.

Hardy and relatively pest- and disease-free, delphiniums flourish in all of Canada except the Arctic. They grow rapidly after a long winter dormancy to flower for three or four weeks in June, a boon for gardeners on the Prairies, with its short growing season. And if they're cut back to the crown after flowers fade, nearly all will rebloom in late summer.

Ideally, tall delphiniums need a spacious garden to do them justice and to allow admirers to stand back and enjoy their magnificent spikes. But they also look at home jammed into English-style cottage gardens, towering loftily over cosmos and shasta daisies, or rivalling hollyhocks in height. Planted in groups of three of one colour behind medium-height perennials, they give a regal touch to a sunny bed, creating waves of blue, pink or white in a summer breeze.

The flowers in the Fountain Series look deceptively delicate. In fact, they're exceptionally hardy. Tall hybrid delphiniums are the perfect backdrop in perennial borders.

↑ *D. elatum* Fountain Series

Delphiniums

They stand tall and beautiful in Canadian gardens BY GILLIAN PRITCHARD

Hardiness	Growing conditions	Colour range	Bloom time	Size
Zones 4 to 6, depending on variety	Well-drained but moist, rich, friable soil; full sun	White to cream; pink to rose; light and deep blue, mauve, purple	Mid to late July	30 centimetres to nearly metres, depending on variety

. elatum (variety unknown)

To dry delphinium stalks, cut them in full bloom and hang them upside down in a dry basement equipped with a ceiling fan and a dehumidifier.

Growing

Delphiniums grow best in full sun and well-drained, friable soil with sufficient nutrients to last for years—plants don't like to be moved. Space them 30 centimetres apart in soil that's amended with compost and/or well-rotted manure; the fibrous roots grow just beneath the surface, so the top 30 centimetres are crucial. Plant far enough away from fences or hedges to allow good air circulation.

Dig well-rotted cow manure or compost into the planting bed in the fall for spring planting, allowing soil to settle over winter and early spring. Set out young plants in May, making sure the crowns are at ground level and firming the soil around the roots so no air pockets remain. Keep plants well watered until they're established and use a weak solution of 15-30-15 fertilizer every two weeks through the growing season. In the fall, stems that have fallen over the crowns can be left in place to collect snow.

Cuttings are the most reliable way to get true-to-type plants (cuttings are sometimes available from horticultural society plant sales or perennial growers; most plants sold in nurseries are started from seed by wholesale growers). But growing delphiniums from seed is economical and not difficult. Because seeds sold today are many times removed from the original named varieties, many enthusiasts get seeds from the British Delphinium Society, which has some of the best new cultivars.

Start with fresh seed; store unopened packages in the refrigerator until you're ready to plant. Start seed in January under lights, using sterilized potting soil and covering seeds with a dusting of the soil. Keep seeds moist but not wet, and cover them

Staking

Tall delphiniums need support to survive wind and heavy rain. The most common way to stake plants is to insert three 120-centimetre bamboo poles 15 centimetres into the ground in a triangle around each plant as soon as shoots grow to about 20 centimetres in the spring. Make the triangle large enough to allow air to circulate. Tie a circle of twine around the three poles about 30 centimetres above the ground. Later in the season, add a second circle of string just below the flower spikes.

For extra sturdy support, rebar stakes can be used. Cut 6-metre lengths of rebar into three pieces and weld two rings taken from a chain to the rebar at the top and 60 centimetres below it. Place three rebar stakes around each plant, then thread bracing wire through the rings and twist the ends together, creating a sturdy cage.

Larkspur: The Annual Delphinium

Larkspurs (*Consolida ambigua* and *C. regalis*) have feathery leaves and several branching flower spikes in colours ranging from deep purple to pink, rose, salmon, white and, of course, blue. At one time larkspurs were classified as a species of delphinium, and their current genus name comes from the Latin word *consolidare* because herbalists believed the plants helped close wounds.

Larkspurs resent transplanting, so seed should be sown directly in the garden as soon as the ground is thawed. Plant in full sun and in rich soil. They perform best when summers aren't too hot. Plants can reach 120 centimetres and may need staking.

If conditions are favourable, larkspurs self-sow. Deadhead frequently to keep plants blooming, although this eliminates self-sown seedlings.

until they germinate—usually in one to three weeks. When seedlings have two sets of leaves, transplant to 10-centimetre pots and grow under lights or in a greenhouse or sunroom with lots of light. Harden plants off in a cold frame or by leaving them outdoors in a protected, shady place for increasing lengths of time each day; plant outside in mid-May.

It's also possible to propagate plants by taking cuttings from mature plants. Before fertilizing in the spring with 20-10-20 and when new growth is about 6 centimetres high, take cuttings from shoots 6 millimetres thick. Don't use stems that are hollow, and be sure to make your cut at crown level. Treat the cut end with a fungicide and a rooting hormone for softwood cuttings, sometimes labelled No. 1, and plant cuttings in a mixture of equal parts perlite and vermiculite in 10-centimetre pots. Once cuttings have developed roots, harden them off and plant as above.

Although generally sturdy and healthy, delphiniums are susceptible to slugs and mildew. Keep the area well weeded and mulched with wood chips to discourage slugs, which feed on leaves and new shoots. Some gardeners start applying slug bait while the plants are dormant; an organic alternative is to remove a bit of soil from around the crowns of the plants and replace it with a thin layer of sharp sand. A solution of 15 millilitres of Epsom salts in 4.5 litres of water sprayed on leaves and stems three times a year also deters slugs, snails and earwigs.

Bud-eating caterpillars are a particular problem for Prairie gardeners. They're the larvae of a moth (*Polychrysia moneta*) that normally feeds on native larkspurs but also likes delphiniums. Hand-pick larvae in summer and destroy.

Mildew is most likely to appear on leaves in midsummer, when nights are hot and steamy. Apply a fungicide according to package instructions, and promote good air circulation by thinning out half the shoots of mature plants when they appear in the spring, retaining the strongest four or five per plant.

Recommended varieties

Not all delphiniums are towering giants: some reach just a few feet and look more in scale in small gardens—they don't require staking, either. Most have finely dissected foliage. A favourite since it first appeared in 1907 is 'Blue Butterfly', a cross of *Delphinium grandiflorum* and *D. chinense*; it has large mid-blue flowers with green centres that bloom on bushy 30-centimetre plants. Long-blooming, light blue, single 'Belladonna', a cross of *D. grandiflorum* and *D. elatum* hybrids, is 60 centimetres tall; and because it's bushy, it doesn't require staking. In the same series is 'Bellamosa' (dark blue), 'Casa Blanca' (white) and 'Cliveden Beauty' (light blue).

The Pacific Giants hybrids bred one hundred years ago, which included the Round Table Series, were well known for dramatic colour and height. Although they're still available, seed quality has deteriorated and many plants bear little resemblance to the originals.

Slightly taller—75 to 90 centimetres—are hybrids in the exceptionally hardy Fountain Series, available in shades of brilliant blue, violet, lilac, rose and cream. Most can be found in nurseries, or can be started indoors from seed.

But the delphiniums that always draw the most attention are the tall hybrids of *D. elatum,* first bred in the early 1800s. Further breeding at the turn of the century produced more hybrids, but it wasn't until a Californian breeder, Frank Reinelt, developed his series of tall, dramatically coloured Pacific Giants in the 1950s that the *D. elatum* hybrids caught gardeners' fancies.

Until Pacific Giants came along, North American gardeners relied on the British and European hybrids (which were mainly blue or white); they were long-lived perennials in those parts of the world, but not so robust in North America. When grown in cold climates or where summers are hot and dry, they lasted only a few years. Reinelt's aim was to breed new hybrids with excellent double flowers that would come true from seed, while also expanding the range of colours in a seed strain. The best-known Pacific Giants, more than 2 metres tall, are in the Round Table Series—'Black Knight', dark blue with black centres; white 'Galahad'; mauve 'Guinevere'; and 'King Arthur', violet with dark centres.

Unfortunately, the seed quality of Pacific Giants wasn't maintained over the years, and plants grown from seed sold commercially today bear little resemblance to the originals. Their colours may be true, but plants sometimes produce irregular bloom spikes, or single or poorly formed flowers. But British horticulturists have built on Reinelt's work to produce their own new cultivars in a wide range of colours; today amateur growers have largely taken over the task of developing new delphiniums, with British amateurs leading the pack.

↑ Maiden pink (*D. deltoides*)

Dianthus

These scented, old-fashioned favourites are sturdy, no-fuss plants BY JO ANN GARDNER

Dianthus plants, commonly known as pinks, have long been cherished for their delicate beauty and spicy fragrance of sweet cloves. Their masses of flowers and handsome silvery blue or green foliage continue to find a welcome place in our gardens.

Wild species, antique pinks and older hybrids offer a variety of landscaping opportunities in beds, borders, rock gardens and containers. Breeders continue to create more heat- and drought-resistant, earlier- and longer-blooming forms. Fortunately, their characteristic spicy perfume has not been bred out of most new cultivars.

Belonging to the genus *Dianthus*, which comprises about 300 species, most of them from Eurasia, pinks thrive in full sun and light, well-drained, slightly alkaline soil. They bear flowers with crimped petals whose edges are fringed or serrated, as though cut with pinking shears, which may account for their common name.

Hardiness

Zones 2 to 5 depending on variety

Growing conditions

Full sun; light, well-drained slightly alkaline soil

Colour range

White; pink, rose, salmon, carmine, red; violet, purple

Bloom time

Late June, early July

Size

15 to 70 centimetres, depending on variety

↓ Sweet William (*D. barbatus*)

Dianthus are also called gillyflower, from the French *girofle*, for "clove." They were often grown by tavernkeepers, who used them to boost the flavour of wines.

'Snowfire', an annual Indian pink

D. gratianopolitanus 'Bath's Pink' ↑

History

The history of clove pinks (*D. caryophyllus*)—from which carnations are descended—is preserved in their colourful name. One of a group of scented flowers known generically as gilly flowers (from the French *girofle* for "clove"), they were prized by tavernkeepers, who raised them as a cheap way to flavour wines; they also came to be known as sops-in-wine.

Of European origin, cottage pinks (*D. plumarius*), introduced to England with the Norman Conquest, are sprawling plants suited to cottage gardens (as their name suggests). Blooming once in early summer, they bear a profusion of 2-centimetre-wide, feathery pink flowers on stems up to 23 centimetres tall, on clump-forming, bluish green foliage. Amateur breeding has extended the range of available colours, creating blooms with contrasting bands of colour around the edges and in the centre—forming a dark eye—and increased the number of petals.

Two noteworthy antique pinks are the 18th-century 'Inchmery'—rare but worth hunting for in specialty plant nurseries—with its double blooms of delicate blush pink and tolerance for heat and humidity (30 centimetres tall, Zone 4); and the legendary 'Mrs. Sinkins', a 19th-century double white with an almost overpowering fragrance and petals so profuse the flowers resemble little cabbages (20 centimetres tall, Zone 5).

↑ Sand pink (*D. arenarius*)

↑ *D. superbus* var. *longicalycinus* 'Primadona'

Pinks took on new life in the early 1900s when an English breeder, Montague Allwood, crossed cottage and clove pinks to some up with border pinks, botanically known as *Dianthus* x *allwoodii*. They come in a range of colours and forms, and are long blooming and beautifully scented.

Less hardy than cottage pinks but ever-blooming, carnations (named for their use in coronets—ornamental wreaths worn by women on formal occasions) are stiffer, taller (to 60 centimetres) and more erect, with narrow, grey-green leaves appearing at swollen intervals along wiry stems. The larger double flowers—in red, pink or white—held in a puffed calyx, are broad-petalled and serrated at their edges. Of Mediterranean origin, carnations are largely bred in North America as long-stemmed, and frequently unscented, florists' flowers. An exception is the *D. caryophyllus* Grenadin Series, hardy to Zone 5. 'Grenadin White' and 'King of the Blacks' (very dark red) are especially fragrant (both grow 50 centimetres high).

In the early 1900s, pinks took on new life when Montague Allwood, an English nurseryman, crossed cottage and clove pinks to produce border pinks (*Dianthus* x *allwoodii*). Though not quite as hardy as cottage pinks, they combine the best characteristics of both: large, carnation-like fringed flowers, long-blooming and well scented, in a range of colours and forms, some eyed and banded. Classics worth looking for are 'Doris', soft pink with a rose eye, and 'Helen', a luscious salmon-pink, vigorous and free-flowering, both 25 centimetres tall and hardy to Zone 3.

Growing

Pinks are short-lived perennials or biennials, so new plants need to be raised every few years, either by seed or, in the case of named cultivars, by division or cuttings.

Start seedlings indoors 8 to 10 weeks before planting outside. Cover lightly with soil or commercial seeding mix and maintain a soil temperature of 20°C. Freezing or soaking seeds is sometimes recommended, but seeds that are lightly covered with dampened soil, covered with thin plastic to maintain moisture and heated from below will germinate in 7 to 14 days.

Space plants outside according to their expected height and width. Add fine gravel to the soil to improve drainage and lime to reduce acidity, if necessary. Once plants are established, trim them carefully in early spring to encourage fresh growth. Clip stems after flowering to keep foliage fresh and stimulate rebloom.

To propagate from cuttings, pull off (don't cut, as this discourages rooting) side shoots after flowering, taking a bit of the main stem. Remove lower leaves, dip stem ends in rooting hormone powder and plant in a pre-dampened, light soil mix, then cover loosely with plastic and place in indirect light; shoots should root in about six weeks. (Check periodically to ensure moisture is being maintained.) Remove plastic and, after plants are growing well, transplant them to a cold frame or protected area outside for the winter, and then plant out the following spring.

↓ Cottage pinks (*D. plumarius*)

← *D. x allwoodii* 'Doris'

Quicktips

Pinks are low-maintenance plants, requiring only deadheading after their first flush of bloom to encourage reblooming. I have been growing them for more than 30 years and have never encountered disease or insect problems. Just keep the following in mind:

- Where summers are very hot and humid, give plants good air circulation by thinning overgrown clumps that could shelter insects.
- Never mulch pinks; this encourages moisture around the root crown and leads to untimely death.
- Protect plants over the winter with a covering of evergreen boughs.
- Plant in well-drained soil in open, sunny conditions.

Recommended varieties

For 25 years, I explored and experimented with pinks in my Zone 4 garden on Cape Breton Island. I've found that modern hybrids are hardier and more adaptable to unfavourable soil conditions.

D. plumarius Ballade Strain syn. *D.* 'Ballad Blend' formed vigorous clumps of silvery blue foliage in my garden, where soil was heavy, on the moist side and somewhat acidic—conditions that discourage true cottage pinks. By early summer, Ballade Strain had sent up a mass of straight stems reaching 38 centimetres, with flowers in a broad colour range—salmon, rose, red, pink and white—some banded, all with dark eyes. Very different from the petite, sprawling cottage pinks, these bold plants have a fragrance that's enticing, though not quite as heady as the cottage pinks. Their early-summer bloom complements the blues of lavender and catmint and the pink hues of old roses; there's modest rebloom in late summer. The spiky blue foliage is attractive throughout fall and winter.

I grew fringed pinks (*D. superbus*) and 'Rainbow Loveliness' (*D. allwoodii* x *D. superbus*) in containers by our front porch to enjoy their enveloping jasmine-like aroma (both varieties are 30 to 38 centimetres tall, Zone 3). Fringed pinks have feathery flowers ranging in colour from delicate lilac to white. Hybrid strains bear flowers so deeply fringed they appear as a haze of carmine, pink, lilac or white, some banded, all intensely fragrant.

Maiden pink (*D. deltoides*) makes up for its lack of scent by unstinting, dazzling bloom and a tough constitution; hardy to Zone 3, maiden pink blooms even in partial shade. Growing 15 centimetres tall from a low-growing, wide mat of tiny, bright green leaves, it erupts into a sheet of small, neon pink flowers in early summer that spill over rocks and the edges of my perennial border. Recent introductions, all hardy to Zone 3, have given this old favourite a new look and ever-blooming habit: 'Arctic Fire' (20 centimetres tall) is a dainty white form with a glowing cherry red eye; 'Flashing Light' (30 centimetres tall) is bright crimson with striking bright green foliage; 'Microchips Mix' (15 to 20 centimetres tall) blooms the first year from seed and displays masses of white, pink and purple flowers, all with dark eyes.

Similar pinks include the 20-centimetre-tall sand pink (*D. arenarius*), with fragrant, fringed white flowers, and the 30-centimetre-tall cheddar pink (*D. gratianopolitanus*), silvery blue foliage topped by a mass of clove-scented pink blooms, or rose in the cultivar 'Tiny Rubies' (10 centimetres tall).

Sweet William (*D. barbatus*) is distinguished from other pinks by its compact heads of tightly clustered, phlox-like flowers on stiff stems to 70 centimetres tall. Colours are brilliant shades of crimson, pink or white, often edged and eyed with contrasting colours; scent is light. Although it's a biennial—blooming the second year from seed—gardeners have observed that some strains grow as short-lived perennials and are more scented than others. A friend in Ontario reports that 'Newport Pink' (50 centimetres tall, Zone 3), an old strain, has survived five years in her garden and has a noticeable sweet aroma. Semi-dwarf 'Early Spring Messenger' (45 centimetres tall, Zone 3), blooming the first year from seed, is a boon where summers are short and windy.

A recent breed of hardy pink, a cross between sweet William and annual China pink, the Ideal Series has been widely acclaimed for its early bloom (10 to 15 days earlier than annual pinks), heat tolerance and ability to survive subzero winter temperatures as a biennial or short-lived perennial. In the Ideal Series (Zone 2) there is a wide range of colours, including splashy carmine, violet, pearl and salmon, as well as flowers with contrasting bands. Plants grow to 25 centimetres and look great at the front of a border. Shearing encourages a moderate bloom in late summer. 'Melody Pink', blooming the first year from seed, is a 2000 All-America Selection winner that grows to 45 centimetres over a mound of handsome green foliage, has spicy-scented fringed flowers of soft antique pink that bloom all summer into fall, and is resistant to heat and cold.

↑ Sweet William (*D. barbatus*)

Pinks grow as short-lived perennials (which means they last only a few years) or as biennials (which bloom their second year of growth and then die). For a continuous show, start new seeds every couple of years or propagate with cuttings.

↑ Yellow trout lily (*E. americanum*)

Hardiness

Zone 4

Growing conditions

Loose, moist soil enriched with humus

Colour range

White; light yellow to orange; rose to violet-purple

Bloom time

April and May

Size

20 to 30 centimetres, depending on variety

favouriteperennials

Erythroniums

Dainty flowers, dramatic foliage—what more can a spring garden ask? BY JOAN DE GREY

Erythroniums have inspired many rather peculiar common names, such as dog's tooth violet (although the plant is not a violet), trout lily, adder's tongue and fawn lily, but whatever you call them, they're terrific plants. They're underused garden treasures, and it's high time more attention was paid to them.

The name "erythronium" is a case of mistaken identity. It was originally the name for another plant, and is derived from the Greek word *erythros*, meaning "red," which has nothing to do with the colour of the plant's flowers.

They may look delicate when they're in bloom, but erythroniums are tough and long-lived. They love shady, woodland conditions, where they come into their own.

↑ *E.* 'Kondo'

↓ *E.* 'White Beauty'

Although they appear dainty and delicate in flower, erythroniums are tough, reliable and long-lived. Many in this family of perennial, spring-blooming bulbs are hardy to Zone 3. In shady locations, where other spring ephemerals struggle, erythroniums come into their own. Planted in rock or woodland gardens or under deciduous trees, they naturalize quickly in dappled sunlight or light shade and cover the ground with masses of blooms.

The foliage alone would be reward enough to grow these marvellous plants: the two strap-like broad leaves, which appear at ground level, are usually marbled or blotched with a contrasting colour. When the lovely, sometimes fragrant flowers appear, the plant really puts on a show. Each flower's six-pointed, recurved petals may be white, or shades of purple, pink or yellow; up to 10 pendant, lily-shaped blooms perch on top of each slender, arching stem. Try combining them with hellebores, ferns, trillium, moss, wood anemones, foamflower, bloodroot or other spring bulbs. Blooms can last as long as two weeks.

↑ *E.* 'Pink Pagoda'

↑ *E.* 'Pagoda'

Growing

Plant bulbs in late summer or early fall. Look for plump, fresh bulbs and plant as soon as they're purchased; do not let them dry out. Choose a partially shaded location with moist, humus-rich, well-drained soil, and plant with the bulb's pointed end down, 8 to 10 centimetres deep and 8 to 13 centimetres apart. Water erythroniums frequently and well during spring, less often in the summer when the plant is dormant.

Divide established plant clumps after they have flowered and the leaves have died down, generally by midsummer, or try propagating plants from seeds. Allow the seed pods to mature and the seeds to fall to the ground to self-sow, or pick the seed pods as soon as they have ripened. If picked, plant the ripened seeds in pots or a flat as soon as possible. Water sparingly during the summer months and plant where they are to grow in the garden after they've germinated and grown a set of true leaves. Be patient. Seedlings may take three to five years to mature and flower.

Erythroniums are relatively pest- and disease-free, though rust and fungal spots can occur. Squirrels are attracted to the buds and slugs enjoy munching on the leaves—your local garden centre or master gardener's association will have recommendations for protection against these unwelcome pests.

Recommended varieties

The original habitat of **European dog's tooth violet** (*E. dens-canis*) ranges from Europe through Asia. The plants have heavily marbled green-and-brown leaves with gorgeous, solitary flowers in white or shades of pink or lilac. They grow 10 to 15 centimetres tall and bloom in early spring; they are hardy to Zone 3.

Eastern trout lily, yellow adder's tongue and **yellow trout lily** are all common names for *E. americanum*, a short North American native with slightly to fully reflexed solitary bright sulfur-yellow flowers. It's considered one of the most beautiful examples of the species. The mid- to deep green leaves (10 to 15 centimetres tall) are mottled with rust brown markings. It blooms in early spring and is hardy to Zone 3.

E. tuolumnense is a California native that displays the brightest yellow flowers of any of the erythroniums, and puts forth up to four flowers per stem. The leaves of *E. tuolumnense*, which are pale to mid-green, are slightly mottled with brown. It grows to 20 to 35 centimetres, blooms in early spring and is hardy to Zone 3.

The cultivar 'White Beauty' has upright stems, each bearing up to three spectacular white flowers. Red dots form a ring around the stamens and mark the inside of the flowers. Leaves are dark green, mottled with purple-brown. 'White Beauty' is an exceptionally decorative addition to any semi-shaded garden. It grows 20 to 35 centimetres tall and blooms early to mid-spring; it's hardy to Zone 3.

'Pagoda', another hybridized

↑ White trout lily (*E. oregonum*)

Erythroniums are lovely little surprises when one comes upon them growing beside a garden path. Plant them under deciduous trees in dappled sunlight or in a rock garden.

Pink fawn lily (*E. revolutum*) →

variety, is readily available from bulb retailers. It's a vigorous and reliable perennial, with each stem bearing up to five sulfur-yellow flowers. The plant's leaves are a glossy deep green with a modest mottling of bronze. 'Pagoda' has distinctive brown markings around the stamens on the inside of the flowers, grows 15 to 25 centimetres high and blooms in mid-spring; it's hardy to Zone 4.

The natural habitat of white fawn lily, also commonly called white trout lily (*E. oregonum*), ranges from Oregon to British Columbia. It quickly creates a massive display of stunning, creamy white flowers with yellow centres. Each stem bears up to six flowers, which appear to float above the plant's green-and-brown mottled leaves. It grows 15 to 35 centimetres tall and blooms mid- to late spring; it's hardy to Zone 3.

The hybridized 'Kondo' has scented, pale lemon-yellow flowers that make it a wonderful addition to the garden. Its flowers, up to 10 per stem, dance above the plant's attractive, mid-green leaves, which are marbled with bronze. 'Kondo' is vigorous and can be invasive. It grows 15 to 35 centimetres tall and blooms in mid-spring; it's hardy to Zone 4.

Western trout lily, or pink fawn lily (*E. revolutum*), ranges in natural habitat from southwest British Columbia to northern California and it's considered to be one of the most beautiful erythroniums. Up to four lilac-pink flowers are carried per stem, and the handsome leaves are deep green mottled with brown. It grows 20 to 30 centimetres tall and blooms in mid-spring; it's hardy to Zone 5.

↓ *E. tuolumnense*

Native Erythroniums

As members of the lily family, erythroniums comprise a genus of about 20 species of rapidly spreading, clump-forming perennials. Most species are native to North America, with the exception of *E. dens-canis*, which is native to Europe, and *E. japonicum*, which is native to Japan.

E. albidum was once plentiful in central North America, but is now quite rare. Imagine early explorers encountering masses of native erythroniums in full bloom. In western North America, *E. revolutum* and *E. oregonum* have also become increasingly rare, while *E. propullans* and *E. elegans* are currently on the American endangered plant species list. These native plants should not be collected in the wild. Fortunately, cultivated erythronium bulbs are readily available from retail bulb suppliers and will perform better in your garden.

Groundcovers serve many purposes in a garden, from masquerading as a carpet to providing greenery and texture under a canopy of trees where grass won't grow.

↑ Green-and-gold *(Chrysogonum virginianum)*

SUGGESTIONS FOR SPECIAL LOCATIONS

Shade

European ginger; foamflower; sweet woodruff

Sun

Pussytoes, prairie smoke, thymes; prickly pear cactus

Colour

Creeping Jenny 'Aurea' (yellow foliage and flowers); bunchberry (white flowers, red berries); bugleweed 'Burgundy Glow' (deep blue flowers, scarlet, cream and green foliage)

Winter texture

Woolly thyme; bearberry; bergenia

Between pavers

Mother of thyme; Corsican mint; chamomile; Irish moss

Irish moss (*Sagina subulata*)

favouriteperennials

Groundcovers

The great problem-solvers of the garden BY FRANK KERSHAW

Groundcovers blanket bare ground in shady areas or in spots where grass won't grow. They keep the soil cool and free of weeds, and they protect the shallow roots and bark of trees from foot traffic and encroaching lawn mowers. They're ideal for difficult-to-mow areas such as steep banks, wet areas and rocky cottage properties. And there are so many groundcovers to choose from you can easily find one that's ideal for your garden.

↓ Sweet woodruff (*Galium odoratum*)

Most groundcovers are easily established and long-lived, spreading by creeping along the soil surface or by underground stems. They're reasonably priced and require little maintenance. Some of the best also exhibit multi-season interest, such as those with winter berries, or have attractive form and texture, or allow specimen plants to grow up through them for visual contrast and multi-tiered effects.

↑ European ginger *(Asarum europaeum)*

↑ Wood anemone *(Anemone nemerosa)*

↓ Bunchberry *(Cornus canadensis)*

Groundcovers look good planted in patches large enough to establish their presence and show texture and colour. For more visual interest, plant a fine-textured variety such as woolly thyme in large drifts with a plant that has bigger leaves, such as the shiny, paddle-shaped auricula primula.

Many species and cultivars, both native and non-native, serve a variety of functions. Groundcovers that weave around trees, shrubs and garden sculptures, for example, are an effective design element, linking these items together to provide a unified look. Used as edging plants, they provide a flowing cohesion in courtyards, pathways or borders.

Some groundcovers make excellent foils for star performers, emphasizing the colour, texture and form of showy plants: the lustrous green leaves of European ginger (*Asarum europaeum*) set off white trillium (*T. grandiflorum*), for example; the scarlet, cream and green foliage of 'Burgundy Glow' bugleweed (*Ajuga reptans*) highlights 'Palace Purple' coral bells (*Heuchera micrantha*); or a sheet of yellow stonecrop (*Sedum acre*) accents the nodding red-and-yellow heads of Eastern columbine (*Aquilegia canadensis*).

Low-growing groundcovers provide interesting contrasts to taller, bolder foliage plants—the tropical-like foliage of Jack-in-the-pulpit (*Arisaema atrorubens*) contrasted with the dainty whorled leaves of sweet woodruff (*Galium odoratum*), or the bold, rounded foliage of bergenia (*B. cordifolia*) floating in a sea of creeping Jenny (*Lysimachia nummularia,* 'Aurea') with its attractive yellow flowers in summer and small, shiny golden leaves. Fountain grass (*Pennisetum alopecuroides,* 'Hameln') and spiky Japanese bloodgrass

(*Imperata cylindrical,* 'Red Baron') look striking erupting out of a bed of ground-hugging mother-of-thyme (*Thymus serpyllum*).

Groundcovers of varying forms, textures and colours planted in large drifts add depth and dimension to a garden, particularly where finer-textured species recede into medium-textured ones. Try planting woolly thyme (*Thymus pseudolanuginosus*) with the waxy, paddle-shaped leaves of auricula primula (*P. auricula*). Or mix it with pink-flowering moss phlox (*P. subulata*) and bugleweed receding into taller barrenwort (*Epimedium* spp.). A favourite of mine is woolly thyme merging into dragon's blood sedum (*S. spurium*).

Not only does mixing groundcovers enhance the presence of each, but the right combination can combat weeds as the plants become established. Bruce Scott, head gardener at Casa Loma in Toronto, says when bearberry cotoneaster (*C. dammeri*) is interplanted with Virginia creeper (*Parthenocissus quinquefolia*), the latter species fills bare spots while the cotoneaster gets established, and thwarts weeds. In the fall, the dark green foliage of the cotoneaster accentuates the purplish red of the Virginia creeper; however, Scott cautions that Virginia creeper must be pruned to keep it from taking over.

On the east and west coasts, where cool, dampish, acid-type soils are common, many interesting native groundcovers can be combined effectively. Low-growing bunchberry (*Cornus canadensis*), a plant that looks like a dogwood tree growing over the ground, with an abundance of red berries in summer and striking purplish red foliage in fall, combines beautifully with other groundcovers such as bearberry (*Arctostaphylos uva-ursi*), wintergreen (*Gaultheria procumbens*), clintonia (*C. borealis*), haircap moss (*Polytrichum commune*) and oak fern (*Gymnocarpium dryopteris*).

As a design element, groundcovers soften rock outcrops, boulders, old walls and stumps, merging them with their surroundings. Climbing hydrangea (*H. anomela petiolaris*) and trumpet vine (*Campsis radicans*) have a similar effect if allowed to wander across the ground. Mayapple (*Podophyllum peltatum*), with its large, umbrella-like leaves, is an attractive foil at the base of a large outcrop of rock.

Gardeners faced with rocky outcroppings sometimes use smaller groundcovers, such as mossy stonecrop, thymes, Corsican mint (*Mentha requienii*), chamomile (*Anthemis nobilis,* 'Treneague') and various mosses, to trace intricate cracks and fissures in rocks that might otherwise go unnoticed.

A groundcover that deserves more attention is moss. Many people consider it something to eradicate rather than encourage, but because moss thrives in damp shade and acid-type soils where grasses generally do poorly, it's ideal for creating a cool, tranquil woodland mood. Use it to edge and fill gaps in flagstone paths, or even as the walkway itself, provided it's not subjected to heavy traffic. Moss also acts as a kind of calendar, responding to changes in moisture and sun and signalling the approach of different seasons. To keep moss looking good throughout the summer, water or mist it several times a week, and pull invasive weeds or tree seedlings, which use it as an incubator.

↑ Redwood sorrel *(Oxalis oregana)*

Growing

Once established, groundcovers generally require little maintenance. But to thrive and spread, plants need their preferred habitat; even aggressive groundcovers won't do well under adverse conditions. Success begins with choosing the right site and preparing the soil properly. It's important to get it right the first time; trying to fix the soil or drainage later is disruptive. Correct plant spacing is also essential for best coverage and to avoid weeds. I tend to plant a little closer than recommended to ensure early, continuous coverage.

Applying a mulch at the time of planting is crucial. A 3-centimetre mulch between newly set-out plants helps to conserve moisture and keep out weeds—critical with slow-spreading groundcovers like bearberry and European ginger. Over the years, I've used many different mulches, but I prefer pea gravel because it's easy to replace, doesn't decompose or take nutrients out of the soil, stays cool and moist on the underside and deters slugs better than wood-based mulches. As plants knit together it becomes invisible. Groundcovers that require a dry crown, such as the pretty green-and-gold *Chrysogonum virginianum* and prairie smoke (*Geum triflorum*), thrive in stone mulches.

Water the plants to promote root and stem spread while they're getting established, but don't overdo it; moisture on the foliage contributes to rot and attracts slugs. If slugs are a problem, particularly with hostas, gingers and bergenias, you may need to set up slug traps or barriers.

In most cases, groundcovers don't require supplemental feeding. In woodland conditions, decomposing leaf litter is often sufficient, and groundcovers also benefit when adjacent turf or perennials are fertilized. If using a gravel mulch, apply a balanced fertilizer once a year.

Winter sometimes takes its toll on shallow-rooted groundcovers like crested dwarf iris (*I. cristata*), bloodroot (*Sanguinaria canadensis*), wood strawberries (*Fragaria vesca*) and coral bells (*Heuchera* spp.). Alternating freeze-thaw cycles can dislodge the roots, bringing them to the surface where they dry out and die. Avoid planting in low spots that collect water. Winterburn, particularly on barrenwort and ivies, also takes a toll if snow cover is minimal. Cover groundcovers with evergreen boughs to reduce damage, and prune out dead foliage in the spring. Be careful not to injure stem tissue, and try not to dislodge plants when raking around them.

Some groundcovers, such as wintergreen, bergenia and thymes, maintain their foliage all winter, although it might take on a bronzy tinge. Others die back but shoot up in spring with tall stems of dainty flowers.

↓ Wintergreen *(Gaultheria procumbens)*

↓ Foamflower (*Tiarella cordifolia*)

↑ Bunchberry (*Cornus canadensis*)

Some groundcovers tend to grow very dense over time, resulting in smaller leaves and a weedy look. Species such as bergenia, armeria, ivies and mayapples may need to be divided to rejuvenate them. Others, like 'Emerald Gaiety' euonymus (*E. fortunei*), may require pruning to remove green leaves of the parent species that often appear on variegated cultivars. A late-summer trimming or pruning also spruces up groundcovers that are getting leggy and weedy. Lamium, aubrieta, anthemis, creeping Jenny, artemisia, arabis, euonymus, ericas and moss phlox benefit from trimming during the growing season to keep them attractive.

Recommended varieties

THE WEST COAST

American barrenwort (*Vancouveria hexandra*), a native plant, grows 30 to 45 centimetres tall, with attractive white flowers (sepals, really) that reflex to reveal yellow stamens, presenting an inside-out look. Its glossy green foliage is divided into three leaflets, resembling maidenhair ferns from a distance. This dependable shade species spreads quickly by underground stems, likes acid-type soils of coniferous forests and combines well with ferns and wildflowers. It's hardy to Zone 7.

Piggyback plant (*Tolmiea menziesii*), an attractive native evergreen groundcover 10 to 25 centimetres tall, thrives in shade to semi-shade in moist coniferous forest conditions. It has five to seven lobed, heart-shaped leaves that resemble foamflower, and small, reddish brown flowers that bloom from May to June, with recurved petals sitting atop 40- to 60-centimetre stems. Buds at the leaf bases often develop into new plants where they touch the ground—therefore, its common name. It's hardy to Zone 6.

'Vancouver Gold' broom (*Genista pilosa*) is a non-native plant, 15 to 30 centimetres tall, that was introduced by the University of British Columbia Botanical Garden. It has striking golden yellow, pea-like flowers in late spring and early summer, which hide the small, dark green leaves. Used extensively on banks and even as a lawn substitute, it thrives in full sun and well-drained soils and is hardy to Zone 4.

Redwood sorrel (*Oxalis oregana*) is a native plant, 5 to 15 centimetres tall, with shamrock-like foliage and white or purple flowers in spring that combine beautifully with ferns, azaleas, rhododendrons and trilliums. It does well in moist, humus-rich coniferous and deciduous forest areas, but can be invasive, spreading quickly by a surface-creeping stem, so be prepared to control it. It's hardy to Zone 4.

Irish moss (*Sagina subulata*) is a non-native, dark green mosslike plant 5 centimetres tall, with small, starlike white flowers in summer. Large sheets of it appear in acid, well-drained conditions. It's useful as an edging plant or between flagstones. It needs some shade, especially in the afternoon; keep moist. It's hardy to Zone 4.

Western wild ginger (*Asarum caudatum*) is 15 to 25 centimetres tall, with heart-shaped, dark green foliage and brownish red, urn-shaped flowers that hug the ground. Once established, this native plant spreads quickly by an underground fleshy stem. Suitable for light to deep shade and moist, humus-rich soils, it's excellent with woodland wildflowers or as a mass planting under a grove of trees. It's hardy to Zone 5.

THE PRAIRIES

Cranesbill geraniums (*Geranium macrorrhizum*) are non-native, up to 30 centimetres tall, with light green, maple-shaped foliage and showy, musky-scented magenta to clear pink flowers in June. This drought-tolerant species spreads quickly by fleshy underground stems and does well in sun or shade. Its tussock shape and textured foliage are attractive through the summer; use in a mass planting or combined with hostas for a bold effect. It also thrives under maples and other shallow-rooted trees and is hardy to Zone 3.

Pussytoes (*Antennaria dioca* var. *rosea*) is an attractive native alpine plant that grows to 15 centimetres, with grey foliage and rosy pink flowers that appear in spring and early summer. A plant that does well in full sun and dry, sandy, low-fertility soils, it's useful in rockeries, between flagstones and sometimes as a lawn substitute. It's hardy to Zone 2.

Prairie buttercup (*Ranunculus rhomboideus*) is a native plant with oval basal foliage and glossy yellow flowers in May. It grows 8 to 20 centimetres tall and does well in full sun and well-drained soils. Sometimes it can be effective on open slopes and in rock gardens; it's often combined with alumroot and prairie phlox. It's hardy to Zone 2.

Prickly pear cactus (*Opuntia* spp.), a native plant, 10 to 15 centimetres tall, has prickly oval pads and brilliant yellow flowers in summer. It spreads by small wiry roots and requires full sun and sandy soils with excellent drainage. A spectacular addition to a rockery, it can also be used on its own in a raised bed. It's hardy to Zone 5.

Alumroot (*Heuchera richardsonii*) does well in open areas and partly shady woodlands, growing up to 60 centimetres. A native plant, it has greenish white flowers on leafless stalks and attractive foliage somewhat similar to foamflower. It's often combined with shooting star, columbine and flowering spurge and is hardy to Zone 3.

Prairie smoke (*Geum triflorum*) is a rugged native, up to 30 centimetres tall, with hairy stems and abundant, deeply cut leaves that hug the ground. Flowers have red sepals and pink petals, followed by showy hairs on fruiting heads that look like a puff of pink smoke. Plants produce blooms and seed heads in May. It prefers full sun and low-nutrient soils with good drainage. Popular as a mass planting at the front of a border, in rockeries or as sheet planting in open areas, it spreads by a woody underground stem that fans out in many directions. It's hardy to Zone 2.

GREAT LAKES REGION

Foamflower (*Tiarella cordifolia*) is a native spring bloomer, 15 to 25 centimetres tall, with showy white flowers and maple-like leaves that turn an attractive bronze in the fall. It spreads moderately fast by

Mother-of-thyme (*Thymus serphyllum*) ↑

Mother-of-thyme (*Thymus serphyllum*), left, is sometimes used in place of turfgrass. It spreads rapidly and thrives in full sun. Once established, groundcovers usually thrive with little maintenance. But they need to be planted in conditions they require—sun or shade, moist or dry soil.

surface-creeping stems and prefers light shade and a humus-rich soil. It combines beautifully with native columbines, ferns, dwarf bleeding hearts, blue phlox and spring bulbs, particularly muscari. It's hardy to Zone 3.

Sweet woodruff (*Galium odoratum*) is a non-native herb, 15 to 20 centimetres tall, with leaves in whorls of 8 and white, starlike flowers in spring. A moderately fast spreader by surface-creeping stems, it favours humus-rich woodland soils, but also grows in dry shade and even clay soils. Its fine texture contrasts well with the bolder foliage of bloodroot, Jack-in-the-pulpit and hostas. It's hardy to Zone 4.

Barrenwort (*Epimedium* spp. and cvs.) is a popular choice because of its attractive heart-shaped leaves that remain on the plant in mild winters. It's non-native, 20 to 30 centimetres tall, with hooded flowers in spring that resemble miniature bishop's hats. Flower colours range from red to white to sulfur yellow, depending on the species and hybrids. It spreads moderately fast by surface or underground stems, again depending on the species, and prefers moist, humus-rich woodland soils, but also does well in dry shade, even under Norway maples. It's excellent for planting on banks with columbines, Virginia bluebells, forsythia, trilliums, spring bulbs and ferns. It's hardy to Zone 5.

European ginger (*Asarum europaeum*) is non-native, 8 to 18 centimetres tall, with dark green, waxy leaves. It spreads quickly by underground stems and prefers humus-rich, moist soils but tolerates dry shade. Ideal for woodland gardens, it's also a good edging plant, combining nicely with Japanese-painted ferns, astilbes and bugleweed. It's hardy to Zone 3.

Green-and-gold *Chrysogonum virginianum* is native to the eastern United States, but worth trying in Canada's more temperate areas. Up to 22 centimetres tall, with showy yellow, daisylike flowers atop a mat of spoon-shaped foliage, this choice species spreads quickly by underground stems, and does well in sun or shade, blooming throughout the summer in sunnier sites. It's excellent for defining cracks in rocks, lining a path or in combination with eastern columbines and trilliums and it's hardy to Zone 6.

Wood anemone (*A. nemerosa*) is non-native, 15 to 22 centimetres tall, with dramatic starry white, rose or purplish flowers suspended above green cleft foliage in spring. It spreads moderately fast by wiry underground stems, and thrives in humus-rich woodland soils in full to part shade. It naturalizes beautifully with trout lilies, red trilliums, Virginia bluebells and spring bulbs and is hardy to Zone 3.

THE EAST COAST

Bunchberry (*Cornus canadensis*), a native plant up to 20 centimetres, looks like a miniature dogwood tree, with showy white flowers (bracts) in late spring, whorled foliage that turns an attractive

Bearberry (*Arctostaphylos uva-ursi*) ↑

Some groundcovers creep along, keeping a low profile a couple of inches above the surface of the soil, while others, such as prickly pear cactus or cranesbill, have a more emphatic presence. Groundcovers can soften rocky outcroppings or bare areas of a garden better than grass and they need no mowing.

Prickly pear cactus (*Opuntia* spp.) ↓

bronze in the fall and brilliant red berries in late summer. Somewhat slow to get established, it spreads by shallow underground stems and forms large colonies in favourable conditions, such as shaded, moist, acid soils, where there are cool root runs. Often it's used with blueberries, painted trilliums, sorrel, laurels and rhododendrons, and around stumps and logs in a woodland garden. It's hardy to Zone 2.

Bearberry (*Arctostaphylos uva-ursi*) is a native, creeping evergreen shrub that can spread up to 4 metres. It has small, paddle-shaped bright green foliage that turns bronze in the fall; bell-shaped white or pink spring flowers are followed by red berries. Requiring dry, sandy soils in part to full sun, it's useful on rocky slopes or in cracks in rocks, and is a good groundcover under pines, spruce and oaks. This plant is slow to get started but worth the wait. It's hardy to Zone 2.

Wintergreen (*Gaultheria procumbens*) is a low-growing native plant, up to 10 centimetres, with glossy, dark oval leaves that taste of wintergreen. Bell-shaped white flowers in late summer are followed by red berries. It spreads slowly by surface-creeping stems, likes full or part shade, and is often used around stumps and logs in woodland gardens or under pines and other conifers. It's hardy to Zone 3.

Purple Labrador violet (*Viola labradorica*), a small but striking native plant, is 10 to 15 centimetres tall, with low tufts of purple-tinged leaves and purple flowers that bloom in spring and again in the fall. It prefers semi-shade and moist, well-drained soils. Often used around rock outcrops and in woodland gardens, it's hardy to Zone 4.

Mother-of-thyme (*Thymus serphyllum*) is a low-growing, mat-like non-native plant that grows up to 5 centimetres tall, with dark green aromatic foliage and dainty mauve to rosy-coloured flowers in summer. A fast spreader—it moves out to 30 centimetres—it thrives in full sun and sandy, well-drained soils. It's frequently used on dry banks and in rockeries, or to fill gaps in flagstone walkways, edge paths or even replace lawns and is hardy to Zone 5.

Troublesome Varieties

Some groundcovers are too successful, flourishing so vigorously that they exclude other plants. Most problematic are those that form underground root mats that choke out other plants and are next to impossible to remove. Consider the consequences before planting Canada anemone (*A. canadensis*), silverweed (*Potentilla anserina*), harebell (*Campanula rotundifolia*), goutweed (*Aegopodium podograria*), lily-of-the-valley (*Convallaria majalis*) or ribbon grass (*Phalaris arundinacea picta*).

Trumpet vine, a native vine with attractive scarlet trumpets, can be a rampant spreader, popping up many metres from the parent plant. But it's useful at dry, sandy cottage properties. It's possible to limit the spread of these rampant growers by burying flexible metal material at least 30 centimetres deep around the roots to confine them.

An emerging concern is the spread of non-native groundcovers such as periwinkle (*Vinca minor*), Japanese spurge (*Pachysandra terminalis*), bugleweed, goutweed and English ivy (*Hedera helix*), which may invade woodlots and displace native plants. Sometimes this happens because people transplant them to their weekend retreats in rural areas, not realizing how quickly they'll spread and threaten other plants. It's important to watch out for this; remove them if it appears they're becoming too entrenched—by digging them out or, as a last resort, using a herbicide such as Roundup to control them. Unfortunately, hand-pulling or even digging doesn't always kill all the roots. Removing seed heads before seeds disperse helps, but there's still the problem of remaining roots. Restore the area as quickly as possible with the plants suited to that environment.

Hellebores

The Christmas or Lenten rose jump-starts the spring garden BY JUDITH ADAM

↑ Christmas rose (*H. niger*)

↑ Christmas rose (*H. niger*)

↑ Lenten rose (*H. orientalis*)

Anticipation is sometimes the greater part of gardening. In winter, we linger by windows searching for emerging green shoots that are still weeks away. But thankfully, some cold-loving plants share our enthusiasm. The hellebores family (*Hellebores* spp.) is one—and just what we need to make an early start on the season.

History

The most widely grown hellebores are commonly called Christmas or Lenten roses, and they have long been associated with magical powers and protection from evil spirits. Clumps of hellebores guarded medieval cottage doors from witchcraft, and cattle were blessed with garlands of hellebore flowers to protect them from spells and diseases. The ancients considered hellebore a cure for insanity, and sad souls afflicted with "the melancholy" were treated with drops of *helleborin*, a toxic derivative of hellebore roots that could end melancholy rather permanently. The poisonous properties of the plant were well known to

Hardiness	Growing conditions	Colour range	Bloom time	Size
Zones 5 to 7, depending on variety	Light or partial shade to moderate sunlight; well-drained but moist soil with added humus	White to pale green; pink to reddish mauve and purple	March to mid-spring, depending on variety; January in Zone 7	30 to 45 centimetres, depending on variety

↑ Not for Calgary climate

Hellebores are native to woodsy, grassy and rocky sites in Europe and Western Asia; only in the past few years have they been readily available in Canada.

nten rose (*H. orientalis*)

↑ *H. orientalis*, purple form

↑ *H. foetidus*

↑ *H. orientalis* 'Ashwood Garden'

Like many plants before them, hellebores have been discovered by hybridizers, and new cultivars of different colours and combinations are slowly becoming available.

the ancients, and its botanical name is taken from the Greek words *hellein* ("to kill") and *bora* ("food"), indicating its toxic effect.

The Christmas rose (*Helleborus niger*) was also known as the black hellebore—"so called because its heart, or root, is black, while its face shines with a blazing white innocence, unknown to the truly pure of heart," according to 19th-century botanist Reginald Farrer.

Hellebores are indigenous to woodland, grassy and rocky sites from central Europe to western Asia, and we can be forgiven for not knowing them better. Gardeners in the mid-20th century had great difficulty locating hellebores and cherished the few fat clumps in their gardens. Louise Beebe Wilder, the garden author who celebrated her suburban lot in a series of books, despaired (in 1931) of acquiring particular species of *Helleborus*: ". . . our dilemma being to lay our hands upon any at all. Indeed, it takes a good deal of scouting about in the dogged way common to gardeners on the trail of a desired treasure." Fortunately, Ms. Wilder's tenacious plant hunting eventually stimulated the market for hellebores, and they are well represented in garden centres and mail-order catalogues today. And what better way to jump-start the gardening season than with the gleaming white petals and golden anthers of the Christmas rose, or the speckled pink-to-plum heads of the Lenten rose (*H. orientalis*).

Growing

When grown in the comparatively mild winters of England and Italy, the Christmas rose lives up to its name by blooming in the month of December. In areas of Canadian Zone 7, the plants may bloom in January. But the deeper frost of Zones 5 and 6 keeps *H. niger* snugly in the ground until early March, when fat white buds burst through the melting snow to open before new leaves are apparent. The Lenten rose follows toward the end of March, extending flower stalks and leaves together to make a graceful clump of nodding flowers that last four to six weeks in the garden.

Hellebores are valued for more than their blossoms. Their deeply divided foliage, with leathery texture and artfully serrated edges, is distinctive all season in garden borders or massed in groups to fill a small space. In spring the Christmas rose is a good companion to the earliest blooming shrubs, its gleaming white flowers standing under the mauve-pink February daphne (*Daphne mezereum*) or the delicate yellow Cornelian cherry (*Cornus mas*). Hellebores are valuable accessories to foundation plantings around windows, steps and doorways, complementing dwarf evergreens such as dwarf Alberta spruce, Globe blue spruce, groundcover junipers and boxwoods. Clusters of small bulbs

↓ *H. orientalis*

such as snow crocus, snowdrops (*Galanthus*), squills (*Puschkinia*) and glory of the snow (*Chionodoxa*) can be clustered with hellebores and evergreen shrubs to make a complete spring display. The Lenten rose is also a strong anchor to slightly later groups of cowslips (*Primula veris*), deep blue Siberian squills (*Scilla siberica*), Virginia bluebells (*Mertensia virginica*) and the checkered bells of snake's head fritillary (*Fritillaria meleagris*).

The availability of various kinds of hellebores has improved in recent years, although named hybrids are slow to appear in the market. The basic white species of *H. niger* is easy to obtain, and frequently subspecies with slight variations in the flowers (pink flushed petals or red markings in the stamens) are sold under the same name. Greater variability is seen in the colouring of *H. orientalis*—pale to muddy pink, deep speckled pink or even darkest maroon. More frequently, the *H. orientalis* hybrids are offered as colour groups indicating basic characteristics, such as pink with speckles, deep red shades or plum-black. To be certain of flower colour, it's best to purchase plants in bloom at a local garden centre, although mail-order plants are true to description. Most *H. orientalis* flower stems have streaks or flushes of colouring, and if the flower petals have fallen, the stems with deepest colouring indicate darker-coloured flowers.

↑ *H. niger*

↑ *H. orientalis*

The gardener's heart fairly leaps to see how comfortable hellebores are in Zones 5 to 7 (and in Zone 4, if positioned out of winter wind), and their resilient adaptability to a wide variety of conditions. They are natural plants of the forest edge and prefer slightly alkaline soil conditions with a pH rating of 7.0. Hellebores are long-lived plants and will successfully produce flowers and ornamental foliage in light shade conditions, as well as partial shade and up to half a day of direct sunlight. Old and long-established clumps can put up 30 to 40 flower stems, but even young plants will give you a stem or two of blossoms in spring.

Like most herbaceous perennials they grow best in soil that is consistently moist and amended with organic material, although they will tolerate gravelly soil or clay with enrichments of compost, aged manure and peat moss. Avoid poor drainage—it can slow plant growth and cause root rot. In heavy soil, improve drainage by digging sharp sand and fine grit or 5-millimetre gravel into the bed.

↓ *H. orientalis* 'Early Purple'

The easygoing hellebores will bloom in light to partial shade or in a spot with up to half a day of sun. They grow in gravelly or clay soil, but thrive with added organic material. Roots will rot in soil that's poorly drained.

Looking after hellebores is simple; they prefer easily obtained organic foods. A 5-centimetre layer of compost or aged manure over their roots in spring and a similar mulch of shredded or small leaves in autumn is all the nutrition they require. Their leaves are semi-evergreen in mild climates, but heavy winter snow cover will damage them enough to warrant their complete removal in spring before the flowers open.

Hellebores will tolerate short periods of drought, but shouldn't be expected to sustain themselves in dry soil for extended periods. Water frequently enough during the growing season to keep their soil sponge-damp. Hellebores prefer to remain undisturbed for many years, but choice, large clumps can be lifted after flower-

↑ *H. purpurascens*

ing and their tuber-like roots cut into divisions. The best method for propagating new plants is by transplanting self-sown seedlings, found around the bases of the mother plants.

Recommended varieties

H. argutifoliu is a 60-centimetre perennial that forms semi-woody stems; it may be short-lived in the garden. Its ornamental leaves are deeply serrated and veined. The pale green flowers appear in early spring. It requires light shade and a protected position with ordinary garden soil and is hardy to Zone 7.

H. atrorubens blooms in mid-spring with outward-facing, dark plum flowers. The 40-centimetre woodland plant grows wild in the northwest Balkan region, and it appreciates moist, loamy soil and partial shade. It's hardy to Zone 5.

H. foetidus is sometimes called the "stinking hellebore" because its broken stems and foliage have a slight odour; it can reach 45 centimetres high. It's native to Britain and thrives in partial shade with rich organic soil, but it can be short-lived in Canadian conditions. The deeply divided, dark green leaves are carried low, with thick flowering stems pushing up in early to mid-spring. 'Wester Flisk' is a famous hybrid with small greenish white flowers held in pendant clusters that is hardy to Zone 6.

H. purpurascens has leaves that die down completely in winter. The flower buds push up in early spring, with blossoms that nod downward and are purple outside with a green flush on the interior. The 30-centimetre plant is found in grassy alpine meadows and regions of Eastern Europe. It grows well in part-sun locations with average garden soil and is hardy to Zone 5.

↑ *H. foetidus* 'Wester Flisk'

Starting from Seed

Hellebores are simple to grow from seed if you understand their ways. Allow the flowers to age on the plant and develop the seed capsules, which eventually bend toward the ground. Keep in mind that seedlings won't be identical to hybrid parents.

The seeds are easy to germinate if they are fresh (but difficult if allowed to age and dry), so watch carefully for the capsules to ripen and crack open. Plant the seeds directly into a prepared garden bed or in small pots with soilless mix, and keep them moist. Germination will occur in about six to eight weeks.

Seeds planted in pots should be put into the ground before winter, even if not yet germinated (sink the whole pot into the soil). Self-sown seedlings from the previous year can often be found under the leaf "skirts" of mother plants, and these can be carefully transplanted to more spacious quarters where they will flower in their third year.

Hens and Chicks

Their precise rosettes, arranged in mathematical whorls, are a pleasure to behold

↑ *S.* 'Purple Beauty'

Echeveria with *Sempervivum* spp. ↑

← *Echeveria* in bloom

Hardiness

Zones 4, 5

Growing conditions

Sun, dry or gravelly soil

Colour range

Leaf rosettes in grey, bright to dull green, and rose to red; occasional flowers in yellow, pink or rose

Bloom time

Flower spikes appear mid-to late summer on established mother plant

Size

4 to 7.5 centimetres tall; spreads up to 75 centimetres

The common name hens and chicks also applies to *Echeveria*, a tender succulent with an otherworldly presence. Like *Sempervivum*, it grows in whorls and builds colonies of baby plants. *Echeveria* is a good edging or rock garden plant, and combines well with *Sempervivum* in containers. But winter plants over indoors, in low light and with minimal water.

BY LORRAINE HUNTER

I've tried many different plants in my clay strawberry pot, but it wasn't until I planted hens and chicks (*Sempervivum* spp.) that I finally achieved success; they grew happily in it all season long.

Hens and chicks—also affectionately known as semps—are delightful plants. These low-growing perennials range from less than 1 centimetre in diameter to more than 10 centimetres, and clumps can spread up to 76 centimetres wide, making them ideal groundcovers. There are well over 60 species, some with white hairs covering their leaves, resembling a dense spider's web. Semps form compact clumps of rosettes in shades of green, red, purple, pink, yellow or grey. They are usually available in the alpine section of your local garden centre from spring until autumn.

Originating in the wilds of southern Europe, North Africa and western Asia, where they live under harsh conditions at high altitudes, semps can withstand temperature extremes. Many are hardy to Zone 4. They present themselves well grown singly or in mixed groups of different colours and will thrive in rockeries, raised beds and even narrow beds beside the house. They also flourish when planted in terra-cotta pots, troughs, old logs, bricks or even the hollow pockets of concrete building blocks. Another good place to grow them is on a low roof, such as a shed. In Germany hens and chickens were grown on the roof to protect the household from lightning, and today they're a common plant used in European green-roofs, which help control rainwater drain-off and add insulation to both homes and business buildings.

Growing

Well-drained soil is essential for semps and can be attained by adding grit (sand or small particles of stone) and gravel to a store-bought potting mix. To deter slugs, top-dress containers or the soil around outdoor pots with sharp grit gently pushed under the rosettes. Semps benefit from a light feeding of fertilizer, such as pelleted chicken manure, once or twice a year, but don't put the pellets on the rosettes or you risk damaging the little plants.

Though semps will grow in shade, they require full sun to bring out the rich colour of their rosettes. Make sure they're not overshadowed by other plants—this may also prevent full colour development. Whether they grow indoors or out, winter is their dormant period, so keep semps quite dry during this period. In spring and summer, water when dry.

Semps have a profound ability to survive drought and display dazzling progressive colour changes throughout the year. Hues fade in winter, but their brilliance returns in sunnier spring and summer weather. Rosette sizes and shapes also vary. Even individual leaf shapes are different; some are fat and globular, others short and pointed, or long and tapered.

Fire-Resistant Semps

The botanical name *Sempervivum* means "always alive." Even rosettes left dry and without soil for several months usually survive and grow rapidly as soon as suitable conditions are provided.

The leaves of *Sempervivum* are succulent and retain water. In Britain they're known as houseleeks because the Welsh used to plant them in thatched roofs to help prevent fire damage. This was also a common practice throughout much of Europe, and is reflected in the green-roof projects of today. In the past, offshoots were planted, with a minuscule amount of soil, into gaps between thatching, lumber or roof tiles; in some areas today whole roofs are planted with small plants, including semps, to prevent fast runoff of rainwater and to insulate the building.

← Cobweb sempervivum (*S. arachnoideum*)

↑ Cobweb bloom (*S. arachnoideum*)

↑ *Echeveria* spp.

Hardy hens and chicks are native to harsh conditions at high altitudes, and can withstand extreme heat and drought. They perform well as groundcovers or in dry areas beside a house, as well as in the crevices between rocks.

Hens and chicks are so named because of the way they reproduce vegetatively. The "mother hen" (the main rosette) is surrounded by small replicas of herself, the "chicks," which are often borne on the ends of long, trailing stems, or stolons. The chicks can either be left to root around the main plant, where they will form a cushion of rosettes, or detached and grown separately.

After two or three years, the mother hen produces a quite spectacular flower spike up to 15 centimetres high, showing white or pink flowers. Once it matures and dries, it can be easily pulled away. The mother rosette dies after flowering, but the chicks eventually become mother hens themselves, producing their own chicks.

Semps hardy to Canada are generally considered trouble-free, long-lived plants without major pests or disease problems. When they're grown indoors, however, they are susceptible to mealy bugs.

Recommended varieties

There are so many species and hybrids that cultivars are often not labelled. However, there are two main species.

Sempervivum arachnoideum, also known as the spiderweb or cobweb houseleek, forms a low rosette that spreads up to 25 centimetres wide and becomes densely covered with cobweb-like, white threads. The plant develops bright pink to rose red flowers in early summer and is hardy to Zone 5. Examples include 'Canada Kate', whose velvety green-and-red leaves have tiny tufts of hair on the tip, and 'Cobweb Capers', whose rich green leaves are tipped with white hair.

S. tectorum is also known as a houseleek or roof houseleek. Its spoon-shaped, bright to mid-green leaves form rosettes up to 7.5 centimetres high. During midsummer it bears purple flowers on 15- to 23-centimetre-high stems and is hardy to Zone 4. Examples include 'Donar Rose', a medium-sized variety with green leaves washed with rose, while 'Purple Beauty' has blue-green leaves shaded and tipped in red.

Irises

An illustrious and dependable family of Old World species and modern hybrids

BY MARLENE ORTON

↑ *I. germanica*, unnamed cultivar

Like Las Vegas showgirls, tall bearded irises sweep to centre stage in June and July with a dazzling explosion of colour. The most spectacular members of the iris family (*Iris* spp.), they stand proudly in colourful borders resembling long, luscious chorus lines—flamboyant lovers of the limelight. You can almost hear the accompanying fanfare.

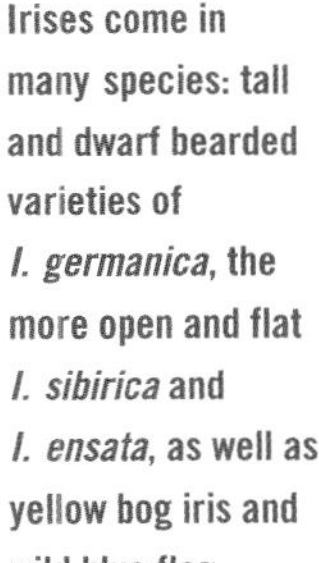

Irises come in many species: tall and dwarf bearded varieties of *I. germanica*, the more open and flat *I. sibirica* and *I. ensata*, as well as yellow bog iris and wild blue flag.

History

Botanically known as *Iris germanica*, tall bearded irises were a favourite of Impressionist painter Claude Monet, who painted them in his famous garden at Giverny, in France, where he settled in 1883. But they're just one branch of a noble and illustrious family. Like Iris, the Greek goddess of the rainbow from whom they get their name, irises come in every shade under the sun, and in more than 20,000 varieties, including Old World species whose lineage is evident in art and heraldry dating back nine centuries or more. (Quebec's flag of blue fleurs-de-lys is actually *I. versicolor*—the wild blue flag iris—that fills bogs and moist meadows in

Hardiness	Growing conditions	Colour range	Bloom time	Size
Most to Zone 3; some to Zone 8	Sun and dry soil or some shade and moist conditions, depending on variety	Many shades and combinations of white, blue, purple, pink, yellow	May to July, depending on variety	20 centimetres to 1.5 metres, depending on variety

↑ *I. germanica* 'Snow Mound'

↑ *I. germanica 'Carnaby'*

Many gardeners are loyal to old favourites, such as the stunning bi-colour on the facing page, an unnamed cultivar. But no wonder—in return, irises offer loyalty in the form of dependable bloom combined with no-demand care.

Quebec and throughout northeastern North America.)

Some modern favourites, such as *I. ensata*, or Japanese iris, have a history, too. Popular on estates on the U.S. eastern seaboard in the late 1800s until the Depression, when the wealthy could no longer afford to pamper the exotic beauties, Japanese irises didn't make their return to North America until long after the Second World War.

Irises have always commanded love and loyalty, it seems—and they're still doing it. Tom Johnson, a dairy farmer in Bashaw, Alberta, 90 kilometres southeast of Edmonton, was captivated by bearded irises in his early twenties when he saw some stunning ones on a catalogue cover. "Irises weren't all that appealing to me when I was growing up," he says. "But that catalogue showed pictures of some of the more modern ones, with all the vibrant blues and yellows. I ordered a few, a couple of them bloomed and I was hooked." He soon discovered they were habit-forming; fortunately, he was able to finance his growing addiction by selling cream from his dairy herd. Today he has 700 varieties of bearded irises—about 300 tall bearded—and such is his devotion to these large lovelies that one American breeder, Paul Black, even named a new iris after him, reckoning that anyone succeeding on such a scale in an area with winters as harsh as Bashaw's deserved the honour. Johnson now breeds irises, working closely with Black in Oklahoma. "Four years ago I started hybridizing, and I have quite a few seedlings going," he says. "A few might be worth introducing in a few years."

Nearly all irises sold in Canada fall into two broad categories: beardless, such as the tough Siberian iris, *I. ensata, I. versicolor* and *I. pseudacorus*, or yellow flag iris; and bearded, which have a fuzzy little tongue on the hanging petals called the falls. Bearded irises are divided according to height, blooming time and flower size. The tall bearded types are the largest, starting at 69 centimetres, and they tend to bloom the latest—right into July in some parts of the country. Other types are miniature dwarf bearded iris, standard dwarf bearded, intermediate bearded, border bearded and miniature tall bearded.

Miniature dwarf beardeds are ideal for rock gardens and beds that aren't spacious enough to accommodate their larger cousins. A varied collection of them, grown in combination with tall beardeds, can also be used to extend the iris season. At 20 centimetres tall, miniature dwarfs are the smallest and earliest to bloom, starting in May in the country's warmer zones. They are followed in sequence by standard dwarf beardeds (23 to 38 centimetres); intermediate beardeds (38 to 63 centimetres); miniature tall beardeds (38 to 66 centimetres); and border beardeds (37 to 62 centimetres).

Bearded irises seem to thrive in most Canadian gardens, even in areas where both cold severe winters and Sahara-like summers are common. When choosing sturdy tall bearded hybrids, Tom Johnson recommends varieties bred in Oregon, Oklahoma and Nebraska, where winters are similar to Canada's. (While some breeding is done in Canada, most big breeders are in the U.S.) "Stay away from California-bred irises," he advises. "There are a lot of modern tall beardeds that won't survive here." Iris catalogues usually name the breeder with each variety.

Growing

Irises are normally planted between mid-July and early September; bearded irises, which have rhizomes resembling small elongated potatoes with roots, should be planted in a shallow hole in full sun. Add well-rotted manure, bone meal or compost. Plant rhizomes in groups of three or five, setting the rhizome atop a small hill in the hole and spreading the roots out before in-filling. Tall beardeds should be planted 30 centimetres apart; miniature dwarfs 15 to 20 centimetres apart. Unless the soil is sandy, the rhizomes should not be completely buried; this might cause them to rot.

Irises' worst enemy is the wormlike iris borer, which burrows in the rhizomes leaving them hollow, mushy and smelly. The borer moth lays its eggs on debris and dead leaves near the plants in late summer. The eggs hatch in early spring, and the larvae enter the sheath of the leaves, tunnelling and feeding until they gradually find their way into the rhizome. Good housekeeping helps eliminate much of the problem. That means trimming the leaves to 15 centimetres after the first fall frost, and removing the clippings to clean away infected leaves, which will also take away many of the eggs that could overwinter. Spraying with Cygon once the leaves reach 15 centimetres in the spring was often recommended in the past, but several years ago Royal Botanical Gardens in Burlington, Ontario, began using an organic program that uses nematodes (available in some garden centres) as a repellent.

Irises are also susceptible to soft rot—characterized by soft, rotting rhizomes—which occurs when the rhizomes are accidentally cut open by careless digging, or attacked by the iris borer. If soft rot occurs, dig out the infected patch, cut away all damaged rhizomes and discard them—but not in the compost. Replant remaining rhizomes in a different spot.

Despite these vulnerabilities, irises are generally a hardy breed, requiring very little coddling and spreading quickly. Ideally, they prefer a dry, sunny spot, and neatness counts in keeping irises healthy. Simply snap off spent flowers and cut off the stems. Don't cut the foliage back until it yellows, allowing plants to store food for the next season of bloom. Don't be dismayed if occasional leaf spots show up once the grand display has wrapped up—the foliage of tall bearded irises can start to look pretty shabby by midsummer. Opinion is divided on whether or not to mulch; some experts advise adding 10 to 15 centimetres of weed-free mulch after the ground freezes in November, and removing layer by layer in spring, allowing the air and sun to dry the surface.

Overgrown clumps of iris lose their vigour, and growth that's too lush can set the stage for soft rot, so clumps should be divided every three or four years, after blooming and before early fall. Use a garden fork to pry out the clump, then clean off soil and inspect rhizomes for damage, rot or borers. Remove withered leaves and trim remaining leaves with a knife or scissors to 15 centimetres in a fan shape.

Discard the old rhizome, and to protect against spreading disease or borers, don't add leaves or root pieces to compost. Cut young rhizomes from the edge of the clumps. Each rhizome should have one or two fans. Dust the cuts with all-purpose fungicide. To minimize the chance of disease, let rhizomes dry overnight to allow any cuts to seal over before replanting.

To plant the new young rhizomes, hold the fan straight against

↑ *I. germanica* 'Summer Wine'

Like all irises, *I. germanica* is easy to grow. All it asks is lots of sun and good drainage. Divide clumps every three or four years to maintain bloom and vigour.

the side of a hole, with the top of the rhizome just above the surface, or build a small mound and set the rhizome on top with the roots draped over the hill, then fill in soil so the top is slightly exposed to the sun. If you have a rich, loamy soil, place rhizomes 2.5 centimetres deep, 5 centimetres deep in sandy soil, which will help prevent heaving during freeze-thaw cycles in late winter and early spring. When planting a clump, face fans in the same direction. Fill in soil until firm and level, and water thoroughly using a light spray so as not to dislodge the soil.

Beardless iris (*I. ensata, I. sibirica, I. pseudacorus, I. versicolor* and the Louisiana hybrids) generally like partial shade, moist conditions and slightly acidic soil. See the categories that follow for specific information.

Types and varieties

Some of the tall bearded iris (*I. germanica*) chosen by the restoration team at Monet's garden in Giverny can be found in Canadian catalogues, including light blue 'Blue Reflection'; deep purple 'Dark Triumph'; 'Ice Sculpture', ice blue changing to white; and 'Mulled Wine', ruffled burgundy with apricot beards. 'Stepping Out' is a hardy, stunning purple-and-white hybrid introduced in 1964.

Other solid performers are 'Supreme Sultan', with a gold standard, erect petals and mahogany falls; 'Sultry Mood', purple with blue beards; 'Vanity', blush pink with tangerine beards; 'Winter Adventure', a ruffled violet-blue with light blue beards.

Japanese iris (*I. ensata*) was developed by the Japanese from the wild iris after 400 years of hybridizing. Like their parents, these irises have exotic flat-topped blossoms of three characteristic petals. Ideal for the gardener who loves to fuss, *I. ensata* has a strong colour range with no yellows. Ensata need a lot of water but they don't like to be waterlogged. They also need acidic soil, a pH between 5.5 and 6.5. Heavy feeders, they require a hit of fertilizer in spring and just before blooming—usually one month after the tall bearded irises. Given at least six hours of sunlight, they grow to 1.2 to 1.5 metres, with large flowers

up to 20 centimetres across. Ensata can withstand winter temperatures to –30°C. Mulch to protect them during freeze-thaw cycles.

Siberian iris (*I. sibirica*) is as tough as its name suggests. Paradoxically resembling orchids, these irises are hardy in Canada to Zone 3, provided there's some winter protection (snow or mulch) in colder areas. Generally pest-free and easy to grow, they bloom in June, after the tall bearded iris but before *I. ensata*. Because of their preference for moist conditions, mulching is beneficial in dry conditions.

Siberian irises have a unique place in Canadian horticultural history. In the 1920s and '30s they were part of a federal breeding program in Ottawa, where Isabella Preston, a botanist renowned for her work in lilies, lilacs and crabapples, also devoted many years to breeding Siberian irises, which she named after Canadian rivers. Her hybrids have since been superseded by others with larger flowers and more vivid colours, but Preston hybrids are still available. They include 'Abitibi', 'Kootenay', 'Mattawin', 'Nipigon' and 'Rideau', all blue and bred in 1932; the azure blue 'Gatineau' (1932); the 'Rimouski' (1938), white with dots of yellow; and the dark blue 'Skeena' (1938).

Louisiana Hybrids, best suited to Zones 6 to 8, were developed from plants native to the American south. Growing 60 to 90 centimetres tall, and in the same wide colour range as the bearded irises, Louisiana irises require acidic soil and plenty of moisture. Like *I. ensata*, they're heavy feeders and require fertilizing. Supplement the soil with peat moss, old manure or compost. They love water, so do well on the perimeter of a pond.

Yellow flag *(I. pseudacorus)* is a bog- or water-loving plant with bright yellow-veined flowers. It's a descendant of the wild yellow flag iris from Europe. Seemingly indestructible, it can grow to astonishing heights, although it doesn't grow as tall in the garden as in a bog. Several new colours have been bred, including ivory and cream. 'Flore Pleno' is a double form.

A descendant of the wild blue flag, *I. versicolor* is violet-blue, but new shades including maroon, purple and violet have been bred. Several crosses are now available too, including a *versicolor* mixed with a *pseudacorus*. Although they adapt to any soil and will even grow in full sun, *I. versicolor* prefers moisture and grows well next to ponds and in moist woodland or other areas that remain damp throughout the growing season, since this is their natural environment.

Yellow flag loves bogs or the edges of a stream, where it will often grow more than a metre tall. It's a descendant of Europe's wild yellow flag and new cultivars have been bred.

ow flag

A Glossary of Iris Terms

Here are some basic terms from the Canadian Iris Society:

Rhizome: the brownish, potato-like, fleshy portion of the plant that grows at or just below the surface of the soil. The true roots that feed and nourish the plant grow downward from the rhizome.

Falls: the lower three petals of the iris flower.

Beard: the fuzzy, caterpillarlike hairs on the falls; may be thick or thin, self-colours or contrasting.

Standards: the upright top three petals of the iris flower.

Style arm: the three style arms rest above the anthers. They may be the same colour as the iris or may be contrasting colours.

Style crest: the upward curving of the top of the style arm. The style crest may be plain, serrated or fringed.

Stigmatic lip: the liplike petal under the style crest, which receives the pollen.

Anther: a stiff, tiny stemlike aperture under the style arm.

Spathe: the papery, eventually brown, covering of the emerging bud. This papery covering eventually covers the ovary of the iris as the flower emerges from bud stage.

Spur: a short side stem that may or may not be near the top of the stem or stalk.

↑ Orienpet #98–114

favourite perennials

Lilies

Spectacular new cultivars and old favourites alike add drama to the garden

BY SUZANNE ANDERTON

Hardiness	Growing conditions	Colour range	Bloom time	Size
Most varieties to Zone 3; some to Zone 2	Sun to semi-shade; humus-rich soil; water in dry weather	Solids and combinations of white, red, orange, yellow, pink, blue, purple	Late spring to early summer	20 to 90 centimetres, depending on variety

↑ Asiatic lily 'Verigold'

Strange as it may seem, some of the best laboratories for hybridizing new lily cultivars are located in Canadian backyards, not in the high-tech facilities of Holland or the U.S. One of these labs is in Dick Bazett's small garden in Kelowna, British Columbia.

Dick and his wife, Helen, have an eclectic—and thriving—garden of perennials, unusual trees, annuals, vegetables and fruits, which is envied by the best gardeners. But serious business takes place in the shade house lined with pots of lilies in various stages of growth, and in the leaf-mulched nursery beds full of lilies—they're a sea of colour from late July through mid-August.

For 30 years, Dick has been tackling the problems of hybridizing lilies specifically for Canadian conditions—especially hot, dry Okanagan summers. Throughout, he has been taking care of his "pets"—spectacularly large, versatile lilies—which are the results of two kinds of cross-fertilizing: trumpet lilies with Oriental lilies, known as Orienpets, and trumpet lilies with Asiatic lilies, known as Asiapets. In his lily breeding, Dick looks for unique colours, strong scents, stable plants with strong stems, good conformation, lasting blooms that don't fade in hot sun, special markings and textured petals. Some of his lilies are extremely hardy and tower over him at heights of 2.5 metres, with up to 30 blooms per stem.

The Bazetts declare this to be a hobby, which began quite by accident in 1970 while Dick, who is now retired, was working with finances in the government-run Farm Credit Corporation. "My grandfather was a well-known gardener in Victoria, and I can remember him growing tall lilies. So about 40 years later I became mildly interested in attending the local lily show," Dick says. At the end of the show Dick was given an unclaimed bouquet to take home for Helen and its unusual blooms prompted him to dust off his science degree. Just to see what would happen, Dick collected pollen from

↑ Unnamed Orienpet

the bouquet to try to pollinate some of the lilies in the garden.

What happened was a new life. The first seedlings produced magnificent lilies, and before long he was showing them at all the lily shows he could attend. Dick joined the North American Lily Society, which put him in contact with hybridizers worldwide. New challenges arrived with each monthly bulletin. Years after this chance, humble beginning, a huge collection of awards and numerous invitations to speak at lily society events attest to his solid reputation in the world of lily growers.

So what does a lily hybridizer do? Cross-pollinating is the first step in creating a lily with a difference and can be undertaken by the average gardener. But the steps Dick takes to modify plant characteristics for the commercial market require the patience of a scientific mind. Many hours are spent with eyes trained on a 10x magnifier within a sterile transfer box (fortified along the way with pots of tea brewed by Helen). Green seed pods are harvested some 40 to 50 days after cross-pollination. Next, Dick dissects countless seeds of Orienpet or Asiapet crosses with a surgical blade to find a few fertilized embryos. These are removed and suspended in a nutrient-rich agar gel inside a test tube. The tube is capped, numbered and kept at room temperature for two to four months. When Dick decides it's time to plant the tiny, emerging seedlings, he pots them in a soilless mix. Once established, the seedlings are transferred into a fast-draining soil mixture in 4.5-litre pots and put out into the shade house. There they await their fate—glory in the garden or relegation to the compost heap—though nothing is decided until they've blossomed, which surprisingly can be as early as the second year (they've been known to take four years to bloom). Bone meal is added to the plants selected for growing in the nursery beds, and—apart from good drainage and annual applications of a balanced fertilizer—that's all they need.

Both bulb scales (the fleshy,

↑ Asiatic lily 'Fireglow'

modified leaves that make up the bulb) and bulblets (which grow on the stem near the soil surface) are natural means of propagation and will grow into new plants with the same characteristics as the parent plant. By treating bulb scales or very young seedlings (less than a month old) with a diluted solution of either colchicine (also used for treating gout in humans and derived from the colchicum bulb, which blooms with crocus-like flowers in autumn) or oryzalin (a weed killer), cell division is altered. The normal number of 24 chromosomes is doubled to 48, giving the grower a much wider range of characteristics to choose from in the continued search for the perfect lily.

These techniques have enabled Dick to create some entirely new lilies, now being marketed worldwide through the Lily Nook in Manitoba and Valley K Greenhouses in Manitoba. A cultivar named 'Golden Surprise' has been very popular on the Prairies, and four of Dick's Orienpets and about a dozen Asiatics have been registered in England with the Royal Horticultural Society. Dick's personal database is nothing more than a tiny, well-thumbed notebook. "My computer is in my head," he laughs, when asked how he keeps track of everything. He tilts the pale pink blooms of #97-132 toward me so I can appreciate its scent and count the flowers—23 on one stem! Now named 'Lady Di', it and other Orienpets have been selected for propagation and sent to Oregon for two to three years of field trials. If it survives all this, 'Lady Di' will become one of the new lilies we drool over in the fall catalogues.

I have to admit, I'm keeping my fingers crossed for this one.

Growing

Lily bulbs are never completely dormant and should be planted as soon as purchased. Fall is the best time to plant, except for the madonna lily (*Lilium candidum*), which must be planted in midsummer, when bulbs become available. Don't

↑ Unnamed trumpet hybrid

allow bulbs to dry out before planting. If immediate planting is not possible, store bulbs in the fridge in damp peat moss.

Lilies look good planted in triangular groups of three of the same variety, about 30 centimetres apart, but single specimens of a tall variety also stand out in a bed of low perennials.

The plants need direct sunlight for most of the day—all day, if possible. Well-drained soil is crucial, and a medium sandy loam soil fortified with humus is ideal—if necessary, plant them in raised beds. Lily roots do not like competition and the plants need good air circulation, so place your bulbs 30 to 45 centimetres away from other perennials.

When preparing the bed, it's a good rule to dig deep enough to allow the top of the bulbs to sit at twice the depth of the bulb itself. If the excavated soil is heavy, lighten it with coarse sand and peat moss or compost. Add a small handful of bone meal to the bottom of the planting hole and place bulbs 30 to 45 centimetres apart, spreading the roots outward. Add excavated soil to the planting hole and firm to remove air pockets. Water the area well so roots can get established before winter begins. Apply about 5 centimetres of organic mulch to keep stem roots, which grow just below the surface, moist and cool. If you top dress with manure, use only well-rotted manure or risk damaging the bulbs.

In spring, just after growth starts, fertilize with a balanced bulb fertilizer, such as 13-16-10. When flowers are spent, fertilize again and remove the seed head but not the stalk: the leaves are needed to manufacture food for next year's growth. Do not fertilize late in the season—bulbs could become soft.

In fall, remove old and yellowing stems by gently tugging on them; the stem bulblets can be removed and replanted (this helps extend the time before dividing is necessary), but discard the old stems. Fall is the best time to divide clumps, and lilies should be divided every three to four years. Use a spading

† Orienpet 'Grenadine'

fork and carefully lift the bulbs from underneath, being careful not to damage them. Carefully separate the larger bulbs and replant as soon as possible into freshly amended soil. Plant the small bulblets about 5 centimetres deep. Mark the location where bulbs have been planted to avoid breaking new shoots during spring cleanup.

Botrytis, a fungus disease that affects the leaves, is caused by excessive moisture and warm temperatures. The first signs are white spots on the leaves. In severe cases the whole leaf and stem is infected and the plant decays. Injury from frost or hail makes plants vulnerable to botrytis spores. If a plant becomes infected, spray weekly with a copper spray or a baking soda mixture (1 millilitre per litre of water). Good air circulation helps prevent botrytis.

Plants may also suffer from basal rot, especially in warm, moist soils. Plants show streaky yellowing on the foliage. Avoid overwatering during warm summer months and provide good drainage. Remove infected scales, dig up bulbs and dip them in a fungicide solution of Benlate, readily available to homegrowers.

Bruising or mechanical injury can cause a harmless mould to form on the injured part of the bulb. If you notice this while transplanting or planting new bulbs, carefully cut away the affected part, dust the bulb with a fungicide powder and plant as usual.

Lily viruses are transmitted largely by aphids. Irregular mottling and flecking of the leaves as well as reduced growth, or twisted and contorted growth, occurs. Other symptoms include colour breaking in the flowers and leaves, and brown ring patterns on bulb scales. To control viruses, completely destroy clumps of lilies that show severe infection. Remove plants showing infection early in the season. Control aphids.

The lily beetle (*Lilioceris lilii*), long a scourge in Europe, has made its presence known in eastern parts of Canada. Both larvae and adults feed on the lily leaves, and both have

voracious appetites and soon devour entire plants. The larva, a yellow grub with a dark head, finds its home in the axils of leaves and stems and covers itself in dark, slimy excrement that can be mistaken for a small clump of earth. The adult, about 8 millimetres long, is bright scarlet with black legs and antennae. It's hard to miss its presence on the leaves. Tiny yellow eggs are laid on the underside of the foliage. The lily beetle is hard to eradicate because it's so prolific. The most environmentally friendly way to control an infestation is to catch adults and squish them, although this must be done several times a week. Many gardeners report that spraying with neem oil every week or so controls larvae and egg infestations. Be sure to spray under leaves, and on the ground around the plant. Also avoid transporting infested soil to other sites.

Recommended varieties

Lilies are a staple in the Canadian garden, and there are many more types available in addition to the Orienpet and Asiapet cultivars. Three families of lilies can take a garden almost through the summer: the cheerful asiatics, which carry up-facing blooms in late June and early July; the taller trumpets, with fragrant outfacing flowers in mid- to late July; and the Orientals, with large, perfumed, generally ruffled and showy blooms a bit later in the summer.

Asiatic lilies are derived from species originating in Asia and are very hardy. Most are early-blooming, brightly coloured and unscented. Pastel colours such as salmon, lavender, cream, lemon yellow, pink and white are available. They reach 90 to 120 centimetres. Tiger lilies (*L. tigrinum* syn. *L. lancifolium*) are probably the most familiar of this group; they are hardy from Zones 2 to 7.

Trumpet lilies are easy to grow and very rugged, though less hardy than Asiatics. The regal lily (*L. regale*) is probably the most familiar trumpet type. Their tall pyramids (some reach almost 2 metres) of waxy, fragrant flowers bloom in July and August and are hardy from Zones 4 to 7.

Oriental lilies are less hardy and more difficult to grow. 'Star Gazer' is one of the best known of this group and was the first upright Oriental hybrid. They need well-drained, rich, moist soil and prefer a mild, coastal climate. They bloom from July to September and are hardy from Zones 4 to 8.

Species lilies native to countries in the northern hemisphere include the madonna lily (*L. candidum*, Zones 6 to 7), the common turkscap lily (*L. martagon*, Zones 3 to 7), *L. henryi* (Zones 4 to 7) and the American turkscap lily (*L. superbum*, Zones 4 to 7). Many true species, like most wild plants specifically adapted to particular conditions, don't do well when planted in domestic situations. Zones vary widely.

Choicepicks

Here are some recent introductions to the lily family recommended by the Lily Nook and hardy to the Prairies (Zone 3):

'Firey Belles', an Asiapet with flared orange petals reversing to brownish purple. Grows to just over a metre tall, blooms late, usually August.

'Northern Carillon', a Manitoba-bred Orienpet with curving white petals flushed with reddish purple in the centre. It grows to about 1.2 metres tall and blooms late, usually August.

'Easter Morn', a Longipet that's also bred in Manitoba. It has huge white blooms with pinkish edges, soft yellow centres and dark maroon reverse petals. It's disease-resistant and grows about a metre tall, blooming in mid- to late season (July into August).

'Shocking' is a Dutch-bred lily with large up- to side-facing bright yellow blooms with a centre red flare. An August bloomer, it grows to about a metre.

'Red Dutch' is also Dutch bred. It has candy-apple red blooms banded in creamy yellow. A July-August bloomer, it grows just over a metre tall.

)rienpet 'Regal Star'

Mullein

A stately roadside native with some pretty attractive cousins BY PATRICK LIMA

Apart from shrubs and trees, mulleins are among the largest flowering plants you're likely to see. It's difficult to overlook them; harder yet to be neutral about them. Meeting mulleins face to flower in our garden, people respond with either surprised enthusiasm ("Magnificent, but what exactly are they?") or quizzical hesitation ("Those aren't weeds, by any chance?"). The difference

Hardiness
Zones 4 to 6

Growing conditions
Full sun; average, dry soil

Colour range
Yellow; white; rose to purple

Bloom time
Midsummer

Size
1 to nearly 3 metres

↓ *V.* hybrid 'Wega'

Mullein is the common name for *Verbascum*, which was originally *Barbascum*, an old Latin word for "bearded." The genus contains 360 species native to Europe, North Africa and central Asia.

V. phoeniceum →

↓ Hybrid purple mullein

↓ Twiggy mullein (*V. virgatum*)

Mullein has had several spellings over the years: *molleyne*, *mollen*, *wulleyn* and *woollen*, all of which described the soft, furry texture of the leaves.

Turkish mullein (*V. bombyciferum*) →

may depend on whether you think "imposing" is a compliment or a criticism when applied to plants. It may also depend on the time of day. Seen at dawn or in morning light, mulleins stand fresh and radiant, their leaves perky, flowers fully open. By mid-afternoon on a hot July day, they can look a bit bedraggled, flowers closed or fallen, foliage like flannel in need of a pressing. Still, few plants compare for bold form, soaring height and long flowering time.

Mullein is the common name for *Verbascum*, a genus of 360 species native to Europe, North Africa and central Asia. Originally *Barbascum*, an old Latin word for "bearded," the genus name refers to the beard of fine hairs covering the leaves, stems and flower stamens. Fuzziness extends to the rest of the plant as well. Mullein was at one time spelled *molleyne* or *mollen*, and before that *wulleyn* or *woollen*, which described the downy or furry texture of mullein leaves.

Although no mulleins are native to Canada, one species, *V. thapsus*, common mullein or flannel plant, has made itself at home throughout the land. *A Field Guide to Wildflowers: Northeastern and North-Central North America* by Roger Tory Peterson gives its habitat rather pathetically as "roadsides, vacant lots, poor fields, waste places." Common mullein sends up a single stalk showing several widely spaced flowers at a time. But I learned one summer just what beauty this exclamation mark of a plant can bring to vacant lots, when a recently bulldozed building site changed naturally into a wildflower garden as yellow mulleins, blue viper's bugloss (*Echium vulgare*) and white field daisies sprang up in the rocky rubble. There was something nautical about the straight mullein masts swaying over a blue sea of bugloss and daisy whitecaps.

Growing

Mulleins are not standard offerings at nurseries (although this is changing as they become more popular), so growing from seeds may be the best way to obtain plants. For all their eventual bulk, mulleins have seeds that are mighty small, like a grind of pepper. Start with a bulb pot—wider and shallower than an ordinary flowerpot—filled with a light soil mix. Scatter seeds thinly over the surface, press them in lightly and cover with the finest dusting of soil. Water from below by sitting the pot in a basin of water. In a warm, sunny place, seeds should sprout in a week to 10 days.

As the seedlings grow, thin them so that each has 3 to 4 centimetres of room to stretch. After a couple of true leaves have formed, gingerly lift and transplant seedlings into individual 10-centimetre pots. Keep them growing in the sun—on a windowsill, in a greenhouse or cold frame—until they look sturdy enough to fend for themselves outdoors, then transplant about 30 to 50 centimetres apart, first hardening off indoor plants by setting them out in a protected location for longer periods each day.

In the summer sun, the first-year mullein rosettes expand quickly in preparation for next year's flowering. With luck, mulleins will take to your garden and come back on their own from seed, saving you the work. If you grow two or more kinds, be prepared for spontaneous cross-pollination and surprises.

Mulleins are upright plants, often soaring to 2 metres or more. Although there are several white ones, and an oddball purple, most flower clear yellow. Leaves are long, wide and smooth-edged, ending in a sharp point; a broad rosette at ground level gives way to foliage up the length of strong stalks. Countless tiny hairs give the leaves of many species a grey shading, from silvery white to olive green. Leaf fuzz (not a botanical term) traps airborne moisture and slows evaporation, while silver deflects the sun's hottest rays—like wearing light colours in summer. Wild mulleins grow in sunny places where summer rainfall is sparse and drainage is fast. For gardeners, this is a clue. Put them in full sun in average soil where no water stands. If you are looking for candidates for xeriscaping—gardening without watering—let me make some introductions.

↑ Greek mullein (*V. olympicum*)

Some varieties have smooth, dark green leaves and grow shorter than the imposing yellow-flowered Greek mullein. Purple mullein grows about a metre tall and has flowers in roses and purples.

Recommended varieties

The first mullein I ever met was in an English country garden years ago, where masses of Greek mullein (*V. olympicum*), radiant on an overcast day, had been left to self-sow through a sunny space surfaced in gravel. This 2-metre-tall Greek native has lived in our garden ever since, against a split-rail fence at the back of a sunny, sandy border. Compared with the common roadside mullein, with its single stalk and sparse bloom, Greek mullein branches out into giant candelabras lit with hundreds of yellow flowers. Starting in late June with the last of the irises, the illumination continues through the better part of July. The association with light goes back a long time: candlewick plant, hag's tapers and torches are old names, and the German name *königskerze* means "king's candle." At one time, mullein stalks were dipped in tallow and set ablaze for illumination—giving garden lighting a whole new slant.

Like many *Verbascum*, Greek mullein is biennial—a rosette of leaves the first year, flowers the next, end of story. Luckily for lazy gardeners, the plant takes care of its own propagation, dropping seeds and sprouting new plants nearby. Small seedlings can be carefully lifted and shifted to a new location. If too many pop up, I remind myself—while pulling them up—that this is probably a big old weed on its home turf. It's been 20 years now, and so far the Olympian hasn't managed to run or jump out of bounds.

Few plants have foliage as woolly white as the biennial Turkish mullein (*V. bombyciferum*), sometimes sold under the cultivar names 'Arctic Summer' (also known as 'Polarsommer') or 'Silver Lining'. The down is so thick you can gather it up like cotton wool in your fingers. When summery yellow flowers appear on the snowy stalks, you have a plant of great interest and distinction. Not as tall as its Greek cousin, Turkish mullein is best near the front of a sunny bed where it can be seen from tip to toe. It grows to about 120 centimetres. As easy as every other mullein to raise from seed initially, Turkish mullein usually self-sows.

A departure from yellow-flowered biennial mulleins, the white perennial mullein (*V. chaixii* 'Album') is probably the most refined of a sometimes rough lot. Coming true from seed, and flowering from the second year onward, it sends up a crowd of slender, branching stems thickly set with white blooms centred with fuzzy purple filaments tipped with yellow pollen. This green-leafed mullein blooms for weeks in midsummer and returns from underground each spring. Unless they get carried away, self-sown seedlings are a bonus and can be left in place or moved when small. Standing about 1.5 metres tall, this mid-border mullein associates well with lilies, phlox, bellflowers, yarrows, coneflowers and grasses. Where daylilies dominate, the white spires provide vertical contrast.

Smooth, dark green foliage is not the only trait that sets the **purple mullein** (*V. phoeniceum)* apart. At only a metre tall, it is short stuff in mullein company. Flowers in shades of rose and purple appear not on stout clubs but on thin, willowy stems. As perennial as a mullein gets, this one may live for three to four years, spawning a batch of seedlings in the process. Easily raised from seed—usually mixed hybrid colours—this is the mullein for gardeners who shy away from the big, hairy, yellow brutes or feel their Olympian bulk is too big for their gardens.

English gardeners have appreciated the species for a long time and over the years have bred **hybrid mulleins** with larger flowers in different shades. In spring I make a habit of checking nurseries in case a new name appears. 'Banana Custard' and 'Wega' are large-flowered yellows, impressive as singles or massed; 'Snow Maiden' is a white mullein that comes true from seed. The purple mullein *V. phoeniceum* is one parent of some intriguing hybrids: 'Cotswold Beauty', pale peachy bronze; 'Cotswold Queen', apricot with purple stamens; 'Pink Domino', dusty light rose. Reaching 130 centimetres, they are most effective in groups of three or more.

Greek mullein (*V. olympicum*) →

Mullein Surprises

Mulleins are not shy about sharing pollen—not that they have any choice, with bees working the flowers incessantly. In our garden the various kinds occasionally interbreed, giving rise to interesting new plants. How else to explain the spontaneous appearance of a tall, branching yellow mullein bearing a striking resemblance to Greek mullein, with the purple "eyes" and perennial habit of *V. chaixii* 'Album'? However it came to be, it decorates the back row of a wide border in company with false sunflowers (*Heliopsis* spp.), sneezeweed (*Helenium* spp.) and hollyhocks. Although our mystery mullein has survived for three years, I don't trust its perennial nature and have started new plants by trowelling away pieces of the crown—a few leaves with roots attached—from the outside of the clump.

↑ *P.* hybrid 'Rich Ruby'

Penstemons

Beauty of form, long bloom and brilliant colour make a touchy plant worthwhile

BY PATRICK LIMA

↓ *P. digitalis* 'Husker Red'

Hardiness

Zones 3 to 7, depending on variety

Growing conditions

Well-drained, moderately fertile soil; good sun and air circulation

Colour range

White; brilliant pinks, reds and purples; clear blue

Bloom time

June and July, often beyond, depending on variety

Size

30 centimetres to 1 metre tall

Penstemons aren't long-lived plants but the shimmering colours of their flowers, which last for weeks in June and July, bring a gardener much pleasure.

When gardeners talk about perennials, the various species of *Penstemon* seldom enter the conversation. Nurseries and catalogues are not crowded with them, so they are easy to overlook. It was only after 20 years of collecting perennials of every kind that we finally planted one. And a pleasant surprise it was. Now, we try any that come along.

White *P. digit*

"Try" is the operative word, for even after you have a penstemon or three in the garden, experimentation remains the name of the game. But this much is certain: every penstemon we've grown has been a beauty; not always long-lived, but more than worth the space for the time it stayed.

Why make the effort for such uncertain perennials? The first reason is colour, not so much range as intensity. Few other perennials match the saturated hues of penstemons: shocking pink, ruby red, pure purple, strong magenta, clear blue; even the whites have a pearly sheen. Then there is the appealing form of the dainty pendant bells—you'll think I'm cracked as an old bell if I say there's something musical about penstemons as they jingle and sway on their thin stems, but it's true. And last, the sheer length of bloom—weeks and weeks in June and July, and often beyond.

↓ *P.* hybrid 'Snow Storm'

Penstemons in large clumps combine well with drifts of plants that match or complement their intensity, such as lemon yellow 'Moonshine' or pink yarrow, hardy salvias, veronicas or dwarf delphiniums.

The name "penstemon" (pronounced *pen-stay-mon*) comes from the Greek *pente*, meaning "five," and *stemon*, meaning "a thread." Besides having five threadlike stamens, the typical penstemon flower is a narrow, tubular bell, flared at the mouth; one of a line of blooms that open in succession, bottom to top, on thin stems. If there were a fairy tale where an elf proclaimed, "Honey, I shrunk the foxgloves!" you'd end up with a penstemon. The two are related, as both are members of the *Scrophulariaceae*, or figwort, family, which also includes snapdragons, toadflax and mulleins. One of its common names is beard-tongue—that could be the troll's name in our fairy tale—which refers to tiny hairs on a sixth sterile stamen that catch pollen as bees crawl by in search of nectar. But today it's generally known in common usage by its botanical name.

Growing

Penstemons are superb dryland plants that revel in drought. They like fast drainage, adequate sunlight and good air circulation, so hardiness may be a problem in very cold, damp or clay-bound gardens.

Penstemons prefer light, moderately fertile soil, hovering around neutral on the pH scale. Wet feet are the kiss of death, while a sheltered spot in the sun keeps them happy in summer. The upper ledge of

P. barbatus syn. *Chelone barbata* 'Elfin Pink' →

↑ *P.* 'Andenken an Friedrich Hahn', also named 'Garnet'

a sunny rock garden is a good site, for example: drainage is assured, and the stones help buffer winds and hold heat. On level ground, clay soil needs a lot of coarse sand or grit to warm and loosen it.

In our sunny, sandy garden, penstemons grow without fuss at the front of ordinary perennial beds, where, depending on quirks of nature beyond our comprehension, they may or may not survive the winter. Our approach is to leave all penstemons in the ground for the season—just in case. Sometimes they only partially die out, a full clump being reduced to a few tufts of green by spring. If these tufts are trowelled out of the ground as early as possible, potted individually and set in a sunny, protected spot—windowsill, greenhouse or cold frame—they grow into garden-ready plants within a month, at a fraction of the cost of replacements.

↑ *P.* hybrid 'Rich Ruby'

Hybrid penstemons are often on the tender side, but they could be used in containers or planted in the garden as annuals expected to last only one summer.

Recommended varieties

Having planted seeds of doubt about the hardiness of penstemons, let me backtrack and point to one species, and one notable cultivar, that comes through the winter without fail (or should that read so far?). Native to Arkansas, the metre-tall *Penstemon digitalis* (Zone 3)—there's the foxglove connection again—is a strong, upright perennial that decorates a sunny flower bed in midsummer with glossy, dark green leaves and wands of showy, white, open-mouthed flowers that face out rather than down. It's tempting to find new nooks for this reliable penstemon—a place in the sun near yarrows, lilies, hardy salvias, bellflowers, veronicas, dwarf delphiniums or other flowers of the season. With fine foliage from the ground up, this tallish species belongs in the front row as an effective screen for something scruffier or more transient behind.

The red-leafed cultivar 'Husker Red'is *P. digitalis* in fancy dress. In some settings, its wine red foliage adds to the plant's ornamental value. To my eye it looks as if the tint of the leaves has seeped into the white flowers, giving them a faint pinkish cast. Like its parent, 'Husker Red' is best in a group of three or more plants, set about two handspans apart. Seen in a fluttering mass, the small, individual blossoms create a light, airy effect. Of all the penstemons we've grown, these two are the hardiest, enduring in one spot for many years. Both can be lifted and carefully divided in early spring for the propagation of new plants. If they are thriving and surviving, though, we leave them be.

Marginally less hardy is **beardlip penstemon** (*P. barbatus* syn. *Chelone barbata*). Said to overwinter to Zone 4, this Colorado native with pink-tinged scarlet flowers has spawned several bright cultivars, including the deep scarlet 'Coccineus' and the light rose 'Carnea'. A favourite in the group is 'Elfin Pink', 50 centimetres tall, as sprightly as its name and generous

An Extended Family

Botanists have yet to agree on the number of penstemon species found in the wild: 250 to 300 is the usual estimate. All but one are native to North America. In fact, the genus Penstemon is the largest on this continent. Wild penstemons flank both sides of the American Rockies, mainly in the southwestern U.S.; some wander south into Mexico and Central America while quite a few extend into Canada.

with bloom—crowded stems hung with scores of intense pink bells that ring for weeks. Planted in late April or early May, 'Elfin Pink' accomplishes a feat of prodigious flowering by July. In my experience, this holds true for other penstemons: set out in spring, they give a full flower show the same summer. Another shared trait? All penstemons die well, dropping their flowers cleanly to the ground, as if to make room for the next batch.

Quicktips

Like many plants accustomed to drought, penstemons make massive amounts of seed after the first flowering. Plants must be kept from expending all their energies to produce seed at the expense of new basal growth, which is insurance for next year. In his book *Penstemons*, Robert Nold advises us to remove the flowering stalks from the plant as soon as flowers have faded, leaving only a few to produce seed capsules, and then removing most of those.

In a semi-circular bed in front of the stone-clad wall of our garden shed 'Elfin Pink' rubs shoulders with 'Red Fox' veronica; *Campanula lactiflora* 'Pouffe', with lots of pale lavender bellflowers on waist-high stems; and inky 'Miss Indigo' salvia, a superb perennial sage that could be interchanged with *Salvia nemerosa* 'Ost Friesland'. In the picture, too, are *Scabiosa columbaria* 'Pink Mist', a low-growing, long-blooming pincushion flower, and the metre-tall *Monarda didyma* 'Marshall's Delight', a deep pink version of bee balm. A few mauve opium poppies, self-sown the summer before, sprout through. In the same setting, the deep crimson penstemon 'Andenken an Friedrich Hahn' (syn. 'Garnet', Zone 7) fits nicely, as does purple-flowered 'Prairie Dusk' (Zone 4). The latter penstemon is equally effective next to lemon yellow 'Moonshine' yarrow. If we get a second or third summer from any of these cultivars, we count ourselves lucky. If not, we don't feel cheated, since they give a lot of pleasure while they last. All stand from 30 to 60 centimetres tall and are best positioned in the front row.

Then there is the unidentified penstemon, a wild-looking thing of plain green leaves, clear magenta blooms and sturdy constitution. Tagged as *P. strictus*, Rocky Mountain penstemon, it doesn't quite match the description of grey-green foliage and lobelia-blue flowers given for that species. No matter, our magenta mystery seems to like our garden, and we like it, too, in a group in the sun next to blue-spiked veronica or in front of Siberian irises. Whatever its real name, this penstemon puts up with careful spring division and has proven hardy so far for seven years.

Last summer, a flurry of pearly white 'Snow Storm' (Zone 6) decorated the edge of a perennial bed in front of lilac-coloured yarrow and steely blue sea holly, a subtle, simple grouping that remained in good form for many weeks. When the real snow melted, our summer 'Snow Storm' reappeared in reasonably good shape.

Definitely on the tender side, **other hybrid penstemons** to look out for are the descriptively named 'Sour Grapes' and 'Rich Ruby', as well as salmon pink 'King George'. Any could be used as floriferous container plants or as long-blooming annuals—something different for pots and beds.

And this is just the start with this large and intriguing group of plants. Uncertain over winter, sometimes unclear in their naming, penstemons are not as predictable as peonies. But given some consideration, they may well stay beyond expectations. Whatever the duration, they delight with graceful growth, appealing form and vivid colour. We may not count on penstemons for permanence, but we're always open for a visit—and ready for a surprise.

P. hybrid 'Prairie Dusk'

Seductive yet spunky, poppies fit in any garden

BY LAURA LANGSTON

↑ Corn or field poppy (*P. rhoeas* 'Danish Flag')

Poppies

Hardiness

Zone 3; to Zone 2 if mulched for winter

Growing conditions

Full to partial sun; moderately rich soil with good drainage

Colour range

White; orange; pink to rose, red and purple

Bloom time

Late spring; annuals in midsummer

Size

Annuals, biennials, 20 centimetres to 2 metres; perennials, 60 centimetres to 1 metre

Poppies grow as annuals, biennals and perennials, but they all like lots of sun and well-drained soil. Generally, they're pest- and disease-free.

← Corn or field poppy (*P. rhoeas*)

I can trace my love of poppies back to *The Wizard of Oz* and that field of swaying poppies that puts Dorothy to sleep before the good fairy makes the snow fall. These simple flowers enchanted me even before I first put trowel to dirt.

True poppies belong to the *Papaveraceae* family, which is made up of about 100 species of annual, biennial and perennial herbaceous plants. They produce light green feathery foliage and flowers that look like crinkled silk. Single poppies generally have four overlapping petals that form a cup, while doubles can be dense and heavily ruffled, almost like peonies. Since they vary from petite 15-centimetre plants to the more stately and flamboyant 150-centimetre varieties, there are poppies suitable for every site, from rockeries to meadows, from formal to informal garden beds. All poppies like sun and well-drained soil, but while the annual species do fine in average soil, perennials prefer something a little richer.

↑ Oriental poppy (*P. orientale*)

Plant late-blooming perennials, such as daylilies or coneflowers, near Oriental poppies to hide their fading foliage; it dies back after the plants bloom and can look messy.

Growing and varieties

Annual poppies

Most poppies are easy to grow, and the annual species are no exception. They do well right across Canada, generally blooming in late spring and early summer. Although each flower lasts only a day or two, deadheading encourages plants to issue new blooms for weeks.

Sow seed for annual poppies directly in the garden—they resent transplanting—in full sun and average soil. Since the seeds are very fine, mix them with sand and gently rake the mix into the ground in spring, watering them in. Mark the ground carefully so small seedlings won't be inadvertently weeded out. In mild climates, sow as early as February or March; in cold regions wait until April or May. You can sprinkle seeds on the last of the melting snow and let them find their own spots in the soil, or plant them a little later, when you can work the ground.

Alternatively, start annual poppies indoors in peat pots in mid- to late April and move them, pot and all, into the garden when they're 8 to 10 centimetres tall (the roots grow through the peat pots, minimizing root disturbance). This method prevents inadvertent weeding of germinating poppy seeds and gives plants a head start.

Successive sowings until late spring mean blooms well into summer. Poppy seeds can also be sown in fall, anytime from late September to November; they germinate the following spring.

Whatever planting method you use, thin seedlings to about 7 centimetres apart, which gives plants room to grow but allows them to support each other. Allow some plants to develop seed heads; they'll reseed and you'll have annual poppies faithfully appearing in the garden for years.

Poppies are generally untroubled by pests and diseases, and this applies to the perennial and biennial types discussed below. Aphids occasionally appear, but natural predators such as ladybugs usually control them. Sterner measures are needed for spider mite infestations, even though ladybugs offer some control for this pest, too. Regular and forceful sprays of water or water infused with combinations of hot peppers, garlic or onion also work.

Powdery mildew can attack just about any plant in a state of

The Poppy Police

Growing opium poppies (*P. somniferum*) in your backyard isn't likely to get you into trouble with the law—but it could. Under the new *Controlled Drugs and Substances Act*, they're illegal.

The act, which came into effect in May 1997, states that anyone found growing the plant could get "a term not exceeding 10 years." The reason? The seed pods yield a milky sap that, when it dries, darkens and turns gummy, is opium. A precipitating agent pressed into the opium turns it into morphine; treated with acetic anhydride, it becomes powdered heroin.

Opium poppies haven't been grown in Canada for the illegal drug trade, and home gardens are rarely, if ever, raided. Still, it's probably advisable not to plant a huge quantity of the poppies in your garden.

Oriental poppy (*P. orientale*)

Medicinal Poppies

Poppies have been used—and abused—for centuries. Native to the eastern Mediterranean, they likely spread east with Arabic traders to India around the seventh century. At that time, petals from the common corn poppy were used as a colouring agent for medicine and wine. They were also used as a sedative and an anti-spasmodic.

It was the opium poppy, however, that was relied on most heavily for its medicinal purposes. Ancient healers in the Middle East and Asia used it as a painkiller, mixing it with wine or smoking it in a pipe. An infusion made from powdered seed heads was applied externally to sprains and bruises, and opium syrup was regularly given for coughs in 11th-century Arabia. Opium was also given to war elephants of the Mogul empire—and to British soldiers to increase their endurance, dull their fear and make them brave, and feel less pain if hurt. By the 17th century, smoking opium was common in China, spurring the violent Opium War of 1839–42.

Sow seeds for annual poppies directly into the ground—they don't like to be transplanted. And sow early; seeds can be sprinkled onto melting snow. Or start seeds in peat pots indoors and plant outdoors, pot and all, when soil can be worked.

↑ *P. rhoeas,* Shirley Series

decline, and since perennial poppies decline by midsummer, they're especially vulnerable. Plenty of air circulation around plants helps. Fungicides, such as Funginex, help control mildew; organic gardeners suggest horsetail tea (made from *Equisetum arvense* and available in health food stores) as an excellent method of control.

The corn or field poppy (*Papaver rhoeas*), immortalized in Flanders during World War I, grows to 45 centimetres and produces a black-centred scarlet flower. A strain of the species is the 60-centimetre Shirley Series; single and double flowers are 5 to 8 centimetres across and come in white, pink, orange and red. Sometimes the petals fade to white at the base. More delicate looking is 'Mother of Pearl', sometimes listed as 'Fairy Wings', which produces pastel blush pink, lavender and peach blooms. The striking 'Danish Flag', sometimes sold as 'Danebrog Laced', grows to 60 centimetres; it has a frilly, single scarlet cup with a vividly marked white blotch in the middle.

Smaller than the Shirley is the tulip poppy (*P. glaucum*), which produces large 10- to 13-centimetre scarlet blooms on 45-centimetre plants. The petals stay semi-erect, which makes them look like giant tulips.

Another annual, the opium poppy (*P. somniferum*), is often grown for its seed pods, striking in dried-flower arrangements. Its large flowers in early summer are complemented by deeply lobed greyish green leaves. The largest of all the opium varieties is

'Hen and Chickens', which can reach 2.5 metres and produce flowers as large as 13 to 15 centimetres in diameter in colours ranging from pinks and reds through purples. Slightly shorter, with smaller blooms, is 'Peony Flowered', while 'White Cloud' produces double white flowers.

Perennial poppies

Spectacular **Oriental poppies** (*P. orientale*) are graceful, hardy border plants with coarse, deeply cut leaves and brilliantly coloured, crepelike blooms 15 to 30 centimetres across. Occasionally blooming on the West Coast in early May, they traditionally appear across the rest of Canada in June or early July, and are usually finished by midsummer, when the leaves die back and leave a bit of a gap in the garden.

Whether you grow them from seed or purchase plants, Oriental poppies prefer moderately rich soil with good drainage; avoid damp areas. Allow at least a foot between poppies and other plants. Generally they prefer full or partial sunshine, although some shade is necessary for purple-toned Orientals, which turn a liver-like colour in full sun.

Potted perennial poppies can be planted spring or summer, but a wider choice is available from mail-order nurseries, which usually ship bare-root plants in the fall. Sink the crown 5 to 7 centimetres below the surface of the soil. Water regularly for

↓ Oriental poppy (*P. orientale*)

↑ Iceland poppy (*P. croceum* syn. *nudicaule*)

A Bouquet of Poppies

In spite of what you may have heard otherwise, poppies do make excellent cut flowers—if you condition them properly. Cut when the bud splits and shows its colour, but before the flower opens. Sear the end of the stem with a flame before putting it in water, or immediately put the flowers in extremely hot water. Leave them there until the water cools, then cut the stems a second time, under running water, before arranging them in a vase.

To dry seed heads for dried-flower arrangements, leave them in the garden until they're brown and brittle. Shake the poppy seeds out of the pod and cut the stem.

the first few weeks—the roots need moisture while they're getting established and before the soil freezes.

To grow perennial varieties from seed, follow the instructions for starting annual poppies indoors, and give seedlings a dose of root fertilizer such as 10-52-17 after they germinate. Like annuals, they should go outside when they're 8 to 10 centimetres tall. Depending on the weather, they usually bloom the first year.

After blooming, let the leaves of perennial poppies die back on their own—the health of the plant depends on it. To disguise the gaping holes left in a perennial border once the leaves are gone, plant dahlias, Michaelmas daisies, daylilies or purple coneflowers nearby.

Orientals are hardy to Zone 3—although plants in Zone 2 can usually make it through the winter if protected by consistent snow cover or a straw mulch under and around (but not on top of) the rosette of new growth that appears in the fall. This prevents freeze-thaw cycles in late winter, which can be damaging. Water plants well in the fall. If the ground is really soaked, it'll freeze like a block and never dry out until the final thaw in spring.

Divide plants every five years to keep them vigorous; late summer or early fall is best because they flower early in the season. Carefully dig up the plant without snapping the roots, and vertically split the mass of shoots into several divisions, making sure each has a bit of the crown and as many roots as possible. Position the divisions a foot from other plants and place the crowns 5 centimetres below the surface. Water well for the first few weeks.

A great favourite is the extra-long-blooming 'Helen Elizabeth', a soft rose-pink with no black dots and slightly ruffled petals. Also popular is 'Field Marshall', white with purplish black markings. For mid- to late-season bloom, consider 'Maiden's Blush', with deeply ruffled white flowers and a 2-centimetre blush edge. An all-white garden would welcome 'Snow Queen', while gardeners looking for magenta might want to try 'Watermelon', with its strong, dark pink petals and black markings.

Biennial Poppies

The Iceland poppy (*P. croceum* syn. *nudicaule*), which is usually grown as a biennial in cold climates but is classified as a short-lived perennial, grows foliage the first year, blooms the second year and then dies. If you let some of your Iceland poppies set seed they'll return faithfully every year; thin them slightly in the spring to give them room to grow.

If seed is started early enough, Iceland poppies may bloom the first year. Since this poppy can tolerate transplanting, start it in flats in late January for mild regions, or early March in cold climates. Bloom usually starts at the end of June, slows during summer heat and, if plants are frequently deadheaded, resumes as fall approaches.

Iceland poppies have clumping, compact leaves and grow 25 to 50 centimetres tall, with 10-centimetre flowers. 'Popsicle Mix' reaches 25 centimetres, while the species grows to 45 centimetres. Both offer a range of colours.

Another perennial that frequently performs as a biennial, or sometimes even as an annual in Canadian conditions, is alpine poppy (*P. alpinum*). Plants produce grey-green, ground-hugging leaves and satiny-petalled flowers on 20- to 25-centimetre stems. Look for 'Alpinum Mix', which comes in a variety of bright colours and blooms quickly from seed. Alpine poppies prefer light, gritty soil—they're perfect for rock gardens. Sow seed in the garden in early spring or, like the Iceland poppy, start it indoors.

When a Poppy Isn't a Poppy

Some plants that look like poppies and are sold as poppies actually belong to separate families. These include the blue or Himalayan poppy (*Meconopsis betonicifolia*), the Welsh poppy (*M. cambrica*) and the California poppy (*Eschscholzia californica*).

The most striking of these is the blue poppy. Challenging to grow just about anywhere except its native Tibet, it can be carefully cultivated in mild climates such as the Pacific Northwest. Impressive drifts of it flourish at Quebec's Les Jardins de Métis in Zone 4a, probably because of the area's winter snow cover and cool summers.

The slightly weedy Welsh poppy comes in yellow, orange and scarlet.

Much easier to grow is the annual California poppy, named after German botanist J.F. Escholtz, who was known for his collection of native California plants. Often listed as a wildflower, it produces bright orange flowers and has finely cut blue-green foliage that grows about 30 centimetres tall and just as wide. Direct seeding is preferred, in a dry, sunny location. Once established, California poppies bloom from early summer until fall and reseed with abandon.

favourite perennials

Primroses

↑ Cowslip (*P. veris*)

↑ *P. auricula* hybrid

Hardiness

Zones 2 to 5, depending on variety

Growing conditions

Shade to part shade; moist, rich soil

Colour range

Yellow; white to ivory; pink to rose; blue; red; purple

Bloom time

April and May

Size

8 to 30 centimetres, depending on variety; some to 75 centimetres

Tiny treasures for the spring garden, too often overlooked BY PATRICK LIMA

Spring holds magic not found in other seasons. For months gardens are dressed in muted tones; except for the flight and squabble of birds at the feeders, the landscape is still. And then an elemental stirring starts, as if some great creature is waking from a long sleep. Gardeners turn eagerly to crocus colours staining the dark earth, along with small blue irises and grape hyacinths, radiant daffodils and tulips, and exotic crown imperials. In many Canadian gardens, bulbs are the mainstay in April and May.

Primroses are also frequently called primulas, their botanical name. Hundreds of species are native to cold and temperate regions around the world.

Drumstick primrose (*P. denticulata*) →

↑ Alpine primrose (*P. marginata*)

↑ *P. auricula* hybrid

P. auricula **has a devoted following of plant collectors who covet its unusually coloured hybrids. Colours can range from soft yellow and rich red to the more rare greys and greens. Many have contrasting centres.**

But where are spring's first roses—the primroses, or prima-roses? Conspicuous by their absence, I would say, judging by my limited snooping in other people's gardens. There may be a misguided assumption that primroses belong to the damp, drawn-out springs of British Columbia or Britain, and won't flourish where winters are severe and springs often dry and fleeting. I have a friend of Scottish origin who once stood gazing down at a bed of primroses in full bloom in our Zone 4b Ontario garden and said, "Ah, primroses, I just love them. Too bad they don't grow in this country."

Old views die hard. True, you can't plunk primroses in any old spot and expect them to thrive. The small plants have definite needs—shelter, part shade and a generous supply of water; winter protection may also be necessary. But a little care is well repaid. Garden primroses are essentially modest flowers—round, simple and easy on the eye. Few flowers display such an array of colours; few are as generous with their gifts of blooms over several weeks, usually from early May to early June. And nothing is quite as fresh and spring-like as a swath of primroses.

Sometime in February big, flashy primroses—the *polyanthus* hybrids—begin to appear in plant sections of supermarkets. Ideal for cheering up the house in late winter, most are questionably hardy outdoors. But you don't have to look too far—possibly as near as a favourite seed catalogue, local nursery or a friend's garden—to come up with the hardier types, sturdy enough to live year-round in a rock garden or shady bed. Supermarket types give a mere hint at the charm and variety to be found.

Botanically, primroses are members of the genus *Primula*, by which name they're also commonly referred to. Hundreds of species are native to cold and temperate regions of the northern hemisphere; the Himalayas are rich in primulas, and many more are native to China and Japan. Over the years, in our sandy, mostly sunny garden less-than-perfect for primroses, we have grown a dozen species and many more cultivars. We have no trouble with pests or diseases, but some gardeners need to battle slugs on the plants. Most of our primroses thrive in a curving bed on the east side of lilac bushes, facing the morning sun and sheltered from prevailing winds; here, snow piles deep and usually stays until spring. Like all gardeners, we have our favourites, plants that impress us with both their beauty and tenacity, and these I describe below. All are hardy to Zone 4; some are worth trying in Zone 3 in a kindly microclimate with winter protection. Many have been with us for 10 years or more, split and re-split, potted up for a spring sale—in short, treated like any other hardy perennial.

Growing

One of the surest ways to bring primulas into the garden is to beg divisions of plants proven hardy in your neighbourhood from friends. In our area everyone grows the wee wine red

↑ Alpine primrose (*P. rosea*)

'Wanda', an indestructible single-stemmed primrose that takes well to the sun. From Wales I once brought home a (soilless) snippet of an unusual pale pink polyanthus with dark purple-green leaves; dubbed 'Pink Wales', it recently turned up in a perennial picture book under the name 'Guinevere'. That one piece is now 5 plants—perhaps 10 by next year.

Lightly rooted and compact, most primroses are easily divided, either in mid-June after flowering or in the cooler days of early September when new leaves begin to emerge. Division is done either to renew aging or crowded plants—three or four years is a good run—or to increase a

↓ Japanese star primrose (*P. sieboldii*)

Seeding Tips

All the primroses mentioned are relatively easy to grow from seed—not quick like radishes, but they do come. For nervous or impatient gardeners—or green-thumbs who are all thumbs like me—the main stumbling blocks are the very fine seeds, slow germination and seedlings that first appear as minute green specks best seen through a magnifying glass.

Don't let this deter you.

Sow seed anytime from April to June for bloom the following spring. Tiny primrose seed usually comes in a small inner envelope inside the seed pack. Two weeks before sowing, open the inner envelope, add a few drops of water and return to seed pack. Put the pack in a plastic bag and place in the freezer. Remove once or twice a week, thaw for an hour and then return to the freezer; the simulated winter and spring cycle breaks the seeds' dormancy. When ready to sow, thaw seed again and dry on a paper towel if damp.

↑ *P. denticulata*

Use clean 12- or 15-centimetre pots and commercial potting soil (sterile and weed-free) with sand or aquarium gravel added to improve drainage. Sprinkle seed on top of the soil, press in very gently, covering with the finest dusting of soil—like flouring a cake pan. Water pots from below with tepid water. Covering pots with glass, plastic or newspapers conserves moisture but may create more problems (fungus, moulds) than it solves. Better to place pots in a cool environment—between 15 and 20°C—out of direct sun, and water from below. When seeds begin to sprout—give them two to four weeks—sift a fine layer of potting soil over them to help anchor tiny roots, and water with a fine spray. Place pots in a brighter indoor location—an hour or so of morning sun is good at this stage. As soon as the first little leaves appear, set pots in a marginally sunnier place, avoiding midday or afternoon sun. Avoid bogging down the seedlings when watering.

When plants are big enough to handle—1 centimetre tall with a couple of leaves—lift each carefully and transfer to an 8- or 10-centimetre pot. When the plants have four or five leaves as big as your thumb, they're ready to live outdoors, either in their permanent location, or better yet, in a shaded nursery bed handy to a water source. In September, or the following spring, shift them to their permanent beds. Beyond the baby stage, all primroses move well if lifted carefully with a ball of soil.

favourite. Lift a clump with a hand-fork or trowel and look for natural dividing lines. Snip and pull into pieces, each with some roots, and replant in soil enriched with compost, old manure, rotted leaves and such. Organic matter not only feeds primroses, it also holds much-needed moisture. In dry weather, water new divisions faithfully every couple of days for several weeks. Even established primroses may go brown and dormant during a hot, dry summer, but as soon as rain returns and the lawn greens up, your primroses will perk up and start to regrow—maybe even flower a bit—in fall.

Seeds, too, open a gate to a number of enticing varieties that you might not otherwise find as started plant. The curious 'Gold Laced' *polyanthus*, for example, is so dark a maroon it's almost black; a fine yellow outline makes 5 petals look like 10. Plants from a package of 'Cowichan' *polyanthus* seed are characterized by hardiness, velvety texture and depth of colour, whether blue, violet, wine or crimson; a packet of mixed 'Cowichan' is sure to yield some outstanding plants that can be tagged for increase. Of all primrose colours—and there are hundreds—I keep coming back to yellows, pale or deep. Planted together with gold-eyed whites, honey browns and rusty reds, in a winding band in the shade of our old lilac bushes, these simple flowers never fail to remind us of the magic of spring.

Recommended varieties

Alpine primulas are for those who love the little gems of the plant world. Among them, *Primula marginata* is an undisputed treasure. A small, tufted thing no more than 8 centimetres tall, its grey-green leaves are leathery and sharply notched; a margin of silver, which looks like frost, gives this charmer its second name. Flowers are a clear amethyst-blue. This is a primrose to place carefully, perhaps in a well-drained crevice between two chunks of limestone. Good loam with a little lime and morning sun are all it needs; that, and a spot away from larger perennials that might smother it.

Judging from affectionate references in old herbals and botanical books, the wee bird's-eye primrose (*P. farinosa*) has been appreciated in English country gardens for centuries. Its leaves, all in a bunch at the base, are narrow, grey and appear to be dusted with white powder like farina. Stems 10- to 15-centimetres long support a parasol of round, lilac-pink blooms, each with a central spot of yellow—the bird's eye. Like most primroses, it needs shade for at least half a day and moisture in spring—preferably after a four-month snooze under snow. A little hollow filled with loam, leaf mould, chips of limestone and a handful of peat moss should keep it content. Bird's-eye primrose looks lost on its own; the close company of small gentians,

P. auricula hybrid

↑ Cowslip (*P. veris*)

Prairie Primroses

Prairie gardeners can grow primroses, too. The hardiest are *P. auricula*, *P. sieboldii* and polyanthus hybrids. Also worth trying, especially in sheltered nooks with reliable snow cover, is *P. denticulata*.

↓ *P. auricula* hybrid

↑ *P.* 'Wanda'

English primroses, cowslips and oxlips are the three wild parents of polyanthus hybrids, which clearly show their heritage in their blooms. They grow in many forms, from single-stemmed yellows reminiscent of English primroses to bunch-flowered types like oxlips.

bellflowers and mossy saxifrages reminds it of its alpine home.

From the mountains of central Europe comes *P. auricula*. Putty in the hands of breeders, the simple yellow flower has given rise to hundreds of cultivars in all shades of yellow, orange and red, often with a dark halo around a light centre; velvet-textured wine, maroon and lilac are in the mix, too. Collectors seek out the unusual green and grey flowers splotched with red or black, or those speckled with silver and centred or rimmed with white.

Flowers appear in bunches on 15-centimetre stems above smooth, thick, grey-green leaves. *Auriculas* prefer an alkaline, rather heavy soil; limestone chips worked into the ground and tucked around their little necks keep stagnant water from pooling and doing damage. A semi-shaded place, preferably where winds are buffered and snow collects, suits these mini-mountaineers.

The last of our quartet of alpines, *P. rosea*, is the tiniest and the most vivid. Always a surprise, its hot pinky red blooms stand out against glossy green leaves tinged with brownish red. A single plant catches the eye, but en masse, perhaps in a damp, low-lying area at the edge of a rock garden, they achieve a brilliance of colour unmatched in their season. *Rosea* loves water and is at home at the edge of a gentle freshet or even standing in very shallow stream-water, but anything deeper than a centimetre would drown the mite.

For sheer splash and show, nothing touches the drumstick primrose (*P. denticulata*), from Himalayan slopes. Officially an alpine, it has taken enthusiastically to our lowland garden in a moist, semi-shaded area. Toothed (that's the *denti* part) flowers of white, lavender, mauve or magenta are packed together in a perfect ball perched on stems up to 30 centimetres tall. Drumstick primroses, one of the earliest blooming primulas, usually in late April or early May, grow lovelier with each passing season; as long as they appear vigorous, we leave them alone, dividing them only to extend the patch. A fall top-dressing of old manure sets them up for spring. *Denticulatas* form their flower buds in fall and start to push above ground at the first hint of spring warmth; if frosts threaten in April or May, we protect them with a flannel sheet draped over sticks poked in among the plants. To date, these are the only primulas requiring such protection.

Drumstick primroses are sometimes sold as spring plants

Primroses for Damp Shade

Not all primroses are short and early. Flowering in late May and June, the **Japanese bog primrose** (*P. japonica*), hardy to Zone 4, closes the primrose season in a beautiful way. Growing up to 75 centimetres tall, its flowers are arranged in ascending tiers—a whorl of blossoms, a length of bare stem, another whorl. The original species is vibrant magenta; hybrids range through all shades of pink to ivory-white. When well situated in rich, damp soil in partial shade, the stellar perennial may seed itself—new plants popping up in surprising colours near the original. Even three plants in the right setting are sure to delight. But gardeners lucky enough to have a slow-moving stream or pond in light shade might plant Japanese primroses in great and glorious masses.

↑ Double-flowered *H. polyanthus* hybrid

↑ Bird's-eye primrose (*P. farinosa*)

either in bloom or (more likely) past it. With a little care, you can raise them from seed much less expensively. A packet of seeds yields many plants. The 'Ronsdorf Strain' has a good colour range and heftier heads than the species. A packet of seeds yields many plants.

Standing as tall but last to bloom, the elegant **Japanese star primrose** (*P. seiboldii*) is a beauty for front-row positions in moist, shady beds. Round, notched flowers—white to apple-blossom pink to dark rose—rise from soft, wrinkly leaves. To my eye, the lighter shades are prettiest and the whites look like cutout-paper snowflakes.

↓ Oxlip primrose (*P. elatior*)

Unlike other primroses, star primroses increase by creeping outward on underground rhizomes. Our first plant barely held its own in a dry, sunny spot; shifted into damper soil in shade, it perked up and stretched into a broad patch. Soil of preference is light and loamy, made moisture-retentive with fine humus. Although our clumps have lived unprotected through at least seven snowy winters, a covering of leaves, dry peat or evergreen boughs is beneficial where winter snows come and go.

Hedgerows and forest edges in Britain and Western Europe are home to three well-loved primroses, all of which flourish for us with minimal care. The **English primrose** (*P. vulgaris*) sports light yellow flowers, one per stem, forming a kind of bonnet of bloom on 20-centimetre plants. **Cowslips** (*P. veris*) bear pendulous, side-swinging bunches of small lemon or light orange blooms atop 25-centimetre stems. **Oxlips** (*P. elatior*) are similar to cowslips, but showier, with larger creamy flowers that tip outward; plants reach 30 centimetres. All have a spirit of wildness about them—and may go wild. In a damp, local meadow, cowslips and oxlips have seeded by the hundreds, and English primroses peek through naturalized daffodils in our old orchard. At the front of a perennial border, cowslips grow thickly between clumps of daylilies, which overshadow them during the heat of summer when the plants have finished blooming. Grape hyacinths, dwarf daffodils and violets make ideal foils in small garden beds.

These three wild primulas have parented a parcel of offspring; **polyanthus hybrids** are descendants of all three. Under our lilacs grow hybrids clearly showing their ancestry: big, single-stemmed yellows reminiscent of English primroses; the same form in mauve, called 'Mrs. King', is smothered in bloom each year; and bunch-flowered polyanthus of many colours. Most were raised from seed years ago and divided time and again. A few rare doubles and souvenirs from travels round out the scene.

favourite roses

Shrub Roses

Robust, long-blooming Canadian-bred roses are finding a place in our hearts BY ROBERT HOWARD

Hardiness

Zones 2 to 4, depending on type

Growing conditions

Full sun; soil enriched with humus; regular irrigation

Colour range

White; yellow; pinks to magenta and red

Bloom time

Late June into July, many with repeat blooms

Size

70 centimetres to 2 metres, depending on variety; most are bushy

Shrub roses are valued for their informal shape and abundant, old-fashioned blooms. But their strongest suits are hardiness and resistance to blackspot and powdery mildew.

↑ *R.* 'John Cabot', Explorer Series

A rose is a rose is a rose is a rose, Gertrude Stein wrote about 80 years ago.

Well, Miss Stein, wrong is wrong is wrong is wrong.

A rose growing in a Canadian garden these days might be a Canadian-bred hardy shrub, a young upstart English rose, a low-growing groundcover rose, or an antique shrub rose with lineage traceable to Imperial China or the France of Napoleon and Josephine. Hybrid tea roses—garden aristocrats grown for their big, solitary blooms that dominated rose beds for decades up until a few years ago—are sharing garden space with all manner of their sturdy, less temperamental cousins.

Roses are more popular than ever, say growers—especially hardy shrub roses and, in some parts of the country, David Austin's English roses. Although there's a lot of renewed interest in antique shrub roses—the albas, the bourbons, the damasks and the

← *R.* 'Henry Kelsey', Explorer Series

↑ *R.* 'Bonica'

'Bonica' blooms lustily in June with clusters of small, double pink flowers, plus a smattering of blooms during summer and a second show in fall. 'Martin Frobisher' is a member of the highly regarded Canadian-bred Explorer Series.

gallicas—growers say it's the newer, Canadian-hybridized shrub roses that are flying off garden-centre shelves.

A large part of the reason for the popularity of shrub roses is their hardiness. Hybrid tea roses can be risky to grow even in the Zone 6 gardens of southern Ontario. Without a great deal of winter protection, they approach endangered-species status in the Zone 5 gardens of Montreal, Ottawa and Halifax. And if they don't succumb during a cold winter, blackspot or powdery mildew often takes its toll.

But many shrub roses, in particular a wide range of Canadian-bred hardy varieties, survive Zone 2 winters. Admittedly, they may die back to their roots during a particularly bad cold snap, but because shrub roses are usually grown on their own roots—not grafted on to hardy root stock, like hybrid teas—they put forth new growth each spring.

Another part of the appeal of shrub roses is their informal growth—it suits the casual, cottage style of gardening that's popular now. But their popularity can also be credited to their inbred resistance to blackspot and powdery mildew.

"Hybrid tea roses are treated like annuals in many parts of Canada," says Barry Poppenheim, owner of Hardy Roses for the North, a mail-order business in Grand Forks, British Columbia. "There's been a great resurgence of interest in shrub roses. They're easy to look after and they fit very well into a mixed border or with the English cottage-garden look. After all, who can afford the time and space of a formal rose bed these days?"

Growing

Select a location that provides protection from strong winds (which lower temperatures and dry out plants), avoiding low spots where frost settles. Roses need as much sun as possible, at least six to eight hours a day. They don't thrive in partial shade, and they produce few blooms; roses in full shade die. Sun also discourages mildew and other moisture-borne diseases.

Improve sandy or clay soil with lots of organic material—leaf mould, compost or well-rotted manure.

Plant bare-root roses in fall or early winter, when their dormant period is just beginning. In the coldest areas, however, bare-root roses fare better if planted in early spring. Plant container roses whenever the soil is workable, although it's best to avoid the hottest, driest days of summer.

The planting hole should be just deep enough to contain the roots or root ball, but at least twice as wide. Spread out the roots of bare-root roses carefully in the hole. Matted roots on the outside of the soil ball of container-grown plants should be gently worked loose.

Determine whether the rose is growing on its own roots or is grafted. To determine this, look for the telltale swelling where the roots and stems meet, which is called the bud union. If you're unsure, ask at the garden centre before you take the plant home. Plant grafted roses with the bud union about 10 centimetres below ground level—except in Zone 8 and higher, when the bud union should be just above ground level. Plant roses growing on their own roots at the same depth as they were growing in the field or in the container. Firm soil around roots or

↑ *R.* 'Martin Frobisher', Explorer Series

root ball so no air pockets are left, and then water thoroughly.

Prune a newly planted rose to several stocky shoots with a few vigorous buds on each. Always prune to outward-facing buds so the interior of the plant remains open when new branches grow.

Mulch roses to keep moisture in the soil, moderate soil temperature and discourage weeds, which steal nutrients from the roses.

Water rose bushes regularly, especially when they're newly planted; give at least 4 centimetres of water each week.

Feed with well-rotted, screened compost, or use a balanced fertilizer or special rose food. Apply early in the season and twice more before mid-July. Feeding later than this stimulates tender new growth that won't survive the winter.

In late winter or early spring, prune the roses again. Remove thin, spindly canes and diseased, broken or crossing canes. Prune the remaining canes to about equal heights, again to outward-facing buds. For tall shrubs or climbers, prune diseased, broken or crossing canes, and thin a few of the older canes to just above soil level.

Recommended varieties

Barry Poppenheim lives in Zone 5, about 485 kilometres inland from the west coast. His company carries 285 varieties of shrub roses and he recommends customers in Zones 2 to 4 stick with Explorer and Parkland Canadian-bred shrub roses, hybrid rugosa roses and, to Zone 4, some of the David Austin English roses, if they're willing to give them extra winter protection.

Among the hardy rugosas, he recommends 'Fru Dagmar Hastrup' (medium pink fragrant blooms), 'Schneezwerg' (small, white blossoms) and 'Blanc Double de Coubert' (white flowers on a large shrub). They're all hardy to Zones 2 or 3. For Zone 2 gardens he also recommends 'Thérèse Bugnet' (soft pink, very fragrant, bred in Alberta in 1950) and 'Hazeldean' (once-blooming, sulfur yellow).

There are, of course, other hardy shrub roses worth considering. 'Harison's Yellow' is often referred to as the original Yellow Rose of Texas. It's a deep yellow bred from 'Persian Yellow' and a Scotch briar rose. It blooms just once, for a few weeks early in the season, and is hardy to

↓ *R.* 'William Baffin', Explorer Series

Zone 3. And 'Bonica' has clusters of small, double, pink flowers early in the season, followed by a smattering of blooms throughout summer, and one last big flush of flowers in fall. It's hardy to Zone 4.

One of the greatest success stories in shrub-rose breeding is Canadian. The Explorer Series of roses, developed by government-funded breeding programs, combines the hardiness of rugosa roses with the repeat-blooming characteristic of tender hybrid teas.

Among the most popular Explorers are 'Martin Frobisher' (soft pink, 180 centimetres tall), 'Henry Hudson' (white flowers with a pink cast, up to 70 centimetres), 'Jens Munk' (fragrant, medium pink flowers, 1.5 metres) and 'John Cabot' (strong pink flowers on canes that reach 3 metres). They're hardy without special protection, disease-resistant and after a burst of extensive bloom in June they continue to flower, if less prolifically, all summer.

Growers say the increased popularity of shrub and David Austin roses doesn't mean hybrids are losing ground—rather, people are just buying more roses. Growers also praise the Parkland Series of hardy roses, bred by Agriculture and Agri-Food Canada scientists at Morden, Manitoba, which hasn't caught on as fast as the Explorer Series. Parkland roses grow from 50 to 100 centimetres tall, with colours ranging from ivory and soft pink to crimson and cardinal red. 'Morden Blush', 'Morden Fireglow', 'Winnipeg Parks' and 'Morden Centennial' are all especially recommended.

Robert Osborne wrote *Roses for Canadian Gardens* in 1991, a time when hybrid tea roses still ruled. He urged Canadian gardeners to consider hardy, disease-resistant shrub roses, such as Explorers, rugosas and even the hardy alba and centifolia roses of the 19th century. In the years since, many Canadians have done just that, and Osborne is feeling some understandable vindication. Shrub roses are tremendously popular in the Maritimes, where hardiness zones range from 6b around Yarmouth, Nova Scotia, to Zone 2 in central New Brunswick. Explorer roses survive Zone 4 winters with no protection, and very little dieback.

In Morden, Manitoba, shrub roses are used extensively, and the tender hybrid teas are sometimes grown as annuals. The hardy shrubs, on the other hand, stand up to almost any winter Manitoba can throw at them, although they don't usually grow as tall and bushy as they do in more southern gardens.

Ian Ogilvie, a rose breeder with the program at the L'Assomption research station in Quebec, says the Explorer Series was developed for the more humid regions of Canada. The Parkland

Canada's Explorer Series of roses was developed by government-funded breeding programs to blend the hardiness of rugosa roses with the repeat blooming of tender hybrid teas.

↑ *R.* 'Henry Hudson', Explorer Series

New Old Roses

David Austin rose 'Constance Spry'

David Austin English roses have reached that benchmark of success peculiar to garden plants: they're now sold in supermarket parking lots.

Some Austin roses are reliably hardy even in Zone 4 gardens, as long as they get some winter protection. 'Mary Rose', 'Redouté', and 'Heritage' (all pink) and 'Winchester Cathedral' (white) may lose up to half their wood in a typical Zone 4 winter, but regrow vigorously in the spring.

David Austin roses also possess the large, dense double form and vivid fragrance of old-fashioned roses, along with the repeat, and sometimes continuous, flowering of modern roses. As well, the more than 80 varieties come in a wide range of colours, including apricot, buff, salmon and primrose, not just the reds, pinks and whites of older shrub roses.

Austin, an English rose breeder, created the new English rose by crossing spring-flowering old garden roses with modern types such as hybrid teas and floribundas. The first Austin rose was 'Constance Spry' (soft pink flowers on a large bush), introduced in 1961. Later introductions include 'Abraham Darby' (coppery apricot); 'Gertrude Jekyll' (large pink flowers, highly scented); 'Graham Thomas' (pure yellow flowers, strong tea fragrance); and 'Mary Rose' (rich pink flowers in small clusters). His roses took England by storm, and soon Canadians were clamouring for the new upstarts of the rose world.

Not everyone agrees on the hardiness of Austin roses. Many others are grafted—for quick growth and to save money—onto vigorous rootstocks. The graft, or bud union, is the most susceptible to cold. Some growers feel they're marginal at best in areas colder than Zone 6 or 7.

If you do decide to plant English roses, here are Austin's planting tips, taken from his book, *David Austin's English Roses*, and adapted for Canadian conditions:

- Mix generous quantities of manure or other humus into the soil before planting.
- Cut back and/or tie canes in early winter just enough to prevent wind from rocking or damaging the bush.
- Protect the plant with soil, mounded or in rose collars, around the base. Don't use soil from around the rose or you'll create a hollow that will collect water and cause root rot.
- In early spring, when the forsythia is in bloom, prune dead wood and weak growth, and cut remaining canes by half or three-quarters.
- Mulch with manure or other humus annually or at least every other year. Feed with rose fertilizer twice a year.
- Spray at the first sign of disease and continue at intervals until it's under control. (Austin roses, like other hybrids, are only disease-resistant, not invulnerable, and are sometimes affected by mildew or blackspot.)

Series, hybridized in Manitoba from a native prairie species rose, is aimed at dry regions, such as the Prairies. Parkland roses are more susceptible to mildew and blackspot than their Explorer cousins.

There are more than just cosmetic differences between Explorer roses. Five of the 16 varieties commonly available are cross-bred from *Rosa rugosa*, a hardy species rose that flourished in Asia more than 3,000 years ago. These—'Martin Frobisher', 'Jens Munk', 'Henry Hudson', 'David Thompson' (medium red, 120 centimetres tall) and 'Charles Albanel' (a groundcover rose, about 50 centimetres tall, medium red flowers)—are the hardiest and overwinter in Zone 2.

Just one climatic zone less hardy are what are known as the Kordesii climber or pillar-type Explorers—'John Cabot', 'William Baffin' (medium red), 'Henry Kelsey' (deep red), 'John Davis' (light pink), 'Captain Samuel Holland' (medium red) and 'Louis Jolliet' (medium pink).

Kordesii shrub and miscellaneous Explorer roses, also hardy to Zone 3, include 'John Franklin' (medium red, 1.5 metres), 'Champlain' (deep red, 1 metre), 'Alexander MacKenzie' (soft red, over 2 metres), 'Frontenac' (deep pink, 1 metre) and 'Simon Fraser' (medium pink, 60 centimetres).

Four new Explorer roses are: 'Quadra', a climber with deep red, double flowers; 'George Vancouver', a medium red shrub rose; 'Royal Edward', a low-spreading, almost semi-miniature rose with mottled pink flowers; and 'Lambert Closse', an upright shrub with pale pink flowers shaped like hybrid tea roses.

Three Kordesii Explorers have undergone field tests in recent years and are now on the market—'de Montarville' (a low shrub with lots of medium pink, mildly fragrant blooms that repeat later in the season): 'William Booth' (a vigorous climber with strongly fragrant single flowers that change from red to deep pink, colourful hips and red-tinged foliage; it's a continuous bloomer many compare to 'American Pillar'): and 'Marie Victorin' (mildly fragrant, semi-double repeating blooms in an unusual pink blend reversing to yellow, on a tall shrub). All are disease-resistant, although 'Marie Victorin' is susceptible to blackspot.

↓ *R.* 'Alexander MacKenzie', Explorer Series

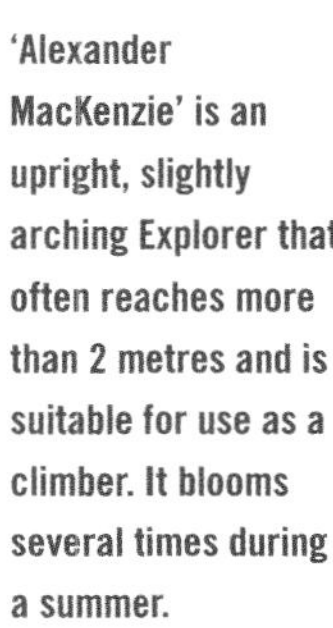
'Alexander MacKenzie' is an upright, slightly arching Explorer that often reaches more than 2 metres and is suitable for use as a climber. It blooms several times during a summer.

↑ Flower Carpet Series, red variety

Groundcover roses aren't a separate species but a group of ancient species, antique cultivars and recently bred shrub roses valued for their spreading habit and frequency of bloom.

Hardiness

Zones 2 to 5, depending on variety

Growing conditions

Three or more hours of sun; loamy soil; regular irrigation

Colour range

White, cream; pink, rose, lavender, red; some yellow

Bloom time

Late June into July; many till frost

Size

Depending on variety: under 30 centimetres to over a metre tall; 90 centimetres to 2.5 metre spread

↑*R.* 'Pierette Pavement', Pavement Series

favouriteroses

Groundcover Roses

They thrive just about anywhere and bloom all season long BY JUDITH ADAM

In gardens where hybrid tea roses already claim pride of place and long canes of climbers scramble up trellises, it's time to consider new venues for roses. Low-growing roses capable of massing, creeping and rambling horizontally are perfect used as groundcovers in less-than-ideal locations, such as corners of borders or alongside driveways and fences, provided they get enough light—at least three to four hours a day. They'll

Flower Carpet Series, white va

↑ *R.* 'Mozart'

'Mozart' is an intensely fragrant hybrid musk rose about 110 centimetres tall with enough substance and width to fill a large area. 'Stanwell Perpetual', with a 2-metre spread, is also a good filler with long bloom and a delicious scent.

flower from late spring to hard frost.

Groundcover roses aren't a special species of rose but a diverse collection of ancient species, antique cultivars and contemporary shrub plants of varying dimensions and styles that are valued for their low and spreading habit, non-fussy cultivation, resistance to disease, frequency of bloom sequence and ability to gobble up space in challenging locations. Tall, leggy beauties such as the grandiflora 'Queen Elizabeth', for example, or the shrub rose 'Westerland' will never be candidates for the job. But modern shrub roses like 'Rosy Cushion' (Zone 4, single, light pink, 90 centimetres high, 90 to 150 centimetres wide) and the *Rosa rugosa* hybrid 'Charles Albanel' (Zone 2, double, mauve-pink, 30 centimetres high, 90 centimetres wide, ornamental hips) have a growth habit that allows them to weave colourful living carpets in sunny gaps and spaces.

Growing

Roses used as groundcovers require much the same planting treatment as do other roses. Dig planting holes 45 to 60 centimetres deep and wide. Mix excavated soil with two parts high-quality loam, one part coarse sand, one part rotted manure. To plant bare-root roses, set the graft or bud union 5 centimetres below the soil surface on a hill of the replaced amended soil. In cold regions (Zones 2, 3 and 4) plant less hardy varieties with the bud union about twice as deep. Container roses should be set with the soil surface the same as it was in the pot.

After planting, keep the soil consistently moist, watering deeply once a week—more frequently if necessary—preferably using a soaker hose. Never allow the soil to dry out during summer droughts. Conserve soil moisture and keep weeds down with organic mulch. Spread 5 to 8 centimetres of finely shredded bark or tree leaves over the soil surface, and replace the mulch as it composts down. Avoid wood chips or rough mulches that can harbour fallen and diseased foliage.

When the first rose leaves open in mid-spring, feed plants with a commercial rose fertilizer, organic fish extract fertilizer, or a combination of blood, bone and kelp meals. Provide subsequent feedings in late June and late July (but no later—fertilizer encourages new, soft growth, which may not harden in time for winter) to keep ever-blooming roses flowering into autumn. Summer-blooming roses with one long flowering period also benefit from the same fertilizer/feeding schedule. Supply a generous amount of rotted manure around each plant in autumn. In colder regions (Zones 2, 3 and 4) place evergreen boughs over and around the plants after freeze-up to hold a protective snow cover through winter.

↓ *R.* 'Stanwell Perpetual'

Recommended varieties

Small spaces require plants in scale with the setting. The Japanese rose 'Nozomi' (Zone 5), smallest of the groundcover roses, is ideal for rambling about in a rock garden or even a large winterized container. The apple green canes of 'Nozomi', which is Japanese for "hope," spread almost prostrate over about 120 centimetres, and the plant has one long blooming time, from early to midsummer. Three plants together make a lovely show in a corner or surrounding a large boulder, with pearly pink, upward-facing, single flowers that wave tiny anthers.

Another diminutive spreading plant, 'Red Cascade' (Zone 4, 45 centimetres high, 120 centimetres wide) covers itself in double, deep red flowers all season. The repeat-flowering Pavement Series of low-growing rugosa shrubs (Zone 2) are disease-resistant and deeply scented, with ornamental hips and a hardy demeanour. 'Pierette Pavement' (dark pink), 'Scarlet Pavement' and 'Snow Pavement' are suitable for exposed locations, growing 75 centimetres high and 120 centimetres wide.

Large spaces require plants of bolder attitude and proportion. 'Raubritter' (Zone 4, 90 centimetres high, 180 centimetres wide) is a modern shrub bred in Germany with medium pink, cupped flowers with incurving petals, an unusual peppery fragrance and a sprawling habit. Flowers of the blush pink to white spinosissima rose 'Stanwell Perpetual' (Zone 3, 120 centimetres high, with a 2- to 2.5-metre spread) are quartered in the antique manner, with frilled edges. Of uncertain parentage—but clearly a rose of impeccable breeding, unfortunately lost to record—'Stanwell Perpetual' was found wandering in a garden at Stanwell, Middlesex, in 1838; for the

↑ *R.* 'Seafoam'

Tips for Roses

For best ground coverage, keep pruning to a minimum, cutti
dead and brown wood in spring.

Take the organic route to treat disease: a solution of 5
baking soda in 1 litre of water applied to foliage weekly i
synthetic fungicides in preventing fungal spot disease
chronic leaf spot disease, remove the plants and tr

Allow some insect damage. If critters threa
use an organic pyrethrum-based pesticide.

↑ 'R. 'Rosy Cushion'

↑ 'R. 'Rosy Cushion'

The modern shrub rose 'Rosy Cushion' grows about 90 centimetres tall with a wider spread. 'Seafoam', an outstanding rose, reaches 60 centimetres and blooms continuously till autumn.

sake of decency, it was allowed into the spinosissima category, where it probably belongs. Its double flowers, deliciously scented with classic tea rose perfume, bloom from late spring to hard frost. Long, arching canes form a dense mass, ideal for filling a major space on a broad hillside or along a driveway.

The wonderfully scented hybrid musk roses 'Ballerina' (Zone 4, single, light pink) and 'Mozart' (Zone 4, single, deep pink and white blend) both grow 110 centimetres high and 180 to 240 centimetres wide, with enough substance and form to fill large areas. Musk roses tolerate lower light and are a good choice for dappled shade or sites with only morning sun.

The familiar polyantha rose 'The Fairy' (Zone 4, 90 centimetres high, 120 centimetres wide), a Victorian style of blossom often replicated on old plates or wallpaper, is ideal for medium-size spaces on a hill or in a house foundation planting. Its jumbled mass of cascading branches are jammed with fat bunches of small, double, pink roses and glossy, boxwood-size leaves. No rose blossoms more enthusiastically—it blooms profusely from mid-May to November—and what 'The Fairy' lacks in fragrance it more than makes up in robust health and generous floral display.

Some groundcover roses are truly snaky and prostrate in habit, forming a low, dense carpet studded with flowers. The species *Rosa pimpinellifolia repens* syn. *R. spinosissima repens* (Zone 3, 60 centimetres high, 120 to 180 centimetres wide) opens small, light yellow flowers for a long summer blooming period.

Most desirable of the low roses is 'Seafoam' (Zone 4, 60 centimetres high, 150 centimetres wide), a gorgeous hybrid featuring slightly scented clusters of 6-centimetre, double, blush pink buds that mature to glistening white. It begins blooming a bit later than other roses, but then flowers continuously until late autumn. Modern groundcover roses are useful for filling niches and gaps in smaller home gardens. The very contemporary Flower Carpet Series of roses (Zone 5) have inbred disease resistance and,

Rooting for New Roses

Roses that like to grow in a down-and-out direction, such as 'Seafoam', can be rooted along their growth pattern to provide a denser field of plants. This is called "pegging" in the world of garden jargon, because you peg the low, arching canes to the ground to form roots over the summer. (With some patented roses this isn't technically a legal procedure, although it's not likely you'd be arrested for rooting plants for your own garden.) To encourage rooting, strip off a few leaves near the end of a cane, bend it over and bury the bare section under 5 centimetres of soil. Choose canes that are still young and soft. Anchor the cane with a large pin fashioned from coat-hanger wire. Set a rock on top to ensure it stays down, and leave the peg and rock in place until roots are evident in late autumn. Some rose growers advocate bruising the cane where it contacts the ground to encourage rooting, but this can present an entry point for fungus; the cane will root without wounding the wood.

given a protected position out of winter wind, make a dense covering in bright sun. They are available in shades of white, pink and cherry red, and grow 60 centimetres high and 120 centimetres wide.

The floribunda rose 'City of Belfast' (Zone 4, semi-double, 60 centimetres high, 90 centimetres wide) is a healthy, ever-blooming plant with scalloped, slightly scented, scarlet-orange to blood red flowers. Its cousin, 'City of Leeds' (Zone 4, double), is similar in size, with deep salmon-pink blooms borne in clusters. 'Essex' (Zone 5, single, 60 centimetres high, 120 centimetres wide) is a Danish shrub rose with large clusters of medium pink flowers and a dense trailing habit, continuously in bloom. Also in the shrub rose category, 'Lavender Dream' (Zone 4, 60 centimetres high, 90 centimetres wide) is a semi-double, lavender-pink rose with growth habits similar to 'Essex'.

A dwarf Scotch rose (*R. pimpinellifolia*), 'William III' (Zone 4, 45 centimetres high, 90 centimetres wide), works well as a front-of-the-border groundcover. Its small, greyish leaves and semi-double, dusty maroon flowers are followed by ornamental, chocolate brown hips.

And saving the best for last, if you select roses by following your nose, the following plants are the sweetest-smelling choices. The shrub rose 'Cardinal Hume' (Zone 5, very double, 90 centimetres high, 120 centimetres wide) has lush, cupped petals of ecclesiastical crimson-purple and a divine fragrance. The essence of Musk roses has long been included in love potions, and you can cook one up with 'Queen of the Musks' (Zone 4, 90 centimetres high, 90 centimetres wide). Its pink-blended, double flowers offer deeply perfumed moments to unbalance the gardener's equilibrium. David Austin, the rose-breeding master of Old World scent in New Age plants, offers his mother's namesake, 'Lilian Austin' (Zone 4, 90 centimetres high, 120 centimetres wide). Its large, double blooms are a celestial—and not garish—blend of pink, lemon and orange captured from the sunset sky and are, of course, highly scented.

'Max Graf' has a wonderful fruity fragrance, but blooms only once during the summer. A vigorous rugosa, it grows 60 centimetres high and about 2 metres wide.

↑ *R.* 'Seafoam'

↓ *R.* 'Max Graf'

↑ *R.* 'John Cabot', Explorer Series

For bloomin' good success, choose the right variety for your garden's conditions

BY JIM HOLE

Few plants can compete with the dramatic impact of colourful climbing roses. Whether winding around a column or adorning a trellis, they add beauty and serenity to any setting. But many gardeners are slightly intimidated by the prospect of growing climbers, which have a reputation for being finicky and especially prone to damage from deep freezes in winter. While it's true many climbing roses need extra winter protection, there are hardy types available that don't. If you're a little daunted by the mythical difficulty of growing these showy plants, take heart: choose the right variety and your rose—not you—will climb the walls with abandon.

favouriteroses

Climbing Roses

Hardiness	Growing conditions	Colour range	Bloom time	Size
Zones 2 to 6, depending on variety	Full sun; soil enriched with humus; regular irrigation	White, cream; pink, rose, orchid, scarlet to deep reds; yellow	June to early July; some varieties bloom sporadically all summer	2 to 6.5 metres tall, depending on variety

R. 'William Baffin', Explorer Series

↑ *R.* 'John Cabot', Explorer Series

↑ *R.* 'Henry Kelsey', Explorer Series

A climbing rose isn't a specific species of rose; in fact, climbers come from the cross-breeding of numerous rose species (which explains why the way they're planted and pruned is similar to the methods used for other roses). "Climber" is a general label for a rose that produces long, vigorous canes that tend to bend under their weight. The difference between bush roses and climbing roses is similar to the difference between bush and staking tomatoes: similar plants, different growth habits.

Climbing roses are categorized as three fairly distinct types: ramblers, trailing roses and true climbers (which include pillar roses). Ramblers are vigorous—they can grow up to 6 metres in one season—and are generally hardy to Zone 4. Traditionally, the blooms of ramblers are small, less than 5 centimetres across, and borne on dense clusters, but some of the newer varieties have larger flowers. The Meidiland Series, in particular, has several lovely cultivars. Ramblers are vulnerable to mildew.

Trailing roses are well adapted to planting along walls or on banks; if not staked, the long canes creep along the ground. Blooms are typically 5 to 8 centimetres across. Trailing roses are quite tough—they do well even in Zone 3. Look for cultivars of *Rosa wichurana*.

True climbers are noted for their large flowers—usually just a few per cluster. Some climbers bloom for a couple of weeks per season; others, often called pillar roses, bloom all season long. There are two main types of climbers: bush climbers and climbing hybrid teas. Bush climbers are the hardier, and bloom continually throughout the season. Both types are described in "Recommended varieties."

Growing

You can plant climbers or other roses any time from spring to fall, but early spring is the best time because plants have ample time to become established before winter sets in. Climbing roses are planted in the same way as other types of rose bushes: dig a roomy hole and mix plenty of organic matter, such as peat moss, well-rotted manure or compost, into the soil. Take the rose out of its container and gently untangle the outer roots with your fingers. (For a bare-root rose, merely place it in the planting hole and spread the roots.) If you're planting a tender climbing hybrid tea in a climate colder than Zone 6, make sure the graft—the knobby part where the rootstock is connected to the rest of the rose—is 10 centimetres below the soil level. For roses grown on their own roots, plant no deeper than the original soil level. Fill in, and firm the soil around the roots and stem; water until the soil is completely soaked.

Throughout the summer until mid-September, water thoroughly once a week, and fertilize every couple of weeks with 20-20-20 or 15-15-30 until the first of August. Follow this regimen each year.

Unlike vines, climbing roses don't have tendrils to wind around and attach themselves to a trellis or

Climbers are roses with long, vigorous and often flexible canes, which allows them to be trained over supports. They come in three main types: ramblers, trailers and pillars. Those from the Explorer breeding program are especially hardy.

arbour, so they have to be tied to their supporting structure. Install a trellis, pergola or arch before you plant so you don't disrupt the plant's roots. Space roses about 30 centimetres from the support—this distance provides good air circulation and enough space to train the rose. Once canes grow long enough to reach the structure, tie them to it loosely, using flexible material such as foam-covered wire, string or strips of cloth. The key to tying roses is to make sure the growing canes have room to expand. Check periodically to ensure branches haven't grown so much the ties are pressing tightly against them.

Every year in early spring, at the first swell of buds, some pruning is necessary to cut out dead, crowded or crossing branches. Since leaves have yet to form, the plant's energy will be channelled to new cane growth. Cut the canes back to the base or, if only cane tips are damaged, back to live wood. Always use sharp, clean secateurs to avoid injuring plants or introducing disease.

In the third and following years after planting, you also want to prune to open the plant up so it gets more sunlight, and to get rid of hiding places for insects or nurseries for disease spores. The timing depends on the type of climber. Prune repeat bloomers in spring, the same time you cut out dead, crowded or crossing branches. Prune roses that bloom once a season after their blooms fade. (Don't prune closer than three or four weeks before the average first frost—pruning stimulates new growth, which is vulnerable to winterkill if done late in the season.) Start by finding the leaf buds just above where a set of five or more leaves are attached to a cane; plants send out new growth in the direction these buds face, so make pruning cuts a short distance (.5 centimetres) above outward-facing buds.

Many climbers bloom on second-year wood, so don't sheer plants off. Some gardeners remove one older cane per year to let younger, more vigorous canes develop.

Recommended varieties

There are several hardy climbing roses available—thanks, in part, to the Explorer breeding program at Agriculture Canada. (In fact, hardy Canadian varieties are now starting to appear in Europe and the United States.) Because I live in Zone 3, I put a high premium on hardiness, so the cultivars I recommend can be grown from coast to coast and down to about Zone 2 with little or no winter protection. Keep in mind that during the first year or two in your garden, all roses are more vulnerable to winter damage than older, more established roses of the same variety. For the first few years, consider untying the canes of new roses to lay them on the ground and cover with mulch, or dig a trench and bury them. Otherwise, you can leave canes tied to their support over winter.

'William Baffin', named for the intrepid sailor who discovered the entrance to the Northwest Passage, is part of the Explorer Series and offers a profusion of deep pink, lightly

↓ *R.* 'William Baffin', Explorer Series

scented, semi-double blooms that appear continually in huge clusters from early summer until frost. Blooms are an average 5 to 8 centimetres across.

'William Baffin' is quite vigorous, reaching heights of 2.5 to 3 metres after just three or four years. Highly resistant to blackspot and powdery mildew, it's a perfect choice for novice rose growers.

'John Cabot', another Explorer Series climber, makes a perfect companion for 'William Baffin'. It has 5-centimetre double flowers that range in colour from a deep orchid-pink to reddish purple. Plants bloom from early summer to frost. Adding to this climber's appeal is a strong, pleasant fragrance. 'John Cabot' reaches 2.5 to 3 metres within three or four years, and has good resistance to blackspot and powdery mildew.

'Henry Kelsey', yet another Explorer, is one of the showiest plants I've seen, with dozens of big, red, double blooms, each about 5 to 8 centimetres across. The plant reaches 2 to 2.5 metres. Blooms appear repeatedly from early summer to frost, and have an attractive spicy scent. 'Henry Kelsey' tends to produce less foliage than other varieties, but its profuse blooms make up for the lack of greenery. The plant has good resistance to powdery mildew. A little less hardy than other Explorers, 'Henry Kelsey' should be grown in a sheltered location, against the south or west wall of a heated building. Pile snow around the base of the canes or lay the canes down and cover with a 20- to 30-centimetre layer of mulch.

'William Booth', a Kordesii Explorer that underwent field tests in recent years and is sometimes compared to 'American Pillar', is now on the market. It has five-petalled, 5-centimetre single flowers, with a strong fragrance, that change in colour from red to deep pink. It's disease-resistant, a continuous bloomer, hardy to Zone 3 and grows to about 1.75 metres.

'The Polar Star' is the largest, most vigorous and hardiest climbing rose I know. It has clusters of small (3- to 4-centimetre) double white blooms that draw people in for a closer look. It's named 'The Polar Star' because the first four or five petals open, lie flat and surround the remaining petals, which remain tightly closed, forming a point aimed at the stars. Plants bloom for about three weeks in early summer. The blooms form on old wood, so be careful not to prune heavily in spring.

'New Dawn' is a pillar rose hardy to Zone 5. It blooms in June and again in September. 'Madame Sancy de Arabere' is a tender, thornless climber. 'Alchymist', a hardy rose, puts on a magnificent display in early summer.

↓ *R.* 'Madame Sancy de Arabere'

↑ *R.* 'New Dawn'

↑ *R.* 'Alchymist'

'The Polar Star' is disease-resistant and grows to 5.5 metres—good for growing on a trellis that extends to the second storey of a house. But be careful not to confuse 'The Polar Star' with a hybrid tea rose called 'Polar Star'.

'Alchymist' is a hardy rose that blooms once in early summer for about three weeks (with sporadic bloom at other times). The showy, fragrant blooms put on a magnificent display—ruffled, 8-centimetre double blooms in shades of pink, yellow, apricot, orange and red. The first flowers to appear have pale, pastel shades; the more vibrant colours appear later in the blooming period. 'Alchymist' reaches 6.5 metres. It's susceptible to blackspot; ward off the fungicide by watering at the base of the plant so the foliage doesn't get wet.

But most climbers are on par with hybrid teas, as far as hardiness goes. If you want to grow a tender climber like 'Joseph's Coat', 'Climbing Blaze' or 'Polka' in zones colder than Zone 6, be prepared to protect them over winter.

Plant **tender climbers** in a sunny location that provides protection against winter winds. Before the ground freezes in the fall, dig a 30- to 60-centimetre deep trench—or more shallow in mild areas. Untie the canes, lay them in the trench and cover them with soil and mulch. The base of the rose is unlikely to bend enough to lie flat, so you have two options: dig up the entire rose, roots and all, to lie flat in the trench, or mound a hill of soil over the part of the plant that protrudes above the soil level. I prefer mounding to uprooting. Be careful not to break off secondary growth when you're laying the canes down; for many varieties, blooms emerge from this growth the following year.

The following climbers are pillar roses (which means they tend to bloom for most of the season) and do best in Zones 5 and up. But if there's one thing I've learned about gardening, it's not to be surprised when someone says, "You call that tender? I've been growing it in northern Manitoba for years . . ." Don't be afraid to try a plant that's said to be too tender for your zone—it's a bit of a gamble, but think of the bragging rights if it works!

'New Dawn' has a profuse number of semi-double, blush-pink flowers with a fruity fragrance; blooms appear in June and September. The plant grows 3.5 metres tall and tolerates some shade. 'White New Dawn' has white blooms.

'Zéphirine Drouhin' grows up to 3 metres in height. It's a lovely rose with very fragrant, semi-double, cherry-pink flowers, and no thorns.

'Altissimo Perfect' also grows to 3 metres, and has showy, bright red, single flowers borne in tight clusters.

The fragrant salmon-coloured flowers of 'America' are a treat; the vigorous rambler reaches 4.5 metres.

'Blaze Improved' has abundant, pure red blooms in large clusters. Blooms have a light tea fragrance and appear all summer on new and old wood. Plants can reach 5 metres in mild areas. Where I live, in Zone 3, it reaches 3 metres.

Hardiness

Zones 2 to 6 depending on variety

Growing conditions

At least 3 hours of sun, or part shade; winter mulch; light fertilizer

Colour range

White, cream; yellow; pinks to magenta and red

Bloom time

June, July; fewer blooms than roses in full sun

Size

30 centimetres to 6 metres (for climbers), depending on variety and amount of sun

Don't overfertilize or overwater roses growing in part shade in the hope of encouraging more bloom. They will naturally bloom less because sunlight is their true food.

← 'Buff Beauty', hybrid musk rose

↑ *R. banksiae* 'Lutea'

Roses *for* Shady Spots

How much sun do roses really need? Believe it or not, some roses tolerate a bit of shade BY JIM HOLE

Roses are gluttons for sunlight. They would bask in the summer sun 24 hours a day if they could. Since gardeners cannot provide such ideal conditions, they must find other ways to successfully grow roses in gardens that include some degree of shade.

Is the term "shade rose" an oxymoron? Quite simply, no. Although roses grown in shade produce fewer blooms than those grown in sun, they offer some advantages. The flower stems are longer, making them excellent for cutting, and the leaves are larger and glossier. Also, bloom colours fade less in the shade.

↓ *R. rugosa* 'Scabrosa'

↑ 'Zéphirine Drouhin', a bourbon rose

For Northern Exposures

The following climbers won't bloom as profusely when grown on sunny walls or fences, but are well worth trying on northern exposures:

'The Polar Star', clusters of small, white double blooms, Zone 5

'Alchymist', fragrant double blooms in yellow, pink, apricot, orange and red, Zone 6

'William Baffin', deep pink, lightly scented semi-double blooms, Zone 2

'John Cabot', medium red double blooms, Zone 3

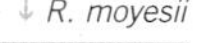

↓ *R. moyesii*

It's difficult to define what constitutes a shady place. Is it less than three hours of direct afternoon sunlight? Less than six hours? And what about those pesky terms like part shade, part sun, full shade, semi-shade and dappled shade? With such a welter of definitions, it can be daunting determining how much sunlight your garden receives and how much sun your roses actually need.

While science hasn't determined a method of growing roses in full shade—that's still about as likely as growing corn at the North Pole—researchers have come close to quantifying optimum light requirements. Using packets of solar energy called moles as a measurement, they have determined that, for excellent growth and flower production, a vigorous rose that covers about a square metre of ground needs from 20 to 50 moles a day. In Canada, the direct light of a sunny day in mid-June provides at least 40 moles to every square metre of ground it touches.

Because there are so many variables, it's difficult to translate moles into an exact number of hours, but assuming that an early-summer day yields about 15 hours of sunlight, it's safe to say that 6 hours of unobstructed direct sunlight daily—preferably afternoon sun—coupled with sufficiently warm temperatures, is enough to keep roses healthy and producing blooms. Warmer afternoon temperatures allow for faster conversion of carbon dioxide to the carbohydrates needed for leaf and flower production. With only half that amount of sunlight—3 hours—roses will still grow, but with less vigour. Even so, by choosing shade-tolerant types and modifying your gardening practices, you can enjoy the beauty of roses in the shade.

Growing

Since shade roses receive less energy from the sun, they produce fewer flowers and leaves. Many rose gardeners try to compensate for this lack of sunlight by applying generous quantities of water and fertilizer, when they should actually be providing correspondingly less: if direct sun is reduced by half (a plant gets half as much sun as one in full sun), cut the water and fertilizer by about the same ratio. Consistent, regular irrigation is vital to roses, but don't be talked into using those special fertilizers that supposedly increase blooms on shaded roses. Sunlight is a rose's true food; fertilizers are simply building blocks.

Feed roses with 28-14-14, either with a pinch in the watering can every time you water, or once every two weeks at a rate of 5 millilitres of fertilizer per litre of water. And, to improve your odds of success and to keep roses healthy, add 5 millilitres of Epsom salts per litre of water to your fertilizer program three times during the growing season. Use the same proportions for a foliar

↑ *R. filipes* 'Kiftsgate'

Roses grown in some shade may produce less bloom, but the flower stems are longer, leaves are glossier, and flower colour doesn't fade.

↑ *R.* 'Mermaid'

↓ *Noisette* 'Blush Noisette'

↓ *R.* 'The Fairy'

R. rugosa 'Charles Albanel'→

R. centifolia 'Cristata' ↓

↑ *R. rugosa* 'Blanc de Coubert'

spray; apply after the leaves open in spring and at flowering time. Epsom salts contain magnesium, an essential element of chlorophyll, the sunlight-capturing compound found in rose leaves. Stop fertilizing after early August.

In an attempt to maximize their reception of sunlight, shade roses produce large, thin leaves that are more prone to blackspot and powdery mildew than the thicker, more robust leaves of plants growing in full sun. That means gardeners need to be extra vigilant when checking shade roses for disease. The fungicides Benomyl and Funginex work well to control the spread of disease if applied early; alternatively, try using 10 millilitres of baking soda with 10 millilitres of Wilson's horticultural oil in 1 litre of water. Brazilian research has shown that cow's milk is also quite effective at controlling powdery mildew. Simply spray affected surfaces with a solution of one part whole milk to nine parts water. The solution dries quickly, leaving no unpleasant odour and a residue no worse than that left by commercial fungicides. (Test this remedy first on a few leaves before spraying all your roses.) Roses in the shade store fewer carbohydrates during the summer than roses in the sun, which leaves them more prone to winter injury. Protect them by applying extra mulch in fall.

Recommended varieties

With a few exceptions, roses that generally don't flourish in shady conditions are hybrid teas, grandifloras, English roses and floribundas. But a number of beautiful and tough roses are suitable for shady situations, even in areas such as Zone 3. Among these are pimpinellifolia (also known as spinosissima) roses, such as 'Spring Gold', 'Double Blush Burnet' and 'Spring Morning', all of which bloom nicely in relative shade. Rugosa roses, which evolved in northerly latitudes with lower light intensities, are also good candidates for shady gardens: 'Charles Albanel', 'David Thompson', 'Moje Hammarberg', 'Fimbriata', 'Scabrosa' and 'Schneezwerg' are especially suited. Also try 'Blanc Double de Coubert'. *Rosa gallica* 'Versicolor', also known as 'Rosa mundi', a species rose that grows on the periphery of its native forest habitat, does quite well in shade.

Centifolias tolerate shade, though not as well as the others. And alba roses, including 'Amelia', 'Félicité Parmentier' and 'Maiden's Blush', do well in partly shaded areas. Also try the albas 'Mme. Plantier' and 'Königin von Dänemark'.

For areas warmer than Zone 3, the following roses are suggested:

Alba/Bourbon 'Mme. Isaac Pereire' (Zone 6), 'Zéphirine Drouhin' (Zone 6)

Climbers and ramblers 'New Dawn' (Zone 5), 'American Pillar' (Zone 5), 'Veilchenblau' (Zone 5), 'Mermaid' (Zone 6)

Damask 'Mme. Hardy' (Zone 4)

Eglanteria 'Amy Robsart' (Zone 4)

Floribunda 'Iceberg' (Zone 5)

Hybrid musk 'Cornelia' (Zone 6), 'Buff Beauty' (Zone 6), 'Ballerina' (Zone 5)

Noisette 'Mme. Alfred Carrière' (Zone 6), 'Blush Noisette' (Zone 6)

Polyantha 'The Fairy' (Zone 5), 'Cécile Brunner' (Zone 6)

Species *R. moyesii* (Zone 6), *R. filipes* 'Kiftsgate' (Zone 6), *R. banksiae* 'Lutea' (Zone 8)

Wichuraiana 'Albéric Barbier' (Zone 6)

Shady Companions

Since roses grown in the shade tend to produce fewer leaves and flowers, try filling in the gaps with these attractive, shade-tolerant companions:

- 'Blue Light' clematis *(grow with climbing roses)*
- Baby's breath
- Foxglove
- Delphinium
- Monkshood
- Lavender *(in warm zones)*

Roses in the 19th century were noted for their intoxicating scent, but perfume was bred out of them in a search for a wider range of colours and a tapered flower shape. Today's hybridizers are bringing back fragrance.

↑ *R.* 'Double Delight'

Fragrant Roses

Choose the right variety and feed and water it well—then swoon BY JUDITH ADAM

On a summer afternoon, when the sweet scent of roses wafts through the air, gardeners across Canada are apt to swoon with pleasure. The Greek poetess Sappho was also overcome by the seductive lure of perfumed petals in the warm sun ("the rose each ravished sense beguiles"), and the rose scents in her seventh-century garden were essentially the same we enjoy today.

Although every rose is desirable, fragrant roses inspire us to particularly industrious planting strategies. Our goal is to find a scented rose for every possible garden situation and to learn the professional tricks of the rose breeder's trade: how best to enhance fragrance and encourage strong growth. We may be northern gardeners, but that's no

↓ *R.* 'Veilchenblau'

↓ *R.* 'Westerland'

OTHER SCENTED PLANTS FOR EARLY SUMMER ROSES

Perennials

Daphne; lilies; peonies; gas plant; lavender; pinks; sweet violets

Annuals

Petunias, especially white cultivars; annual woodruff; stocks; Chinese forget-me-not; heliotrope; sweet peas

← Foreground: *R.* 'Henry Kelsey', Explorer Series
Background: *R.* 'John Cabot', Explorer Series

↑ Circumpolar rose (*R. acicularis*)

On a hot day at the peak of summer, a rose in full sun will take 9 litres of water from the soil. The rose's petals are almost entirely composed of water, and need irrigation to produce scent.

reason to endure sensory deprivation.

Understanding some of the principles of rose scent helps in selecting plants with strong fragrance. The essence of fragrance is stored in tiny chloroplast cells on the undersides of petals. Thicker petals with a velvety sheen have more scent potential than thin, paperlike petals. Colour is also an indicator of types of fragrance. Red and pink petals tend to exude pure old rose perfume, with hints of raspberry and anise, while yellow and white petals are more complex, combining scents of orrisroot, nasturtium, violet and lemon. Banana, citrus, honey and clover frequently perfume orange shades.

Human olfactory abilities are calculated to be 10,000 times more sensitive than our sense of taste, allowing us to appreciate subtle differences in scent between rose cultivars and to remember the fragrance of a favourite rose. When sunlight heats the petal chloroplasts, production of scent-making chemicals is increased and released as vapour to waft through the garden (scented roses give off more fragrance midday, after the air has warmed). Drought and inconsistent watering are the greatest hindrances to the intensity of the scent of fragrant roses. And so, a word to the garden-wise: water in the morning, and swoon all afternoon.

↓ *R.* 'Fritz Nobis'

Trade Secrets

Professional growers accelerate plant maturity by giving roses three growth stimulants:

- When planting roses, use a transplant solution containing vitamin B1 (thiamine). Thiamine increases plant metabolism, helps to avoid transplant shock and increases the plant's ability to absorb carbohydrate nutrients—and grow faster!
- Magnesium sulfate, sold as Epsom salts (9.8 percent magnesium and 6 percent sulfur), encourages new and strong canes to sprout from just above the graft union. These are the main structural canes and will eventually carry many flowers. Apply 125 millilitres of Epsom salts to each plant in early May and again in early July, either dissolved in water or lightly scratched into the soil. Or make a foliar spray of 15 millilitres of Epsom salts to 4.5 litres of water.
- A foliage drench of liquid kelp extract every four weeks, applied early in the day, increases rose scent, cold hardiness and disease resistance. Follow product instructions.

Growing

The day a rose shrub is planted in the garden is the most important of its life. If the hole is inadequate—too small and with poorly prepared soil—the shrub's root development will be truncated and unable to support a strong plant. To create the best hole possible, dig out a 60-centimetre-square area for each rose and remove the soil entirely. Prepare a backfill soil of one part coarse sand, one part peat moss mixed with shredded bark and one part good-quality loam enriched with well-rotted manure. Set the plant's bud union (the bulging green knob just above the roots) 5 centimetres below soil level and backfill with the prepared soil mix. Mulch the soil surface over the rose's roots with 7.5 centimetres of shredded bark or leaves and slowly pour 4.5 litres of water through the mulch and into the hole.

It takes a lot of energy to produce armfuls of scented roses. Plan on providing a meal of rose fertilizer in early May and then again immediately after the June blossoms are finished. A third application can be applied no later than the first week of August to trigger a flush of autumn flowers in reblooming types. Be sure to provide only the amount recommended on the fertilizer package: rose roots are easily burned by excessive fertilizer. In October, give each rosebush a generous meal of one bucket of rotted manure, gently trowelled into the soil over their roots.

Rose petals are almost entirely composed of water; consequently, the size and scent of roses are dependent on adequate and regular water availability. On a hot day at the peak of summer, roses growing in full sun will take 9 litres of water from the soil. Organic mulch around the roses will help to prevent moisture loss, and a regular irrigation schedule (at least twice a week in warm weather) is absolutely necessary for maximum flower production. Avoid wetting rose foliage by watering at ground level, laying a slowly running hose at the base of each plant or using a soaker hose system. Water long enough to moisten the soil to a depth of 30 centimetres.

To prevent blackspot diseases on leaves, spray rose foliage every 7 to 10 days with a solution of 15 millilitres each of baking soda and liquid soap dissolved in 4.5 litres of water. Try to avoid synthetic pesticides—rose flowers and foliage can be burned and disfigured by their overuse, whereas most homemade pesticides are safe and effective.

Kill green aphids and whiteflies with a spray of equal parts water and 3 percent hydrogen peroxide (which can be purchased at a drugstore) applied weekly during dry weather and twice weekly during wet weather. The peroxide also promotes bud sprouting and deepens green leaf colour.

Spray slugs with a mixture of 1 part household ammonia and 10 parts water. Slugs are most active between 10 p.m. and 2 a.m., so bring a flashlight.

To protect plants for winter, after the first hard frost hill up generous amounts of fresh soil and leaves around the canes to a height of 45 centimetres. After freeze-up lay evergreen boughs or recycled Christmas trees over the roses to catch insulating snow.

Pruning for Flowers

In early spring, cut back dead or injured wood. Also remove live wood that is spindly and too thin to carry the weight of blossoms. After each flush of roses, cut back the canes under the finished flowers to an outward-facing leaf axil. This stimulates new growth (and more roses in four to six weeks for reblooming types).

Recommended varieties

Scented roses can be grown in all but the harshest climates. Species roses and Canadian cultivars have the fortitude to cope with harsh environmental conditions or the gardener's extended absences from the cottage. For example, the circumpolar rose (*Rosa acicularis*) is a strongly fragrant species rose, hardy

← 'Alec's Red', hybrid tea rose

Specific Rose Scents

Apple	'Serendipity', shrub, Zone 4
Citrus	'Margaret Merril', floribunda, Zone 6
Clove	'Summer Wind', shrub, Zone 5
Fruity	'Applejack', shrub, Zone 4
Honey	'Troilus', Austin, Zone 5
Lemon	'Heritage', Austin, Zone 5
Licorice	'Sunflare', floribunda, Zone 6
Myrrh	'Constance Spry', shrub, Zone 5
Old Rose	'Gertrude Jekyll', Austin, Zone 5
Tea	'Francesca', musk, Zone 6

to Zone 3, with deep pink, single flowers on 1.8-metre canes. Equally fragrant are the light pink, ruffled flowers of 'Delicata', a disease-resistant and cold-loving, 1.2-metre rugosa hybrid (1898, Zone 2) that also produces large, scarlet-orange hips in autumn. Modern, Canadian-bred roses with superior fragrance include 'Louis Jolliet', with old-fashioned pink flowers blooming continuously from June through September on 1.2-metre shrubs, and 'Henry Kelsey', a 2.4-metre climber that blooms repeatedly and freely, with red petals surrounding its golden stamens. Both are hardy to Zone 3 while other sweet-smelling Canadian cultivars are hardy to Zone 2.

Back in our well-tended home gardens, we can give better care and growing conditions to small-scale scented roses, just the right size to keep company with perennials in mixed borders. Many of the antique rose cultivars are surprisingly adaptable to 21st-century planting beds and have the added benefit of their extraordinary perfume and attractive autumn hips. The fiery red blooms of 'Etna' moss rose (mid-1800s, Zone 5) pair nicely with the dark blue 'Kent Belle' bellflower. The double flowers are deeply perfumed and embellished with tiny, soft, camphor-scented bristles. Notable among the damask roses is the 1-metre-tall 'Jacques Cartier' (1868, Zone 4), a luxuriously double, free-flowering rose with intensely fragrant pink petals, which contrast nicely with annual or perennial purple-flowered salvias. Old roses generally bloom just once, but last for an extended six-week period in early to midsummer. Many are hardy to Zone 5, though some, including *R. gallica* 'Versicolor', also known as 'Rosa Mundi', can be grown in Zone 2 gardens. The striped crimson-and-white petals of 'Rosa Mundi', a rose discovered in the 16th century, bring welcome, bi-coloured gaiety to grey-leafed companions such as 'Valerie Finnis' Western mugwort (*Artemisia ludoviciana*).

Fragrance potential in roses falls into the domain of recessive genes that are difficult to manipulate. The pale antique roses of the 19th century are notable for their intoxicating scent, but many 20th-century roses were hybridized for an expanded colour palette and blossom shape. All too often scent genes were lost along the way. Today's hybridizers have incorporated fragrance into breeding programs to produce roses with strong perfume, smaller plant size and recurrent bloom. Inspired by David Austin's development of modern English roses, European growers have followed by introducing the Romantica, Generosa and Renaissance Series.

The Austin English roses are among the most highly perfumed shrubs and set standards in colour and form. Most are reliably hardy to Zone 6 (Zone 5 with winter protection), though the Canadian Rose Society website recommends 'Graham Thomas', 'Mary Rose', 'Sweet Juliet' and 'Charles Austin' for gardens in Zones 2 to 4. Austin roses are especially attractive when planted in groups of three or five with a complementary underplanting of perennial alpine strawberries. These plants are hybridized cultivars of *Fragaria vesca*, the woodland wild strawberry. Alpine strawberries, which have no runners, are reliably hardy (Zone 4) and form thick, leafy clumps that shade the soil and help to keep rose roots cool in hot weather. The plants produce charming white flowers from May through October and tiny, delicious berries.

The Sweetest Roses

Hybrid Teas

'Alec's Red', to 2 metres, deep red, Zone 5
'Blue Moon', to 1.2 metres, silvery lilac, Zone 5
'Bride's Dream', to 2.5 metres, pale pink, Zone 6
'Double Delight', to 1.5 metres, red and cream blend, Zone 4
'Fragrant Cloud', to 1.5 metres, orange-red, Zone 4
'Just Joey', to 1.2 metres, pink-copper blend, Zone 5
'Medallion', to 1.5 metres, apricot, Zone 4
'Mister Lincoln', to 2 metres, deep crimson, Zone 5
'Welwyn Garden Glory', to 1.2 metres, yellow and copper blend, Zone 5
'Chrysler Imperial', to 1.2 metres, deep red, Zone 5

Floribundas

'Angel Face', 1.2 metres, mauve, Zone 5
'Chinatown', to 2 metres, deep yellow, Zone 5
'Fragrant Delight', to 1 metre, orange and pink blend, Zone 5
'Lavagold', to 1 metre, orange and copper blend, Zone 5
'Lillian', to 1 metre, pastel orange, Zone 5
'Margaret Merril', to 1.5 metres, white, Zone 6
'Radox Bouquet', to 1.5 metres, medium pink, Zone 6
'Sheila's Perfume', 60 centimetres, pink and cream blend, Zone 6
'Sunsprite', 60 centimetres, lemon yellow, Zone 5
'Apricot Nectar', to 1.2 metres, apricot-buff, Zone 6

Climbers

'Albertine', 3 metres, copper-pink, Zone 5
'Dr. J.H. Nicolas', 2.4 metres, rose-pink, Zone 6
'Golden Arctic', 1.8 metres, deep yellow, Zone 5
'Harlequin', 2.7 metres, cream and red blend, Zone 5
'Rosarium Uetersen', 2.4 metres, deep pink, Zone 4
'Seagull', 3.6 metres, white, Zone 5
'Veilchenblau', 3.6 metres, lavender, Zone 4
'Vicomtesse Pierre du Fou', 4.5 metres, copper-pink, Zone 6
'Viking Queen', 3 metres, medium pink, Zone 6
'Clair Matin', 2.5 metres, medium pink, Zone 4

Hardy Shrub Roses

'Bella Renaissance', 1 metre, medium yellow, Zone 3
'Cardinal Hume', 0.9 metres, maroon, Zone 5
'Comte de Chambord', 1.4 metres, bright pink, Zone 4
'Dornroschen', 1.2 metres, deep pink, Zone 5
'Fritz Nobis', 1.5 metres, peach and pink blend, Zone 4
'Hawkeye Belle', 1.2 metres, blush white, Zone 4
'Madrigal', 1.2 metres, deep red, Zone 6
'Westerland', 1.8 metres, apricot-orange, Zone 5
'Applejack', 2.4 metres, rose and pink blend, Zone 4

Austin English Roses

Many cultivars are fragrant and most are reliably hardy to at least Zone 6. Here are some of the most fragrant:
'Charlotte', 1 metre, soft yellow
'Chaucer', 90 centimetres, rose-pink
'Falstaff', 1.2 metres, dark crimson
'Othello', 1.2 metres, deep crimson
'William Morris', 1.5 metres, apricot-pink
'Graham Thomas', 1.2 metres, yellow

Parkland Roses

'Cuthbert Grant', to 1 metre, crimson, Zone 3
'Morden Sunrise', 1 metre, yellow-orange, Zone 3

Explorer Roses

'Charles Albanel', 1 metre, medium red, Zone 3
'David Thompson', 1 metre, medium red, Zone 2
'Henry Kelsey', 2 metres, medium red, Zone 3
'Louis Jolliet', 1.5 metres, medium pink, Zone 3
'Martin Frobisher', 1.5 metres, soft pink, Zone 2
'Jens Munk', to 2 metres, medium pink, Zone 2
'John Davis', to 2 metres, medium pink, Zone 3
'J.P. Connell', 1.5 metres, yellow, Zone 3
'Henry Hudson', 1 metre, white, Zone 2

↑ Unnamed single red rose with lamium

favourite perennials

Rose Partners

Even a bed of roses needs some close friends BY JANET DAVIS

Roses—especially modern roses like hybrid teas, floribundas and grandifloras—are often segregated from other plants in ghetto-like rose beds, unwitting victims of their own high-maintenance reputations and prima-donna bad press. After all, they look their worst in spring after the drastic pruning they need to maintain their vigour. Even in summer, the bottom third of most bushes is devoid of leaf or flower. And won't insect pests and fungal diseases like blackspot and powdery mildew spread to or from other plants, and be that much worse in a mixed border? Besides, isn't it better to appreciate roses on their own, rather than force them to mingle with the hoi polloi such as daisies and delphiniums?

It's time to put these myths to rest. It is true that hybrid teas, floribundas and grandifloras need spring pruning to remove winter-damaged wood and promote vigorous growth and abundant flowering. But as long as sufficient sun reaches the newly pruned canes to kick-start vegetative growth and promote budding, planting low-growing spring perennials and bulbs nearby helps camouflage those clumps of naked, thorny sticks, and won't interfere with the rose's growth. And later, when the roses flower, their gorgeous blooms enhance those of their neighbours and contribute to the garden's overall design.

Thankfully, the rose gardener's palette isn't restricted to these three types of roses. There are thousands of shrub roses, both modern hybrids and old-fashioned species, that require only the same pruning as other flowering shrubs—removal of the oldest canes every few years—making them excellent choices for a mixed border.

As for insects and disease, roses grown in rose beds are, like all monoculture plantings, sitting ducks for pests that thrive on host-specific plants. Spores of the fungus that causes blackspot can easily spread from rose to rose during irrigation or rainy weather, and insects such as the Japanese beetle, aphid, midge, spider mite and leafhopper have no trouble migrating from one bush to the next. But when roses are mixed with other plants, these pests are physically cut off from their next easy conquest. If problems do occur, spot treatments are less onerous tasks than spraying an entire bed.

And isolating roses in special beds to show them off is a practice few home gardeners have the space

Picket fences and arbours are perfect companions for roses, but roses need supportive plant friends, too. Roses grown by themselves in their own beds are sitting ducks for pests and diseases.

↑ *R.* 'Bonica' with lamb's-ears

GOOD PARTNERS FOR ROSES

With yellow roses

Lilac; weigela; purple allium; gold alyssum; purple Siberian iris; blue catmint; white candytuft; yellow 'Zagreb' coreopsis

With soft pink roses

Mauve-pink clematis; blue flax; love-in-a-mist; shasta daisies; 'Bright Eyes' phlox

With magenta and red roses

Silvery grey artemisias; white snakeroot; dark blue delphiniums; Crambe cordifolia; chartreuse lady's-mantle

With white roses

Baby's breath; sweet peas; red bee balm; purple salvia

↑ Unnamed pink rose

Plant repeat-blooming roses with mid- to late-summer perennials for a long-season show. White shasta daisies complement any rose, as do foxgloves, hesperis and rose campion. Annual blue nigella contrasts well with roses in both colour and texture.

↑ *R.* 'Golden Showers'

or resources for these days, especially when roses—in shades of white, cream, yellow and orange, and myriad pinks and reds—make such good companions for perennials, annuals, vines, herbs and ornamental grasses. Here are just a few suggestions for partnerships to enhance both your roses and your landscape.

Species roses

Three spring-flowering species shrub roses with yellow blossoms—pale-yellow Father Hugo's rose (*Rosa hugonis*), semi-double 'Harison's Yellow' (*R. harisonii*) and bright yellow 'Austrian Briar' (*R. foetida*)—bloom early and complement the pinks, lavenders and whites of such spring shrubs as weigela, lilac, fragrant spring viburnums, bridal-wreath spirea, deutzia and tree peonies in a mixed border. Underplant them with late-spring bulbs such as viridiflora or fringed tulips and *Allium aflatuense* 'Purple Sensation', as well as spring-blooming perennials: lungwort (*Pulmonaria* spp.), gold alyssum (*Aurinia saxatilis*), moss phlox (*P. subulata*), *Geranium* x *cantabrigiense* 'Biokova', sweet woodruff (*Galium odoratum*), candytuft (*Iberis sempervirens*) and rockcress (*Aubrieta deltoides*). These plants pay their rent as groundcover later since they all have good-looking foliage.

The red-leafed rose (*R. glauca*, formerly *R. rubrifolia*) is a later-blooming species. The tall, arching, shade-tolerant shrub is grown not so much for its sprays of small, pink single flowers as for its purplish grey leaves and reddish violet stems, which make an effective contrast to green foliage. It's a lovely backdrop in a pink garden scheme, perhaps with mauve-pink clematis 'Hagley Hybrid' clambering over it. In fall, the rose develops abundant clusters of orange-red fall hips, blending in with the season's golds, reds and bronzes and especially useful in naturalistic gardens for attracting birds and other wildlife.

Antique roses

The romantic, often perfumed, old or antique roses—albas, bourbons, centifolias, damasks, gallicas and mosses—and the more modern hybrid perpetuals and hybrid musks offer colours ranging from white and cream through all shades of pink to deep crimson. All look wonderful near plants with silvery grey foliage, such as lamb's-ears (*Stachys lanata*) and 'Silver Mound', 'Silver King' and 'Valerie Finnis' artemisia. The roses' main flush of bloom occurs in late spring or early summer, depending on the region, but a few flower sporadically throughout the season, while others repeat in a second, more modest show in late summer.

Shrub roses combine easily with the huge cast of sun-loving early-summer perennials and biennials that also share the same love of reasonably rich, moist soil. Old roses have a loose, arching habit, perfect for cottage-style gardens where informality reigns, and they can be used in the front, middle or back of a perennial border, depending on their size.

For planting with antique roses such as white 'Blanc Double de Coubert', striped pink-and-white 'Rosa Mundi', pink 'Fantin-Latour' and velvety red 'Tuscany', think of old-fashioned, early-summer perennials in similar hues of white, pink and crimson, such as painted daisy (*Tanacetum coccineum*), shasta daisy (*Leucanthemum* x *superbum*), pinks (*Dianthus* spp.), meadowrue (*Thalictrum* spp.), columbine (*Aquilegia* spp.), gas plant (*Dictamnus albus*) and late-season peonies.

Blue, lavender and purple flowers mix exceedingly well with soft-pink old roses like 'Madame Ernst Calvat' and 'Königin von

Danemark'. Consider blue flax (*Linum perenne*), columbine, lavender, peach-leaf bellflower (*Campanula persicifolia*), Siberian iris, catmint (*Nepeta* x *faasennii*) and false indigo (*Baptisia australis*).

Self-seeding biennials such as foxglove (*Digitalis purpurea*), rose campion (*Lychnis coronaria*) and sweet William (*Dianthus barbatus*) have long been grown in cottage gardens with antique roses. Nurture them in an out-of-the-way spot the first summer as they form their foliage rosette, and then move them into their flowering positions near the roses the following spring.

And if a sweet-scented garden is what you long for, pair fragrant old roses with perfumed lilies such as white *Lilium regale* or Madonna lily (*L. candidum*).

Modern shrub roses

Modern shrub roses are complex hybrids of species roses and/or old roses with modern roses (usually floribundas). They're often hardier and more disease-resistant than old roses, and have repeat or continuous bloom. Some, like the David Austin–bred English roses, extend the colour range into peach and yellow; the popular 'Graham Thomas', a robust apricot-yellow, is a good example.

The Canadian-bred Morden series includes roses like 'Morden Blush' with flesh-pink blossoms that are enchanting near such perennials as purple balloon flower (*Platycodon grandiflorus*). 'Morden Centennial' is a tough shrub with double, clear pink blooms that look great near a summer phlox like 'Bright Eyes', whose light pink flowers with a cerise eye pick up the rose colour.

The magenta-pink flowers of the big Explorer shrub 'John Cabot' or the rugosa hybrids 'Roseraie de l'Hay' and 'Hansa' can clash with hot colours (red, orange and yellow). Instead, pair magenta roses with rich purples like delphinium 'Black Knight' or tall, white-flowered perennials like snakeroot (*Cimicifuga racemosa*) and billowing *Crambe cordifolia*.

All of the early-summer perennials listed as partners for old roses can be grown with modern shrubs, of course, but because of the longer bloom season of modern hybrids, later-blooming perennials and shrubs make enduring neighbours. Consider baby's-breath (*Gypsophila paniculata*) near creamy white 'Seafoam'; blue monkshood (*Aconitum napellus*) near light pink 'Bonica'; purple coneflower (*Echinacea purpurea*) beside pink-and-cream 'Carefree Wonder'; and blue mist bush (*Caryopteris* x *clandonensis*) with single pink 'Nearly Wild'.

Hybrid teas, grandifloras and floribundas

For the most part, hybrid teas, grandifloras and floribundas are shorter than shrub roses, which sometimes reach 2.4 metres. They generally start flowering a little later than old roses, in mid- to late summer, but bloom continuously into fall, making them good companions for annuals and

Roses with Herbs

Since the Middle Ages, when monks tended their cloistered gardens, roses have been grown alongside medicinal and culinary herbs, often in formal parterres. But regardless of the style—a classic knot garden sculpted in boxwood or a casual contemporary planting of rosemary, oregano and thyme—roses and herbs marry exceedingly well.

Shrubby lavender is a familiar rose companion; its blue spikes are especially sumptuous with deep red roses. Giving a similar effect but much hardier than lavender is blue catmint. The frothy chartreuse flowers of lady's-mantle (*Alchemilla vulgaris* and *A. mollis*) look sensational under dark red rose blossoms. Self-seeding borage (*Borago officinalis*) lends a clear blue to enhance yellow, peach or red roses. Sages, including tall blue *Salvia x superba* and cultivars like the deep blue 'May Night', go well with roses and the decorative leaves of golden sage (*S. officinalis 'Aurea'*) provide the added benefit of being an effective groundcover.

Grasses, Tame and Wild

With the growing use of ornamental grasses in gardens and the increasing trend toward naturalistic gardens or meadows, certain types of roses can play an exciting role. Pick a tough species or hardy hybrid rose to help convey an informal look. It's in the nature of roses with a suckering habit—like hybrids of *R. rugosa*, native to grassy coastal sand dunes in Asia—to spread, so they naturally fare better against the root competition of grasses in a meadow garden.

Roses that form hips in late summer create an ornamental effect and provide valuable winter food for birds and wildlife. Hip-formers that also have colourful autumn leaves include *R. rugosa* and its hybrids 'Hansa', 'Fru Dagmar Hastrup' and 'Scabrosa'.

Certain native roses have leaves that colour in fall and also look at home with grasses and wildflowers: small, spreading *R. nitida*, native from Newfoundland to New England, bears single pink June flowers and trails to 4.5 metres; Prairie rose (*R. setigera*) has clusters of single pink blossoms in summer; and tall, pink-flowered *R. palustris* is one of the few roses that tolerates damp soil.

summer and fall perennials, especially low-growing ones that hide their bare lower canes. Best of all, this group extends the colour range of roses into bright yellow, orange and scarlet, creating opportunities to pair them with other hot-coloured flowers.

The yellow daisies of 'Zagreb' coreopsis and 'Kelwayi' anthemis make cheery companions to orange floribunda 'Brass Band' or golden 'Sunsprite', while a taller daisy like *Rudbeckia fulgida* 'Goldsturm' brings out the heat in red floribundas 'Parkwood Scarlet' and 'Satchmo'.

The floribunda 'Iceberg', touted as the best white rose ever bred, is good in an all-white scheme or paired crisply with perennials like red bee balm (*Monarda didyma*) and blue *Veronica longifolia*. And the classic, high-centred pink blooms of the tall grandiflora 'Queen Elizabeth' will still be opening when the pink and white September blossoms of Japanese anemone (*Anemone* x *hybrida*) emerge.

Annuals can be tucked in under roses to provide long-term colour where it's most needed. Generally, those with small, informal blooms like diascia, nierembergia, nemesia, larkspur (*Consolida ambigua*), Chinese forget-me-not (*Cynoglossum amabile*) and love-in-a-mist (*Nigella damascena*) are preferable to stiff, gaudy annuals such as marigolds, red salvia or bedding geraniums, which compete with showy rose blossoms for attention.

Climbing roses

One of the best ways to grow a clematis vine is to let it piggyback on a climbing rose. Large-flowered, late-spring clematis like 'Ramona' and 'Nelly Moser' are beautiful, but their habit of blooming on old wood means that when the necessary spring pruning of roses is done, you must gingerly avoid snipping the clematis. The best choices are summer-blooming clematis that get cut back hard in spring: purple 'Jackmanii', pink 'Comtesse de Bouchaud' or *viticella* hybrids like 'Venosa Violacea' and 'Polish Spirit'. Pair them with modern climbers that flower all summer.

Even a late-bloomer like sweet autumn clematis (*Clematis terniflora*), with its September clouds of tiny white blossoms on 5-metre stems, makes a charming counterpoint to a rambler like pale pink 'Clair Matin', whose long canes reach skyward in fall. Sweet autumn clematis is also cut back in spring.

Certain species of honeysuckle (*Lonicera* spp.) are fragrant and make a heavenly bower with perfumed climbing roses. Passionflower's intricate flowers would steal the show and wisteria is too vigorous to admit enough sun for a rose to thrive, but morning-glory (*Ipomea* spp.) and sweet peas (*Lathyrus odoratus*) are fine annual vines to grow through climbing roses.

A summer-blooming clematis is a natural partner for a climbing rose because the clematis should be cut back hard in spring, the same time you need to prune the rose.

favourite trees & shrubs

favouritetrees&shrubs

The Maple

Forever our favourite tree—here's how to choose the right one BY JUDITH ADAM

Hardiness

Zones 3 to 6, depending on variety

Growing conditions

Light shade to full sun; space to spread

Features

Coloured foliage, especially in fall

Size

6 to 36 metres, depending on conditions and variety

Fall in most parts of Canada means red maple leaves creating a dazzling overhead canopy or a brilliant carpet underfoot. Many of the trees lining our streets are relics from a time when big maples were the only choice.

From the vantage point of any Canadian doorstep you're likely to see a maple tree. In fact, you may see several of your own and enough of your neighbour's to make a small forest. Maples are an arboreal fixation for Canadians. Never has a tree been loved by so many for so long. We have abiding tolerance for the maple's ways and means of spreading progeny, and obligingly allow maple keys to root into every nook and cranny. Several years down the road, when shade begins to spread over the garden, we are still reluctant to remove the saplings. Uprooting these aggressive youngsters is about as acceptable as ruining a sunset. After all, the profile of the maple leaf is firmly affixed to our flag, our national character, and to our lapels when we travel abroad.

In the Victorian language of flowers, maples symbolize reserve, a characteristic that reflects Canadian heritage and values, and is associated with the strengths necessary to build a nation in the North. But before the maple was an image of national pride, it was a tangible asset. We were quick to realize the usefulness of the maple forests, using the wood for axles and spokes, fabricating Windsor chairs, inlaying mahogany, and as a major component in the production of potash fertilizer (maple ash is high in this mineral). The profits from the sugar maple (*Acer saccharum*) also included the manufacture of good molasses and excellent vinegar after the sweet sap was finished.

Many of the maples lining our streets and country lanes are old and weathered relics of a time when big

Sugar maple (*A. saccharum*

trees were the only choices. The garden naturalist William Robinson (*The English Flower Garden*, 1883) thought the big maples—Norway maple and silver maple (*A. platanoides* and *A. saccharinum*)—were "of the highest value. It is doubtful if there is any finer tree than this when old," he wrote, making a point contemporary gardeners might dispute after encountering maple roots in the dahlia bed. The simple logic that large plants should be planted in large spaces seems to have eluded city fathers in many municipalities and has greatly increased the ranks of gardeners who have to deal with dry shade on small city lots. Under ideal growing conditions, big maples can reach 36 metres and live for up to 200 years.

But no tree lives forever, and moderately sized maples can be big assets in smaller gardens. Challenging experiences with large trees shouldn't obscure the valuable features of the maple family or the desirable smaller species that are readily available.

Growing

First, here's some general advice about growing trees in a cold climate. Most gardening books calculate mature growth statistics for hardwood plants on optimum growing conditions in the geographic centre of North America—and that could be a field in Zone 7. The growing season in Canada is considerably shorter,

We're most familiar with the big maple trees that provide shade—plus that delicious syrup, molasses and wood for furniture. But many varieties of graceful, airy Japanese maples offer a wealth of choices for small urban lots.

↑ Japanese maple (*A. japonicum* 'Aconitifolium')

↑ Sugar maple (*A. saccharum*)

↑ Silver maple (*A. platanoides*)

↑ Maple keys

with fewer days of warm growing temperatures. We do have a healthy growing environment and can produce lovely trees, but they will almost always be smaller at maturity than gardening book figures for height and width suggest. (The exceptions to this are the true northern forest trees such as spruce, pine and hemlock.) Keeping that in mind, there are several desirable, small maples suitable for garden use; hybridizers have scaled down some of the large maples with similar reductions in root mass.

Bigness is not a bad attribute in a plant, but there must be space for the bigness without consuming all in its shadow. The Norway maple would be happy in a meadow but makes a terrible obstruction when set down next to a house. Like the silver and sugar maples, it has a thick, fibrous root system that chokes out other plants. Keep them all at least 5 metres away from ornamental plant beds.

Grass won't grow well under the big trees, but three groundcover plants will. Sweet woodruff (*Galium odoratum*), goutweed (*Aegopodium podagraria*) and herb Robert (*Geranium robertianum*) have roots that barely skim the soil and can exist in the dry region under maples. They will need regular watering to keep up a good appearance in competition with the maples.

Recommended varieties

Perhaps spurred by personal experience, plant hybridizers have solved the Norway maple problem to some extent and given us a **columnar maple** (*A. platanoides* 'Columnare') with a possible height of 12 metres and spread of 4 metres (sizes here are based on growth in Zone 6). The shape of 'Columnare' is compact and upright, with branches extending up rather than out. This is a reasonable size for a specimen lawn tree, or a string of trees set along a fence at least 6 metres apart. It would also find good use in the corner of a lot to block out sight of a telephone pole.

Red trees are useful for bringing colour to a green background in the warm months. 'Crimson Sentry' maple (*A. platanoides* 'Crimson Sentry') has deep purple foliage on a frame growing 8 metres in height and 5 metres in width; it's hardy to Zone 4. Its pyramidal form is suitable for lawn placement or at the corner of a house. Both the 'Columnare' and 'Crimson Sentry' maples are generally lower-branched than other maples and this is always a plus in a specimen tree, preventing a hollow blank space under the limbs where grass won't grow. Nurseries sometimes mistakenly limb them up when very young, so search for one that has lower branches intact down to about 1 metre from the ground. Another scaled-down tree with lots of ornamental appeal is the **variegated harlequin maple** (*A. platanoides* 'Drummondii'), with light green leaves, each with a white margin. The harlequin maple makes a showy lawn specimen, growing to 11 metres with a spread of 8 metres. All of the *A. platanoides* hybrids are hardy to Zones 4 or 5.

If you've got a bit more space on a country property but don't want a full-size maple, 'Silver Queen' maple (*A. saccharinum*, hardy to Zone 3) is a more refined version of silver maple, growing to 16 metres with a width of 13 metres, still smaller than its species parent, which can grow to 18 metres high and 15 metres wide. The same can be said for 'Endowment'

sugar maple (*A. saccharum*, hardy to Zone 4), which has a similar height of 17 metres and a narrower spread of 6 metres. 'Silver Queen' turns golden in autumn, while 'Endowment' turns orange-red.

Two mid-size maples perfect for suburban and city properties are the shantung or purpleblow maple and the paperbark maple. The shantung maple (*A. truncatum*) is hardy to Zone 5 and grows about 6 metres high and 5 metres wide. Its delicate lobed leaves are scaled down in size compared with larger maples, and slightly wavy with a lustrous sheen; it will provide dappled shade over a patio or seating area. Leaves are deeply reddish purple as they open in spring and yellow-orange-red in fall. This tree isn't often offered for sale in Canadian garden centres, but only because it isn't well known; asking for it will stimulate the market.

Much easier to acquire is the paperbark maple (*A. griseum*, hardy to Zone 6) and one of the most admired ornamental trees. Its shiny, peeling bark is a warm cinnamon or red-brown colour. This is a good tree to have close to a front door where the bark can be appreciated all year, particularly in snow when it is most beautiful. With a manageable height of 7 metres and spread of 5 metres, it takes on dignity with age. Young paperbark maples show differing degrees of exfoliating bark, and the amount they peel when young is consistent as they age. A young tree with minimal peeling will continue that way as it ages, so be sure to select one with a strong peeling characteristic to ensure it will continue to do so in the future.

A tree we are seeing more of is the very serviceable 'Bloodgood' Japanese maple (*A. palmatum*, hardy to Zone 5), and an ornamental workhorse in the garden. Delicate in structure, 'Bloodgood' reaches 6 metres in height and 5 metres in width, thickly clothed with deepest purple foliage. In a sunny location this colour holds all season, and in shade it is slightly suffused with green. In autumn and early spring it is beautiful when hung with raindrops, and presents a fine, dark profile against snow. Two 'Bloodgood' Japanese maples make a lovely frame for a front door, set 3 metres from both sides of the steps and 2 to 3 metres out from the house wall. Two low and shrubby *A. palmatum* hybrids worth having for vertical accent in a perennial border are 'Butterfly' and 'Seiryu', both hardy to Zone 6. 'Butterfly' is an unusual variegated plant with slightly twisted and curled leaves coloured grey-green, white and pink. It has a stiff, shrubby form with upright branches to 2 metres that are set off and softened by the exquisite foliage. 'Seiryu' is an upright Japanese maple reaching 3 metres, with thin twigs and lacy green foliage, deeply incised and filigreed, that turns orange-red in autumn. Both plants grow well in light shade to part sun, but in brighter light require more water to prevent their fine leaves from scorching. Japanese maples have less fibrous, and therefore less invasive, roots. Pair them with white or pink bleeding hearts in spring and Japanese anemones 'September Charm' and 'Honorine Jobert' in late summer.

The fullmoon maple (*A. japonicum*, hardy to Zone 6) is a lovely tree for a little corner out of the winter wind. Its intriguing, moonlike leaves are chartreuse green turning to rich yellow and crimson in autumn and have wavy edges as though trimmed with pinking shears. Occasionally its fancy-leafed hybrid,

A. japonicum 'Aconitifolium', can be found. It is quite different from the fullmoon parent and possibly the most flamboyant of all Japanese maples, with sharply incised leaves that turn to deepest crimson, earning it the prideful Japanese name of Mai kujaku or dancing peacock. These maples are both highly ornamental and just the thing to have near a seating area or to one side of an entrance, where their fine details will be noticed. They grow well in light shade to full sun, but require more water in stronger light.

Finally, for colder regions, two small, ornamental maples: the striped snake bark maple (*A. pensylvanicum*, hardy to Zone 3), and the amur maple (*A. ginnala* 'Flame', hardy to Zone 2). The striped snake bark maple has a maximum height of 8 metres and spread of 6 metres, and prefers cool, moist soil in partial shade. In spring, its yellow, pendulous flowers glow against the vividly striped bark and young reddish stems. The tree's golden autumn colour is exceptional. The amur maple 'Flame' is a large shrub or small tree reaching 7 metres high and wide, useful to anchor a long cottage garden border at one end or stand at the foot of a country driveway. It has stylized leaves of three lobes compressed into a narrow shape. If grown in strong sunlight, it comes alive in autumn with deep scarlet colour. Amur maple is the toughest of the small maples and will tolerate a dry site and wind, still producing its red display at season's end.

↓ Sugar maples (*A. saccharum*)

Hardiness

Zones 4 to 6

Growing conditions

Deep, well-drained soil for large varieties

Features

Wide range of shapes, leaf forms and colours; some leaves stay over winter

Size

3 to 24 metres, some columnar or weeping forms

↑ Purple-leafed beech (*F.* 'Atropunicea')

The Beech

Its distinctive bark and imposing presence dignify even the humblest of gardens BY TREVOR COLE

In spring, the unfolding leaves of European beech are glossy, new-grass green. The colour changes to dark green in summer and to russet brown in fall. The leaves stay on all winter.

"Among deciduous trees there is nothing quite as majestic or as graceful as the beech." So wrote Donald Wyman, then horticulturist at the Arnold Arboretum near Boston and president of the American Horticultural Society, in his 1951 book *Trees for American Gardens*. Things haven't changed since then; beeches are still spectacular landscape trees that leave a lasting visual impression, perhaps partly because their foliage remains on the tree during winter. Their timber is also valuable, close-grained and easily worked, which may be why one often sees it used for kitchen utensils. It's also used for furniture and flooring.

Of the 10 species of beech worldwide, only two are commonly cultivated by and available from Canadian nurseries, the American beech (*Fagus grandifolia*, Zone 4) and the European beech (*F. sylvatica,* Zone 6).

Growing

Beech trees need deep, well-drained, acidic soil; they will not thrive on wet or compacted soil and they like some shelter from strong winds. Purple-leaf forms generally like some sun, and yellow-leaf varieties prefer a little shade, and all beeches do best in areas with long, warm summers.

Plant container-grown, or balled and burlap-wrapped beech saplings in spring, but if you'd like to try growing from seed, try the European beech. In early fall pick newly ripened seed and sow outdoors; it should germinate the following spring. To start indoors, mix the seed with an equal quantity of just-moist peat moss, enclose in a plastic bag and store in the refrigerator at 5°C or lower for 60 to 90 days to improve the germination rate.

← European beech (*F. sylvatica*)

↑ European beech (*F. sylvatica* 'Zlatia')

The problem, though, is finding good seed. Only two of the many forms of *F. sylvatica* can be grown from seed, and even then the seedlings will differ from the parent plants. Seeds from *purpurea* (a collective name for the many purple-coloured copper beeches) produce plants with purple foliage, but the colour may not be as dark as the parents'; the shape will also likely differ. Named forms of copper beech are propagated by grafting.

Seedlings of weeping beech (*F. s.* forma *pendula*) will most likely have a weeping growth habit, but the branches may hang straight, grow downward from the trunk at an angle or grow horizontally at first, then turn downward. If selecting a weeping beech for a specific location, examine the branch structure carefully before deciding, or you may end up with a tree too wide for your site. The purple-leafed, weeping form *F. s.* 'Purpurea Pendula', with arching branches, makes for a short but wide tree, about 3 metres tall and across.

Both the American and European beeches are highly disease- and pest-resistant but may suffer some dieback if planted close to the limits of their hardiness.

Occasionally, small galls may form on the leaves, caused by a tiny midge laying eggs beneath the leaf surface, but these are not serious and rarely develop enough to warrant spraying; cleaning up the fallen leaves helps keep them from becoming a major problem. There is also beech scale, an insect that attacks beech, and beech bark disease, caused by a fungus that invades the resulting damage, but those are rare unless you live near a forested area containing native beech trees. If necessary, control the scale with sprays of lime sulfur while the tree is dormant.

Inviting Bark

The smooth, grey bark makes beech one of the easiest trees to identify. Even when mature, the bark doesn't become furrowed like that of most trees. Unfortunately, the smoothness tempts people to carve their initials, often in pairs within a heart—a defacement that frequently lasts longer than the relationship.

A tree in Washington County, Tennessee, bore the inscription "D. Boone Cilled A Bar on Tree in Year 1760." This was still legible in 1880, and the scars were still visible when the tree eventually fell in 1916, at an estimated age of 365 years.

Recommended varieties

The **American beech** (*F. grandifolia*, Zone 4) is native from Nova Scotia to Ontario and south to Florida's panhandle. It's a good tree for a large garden but it creates dense shade and has shallow roots, so cultivating grass beneath its branches can be difficult. At maturity, American beech, for which there are no named forms, can grow to 20 metres, with a crown almost as wide. On country properties, plant one for your grand children—it's slow-growing and the kids will enjoy the edible nuts.

The queen of the beech family is the imposing **European beech** (*F. sylvatica,* Zone 6 and sometimes into the warmer areas of Zone 5), which is much less demanding than the American beech and grows in both slightly acidic and alkaline soils. Smaller than the American beech, it reaches a height of about 18 metres. Its main drawback is a high sensitivity to salt, and as such it's not a good choice for siting near the coast or

↓ American beech (*F. grandifolia*)

close to roads that are salted in winter. But it's fairly tolerant of urban pollution, making some of the smaller varieties, such as 'Dawyck', excellent options for city planting.

In spring, the unfolding foliage of European beech is a glossy, new-grass green that changes to a dark green in summer, then to a russet brown in late fall. The foliage remains on the trees over winter until pushed off by the new leaves, giving winter interest and a contrast to the dull green of most coniferous plants.

Although many of the named forms are suitable only for large, open spaces, a few of the smaller ones can be grown in the average garden. 'Dawyck' (discovered in 1860 growing in the forests near the Scottish estate of Dawyck, in Peeblesshire) is a pyramidal beech that reaches about 24 metres high and about 3 metres wide, but gains only about 3 metres in height over a 10-year period. 'Dawyck Gold' is a similar upright variety with yellow leaves in spring that turn to green in summer and then back to gold in fall. 'Dawyck Purple' is also upright but has deep purple foliage all summer long. Its shoot tips turn inward, giving it a slightly more narrow profile than the others. These last two were introduced in 1973, so it's too soon to know their ultimate sizes. Another recent column-shaped introduction (1975) is 'Purple Fountain', which is a lighter purple than 'Dawyck Purple'

↑ Weeping beech (*F. sylvatica* forma *pendula*)

↑ Copper beech (*F. sylvatica*, possibly '*Atropuriicea*')

↑ Fern-leafed beech (*F. sylvatica* forma *lacinata*)

Although 10 species of beech grow in the world, only 2—the European and the American beech—are available in Canadian nurseries. The queen of the family is the imposing European beech, which grows in many shapes, with a variety of leaf forms and colours.

with somewhat pendulous side branches. It's hardy to Zone 5b.

If selecting a weeping beech for a specific location, examine the branch structure carefully before deciding, or you may end up with a tree too wide for your site. 'Purpurea Pendula', the purple-leafed, weeping form of European beech, has arching branches that make it a short but wide tree, about 3 metres tall and across.

The three most readily available cultivars of copper beech are *F. sylvatica* 'Atropunicea', 'Riversii' and *F. s.* forma *purpurea*. Some authorities consider the first and last two to be the same species, but the plants I have seen under these names are different: 'Atropunicea' is cone-shaped, about half as wide as tall, and *F. purpurea* is a mounded form, almost as wide as high. 'Riversii' has a broad crown and slightly pendulous branches, and is likely the darkest selection of all, with the leaves almost black when they open and fading to a dark greenish purple in the summer.

Two final European beech varieties with coloured foliage are 'Purpurea Tricolor'—commonly listed as 'Tricolor' or 'Roseomarginata'—and 'Zlatia'. The former has leaves that are carmine when they first open, becoming pale purple with an irregular pink and white border at maturity. A smaller tree, to about 10 metres high, with a more open crown, it needs midday shade in regions with hot summers to prevent leaf scorch. 'Zlatia' has an almost oval shape with new foliage of a golden yellow that fades to a pale green in summer. It is one parent of 'Dawyck Gold'.

Most European beeches have nearly oval leaves with a smooth margin, but there are several beeches with differently shaped leaves. The fern-leafed beech 'Aspleniifolia' (Zone 5b), for instance, has leaves that are deeply divided, sometimes becoming almost linear, that turn golden brown in fall. Similar is *F. s.* forma *laciniata*, but its leaves are not as deeply serrated.

At the other end of the scale is 'Rotundifolia'. Slender and upright

A Beech Hedge

European beech is a wonderful hedging plant, as demonstrated in many English gardens. Although it doesn't make an instant hedge (which may be allowed to grow to 15 metres or be kept as low as 1.2 metres), it will last for years and is worth the effort. Install young plants in spring about 1.2 metres apart and leave them to become established for one year. Then, cut back to about 15 centimetres above the soil early in the second spring. This will force several shoots to grow from the base, giving a denser hedge. Trim three times a year for the next few years to encourage side branches; thereafter, an annual pruning in midsummer should suffice.

↑ Antarctic beech (*N. antarctica*)

↑ *F. sylvatica* 'Purpurea Tricolor'

↑ *F. sylvatica* 'Rotundifolia'

when young, it forms a low, wide tree with spreading branches, reaching about 20 metres by 15 metres. The small, round leaves are closely set on the branches, usually in pairs.

It's not surprising that there's also a beech with oaklike leaves, given beeches and oaks are in the same *Fagaceae* family. *F. sylvatica* 'Rohanii', first discovered on the estate of Prince Camille de Rohan in Bohemia in 1888, has brownish purple leaves, with rounded lobes that are widest toward the base. 'Rohanii' has been used to produce two new hybrids, 'Rohan Gold', with yellow leaves, and 'Rohan Obelisk', a narrow, purple-leafed form; each has lobed-shaped foliage.

Closely related but from the other side of the equator is the southern beech, *Nothofagus*. Only one of the 35 species seems to be available in Canada: the Antarctic beech, *N. antarctica*. Not as hardy as its name sounds, it grows to Zone 7, reaching about 20 metres high by 2 metres wide. Its small, crinkled leaves turn yellow in fall. Unlike the true beech, this one is very tolerant of salt and wind, making it a good choice for coastal plantings in warmer zones.

Beech Alternatives

A couple of trees commonly grown in Canada are associated with beeches because of a similarity in bark and the way the foliage hangs on into winter, but in fact they're not even in the same plant family, even though their common names suggest otherwise.

The **European hornbeam**, *Carpinus betulus*, is also known as **hornbeech** and **yoke elm**. Beam is Old English for "tree," and this species has wood as hard as a horn. Another explanation for the common name is that it was used to make yokes attached to the horns of oxen. The most widely grown variety is the **pyramidal hornbeam**, *C. betulus*. 'Fastigiata' (syn. 'Pyramidalis'), which forms a narrow column while young, widening to an oval shape with age, reaching 12 metres high by 6 metres wide. This is a tough, Zone 4 tree that will grow in most soil types, provided the soil is well drained. It takes light shade and is tolerant of difficult conditions, such as parking lots and containers. It can also be used for hedging, giving a beechlike hedge where the European beech is not hardy.

Our native **American hornbeam**, *C. caroliniana*, also has a number of common names, including **blue beech** (because of the similarity of the bark) and **ironwood** (because of its hardness). Slightly hardier than the European hornbeam (Zone 3b), it grows best in moist, slightly acidic soils, but will survive in drier ones. In nature it's normally found as an understory tree in woods, so it grows well in shade. It can reach 10 metres or more in height and as much in width. The foliage is bright green in spring, turning dark in summer, then yellow, orange and scarlet in fall.

Both kinds of hornbeam are fairly slow-growing, gaining 3 to 4 metres in height over a 10-year period.

The Crabapple

New thoughts on an old favourite BY TREVOR COLE

Hardiness

Zones 2b to 5

Growing conditions

Full sun; average garden soil

Features

Spring bloom, late summer fruit

Size

2 to 9 metres; some columnar, weeping or spreading forms

When you choose a crabapple tree for your garden, consider how you want to use it. Small fruits are great for attracting birds; bigger ones easier to handle for preserves and jellies. The shape of the tree—rounded or columnar—should also be considered.

In my travels across Canada I've noticed that there are more crab-apples growing than any other single species of tree. No wonder. Starting with bursts of white, pink or red blooms in spring, followed by bright green (and in some cases red) foliage in summer, then green, red or yellow fruit in fall, crabapples are three-season performers. And with the wide variety of shapes, sizes and hardiness levels available, there's a crab that's tailor-made for just about every Canadian garden.

Many species were brought over by early settlers and cross-bred with native crabs to create cultivars with improved characteristics, such as hardiness and a greater range of flower and fruit colours. Unfortunately, many of the older varieties are very disease-prone and, surprisingly, are still frequently offered for sale.

While most people plant crabs for their early spring show, the shape, size and colour of the fruit and the colour of the leaves should also be

← *M.* 'Dolgo' →

taken into account. Smaller fruit will be easier for birds to eat—they'll often descend in clouds to let you know it's ripe—but if you're keen to use the fruit for pickling or for making jellies, bigger ones are easier to handle. And large fruit provide more winter interest. Choose varieties with bright red or yellow fruits, rather than those with green or dull red ones.

The new foliage of many crabs is tinged with a coppery tone that fades as the leaves unfurl; some varieties have leaves that are either tinged with red or are a reddish purple at maturity. Red-leafed trees add visual interest to the landscape during summer but should be used sparingly—too much of a good thing can look overwhelming.

When planning what to plant and where it will go, keep in mind that crabs need full sun. I once planted one in a location that was shaded by the house for part of the day. Although the tree grew well, it never produced fruit on branches that were in shadow. Also take note of the mature size of trees: the cute sapling you have your eye on could be slated to become a monster in 20 years, a monster you may not have ample room for.

Growing

You can plant crabs in spring or early fall, but if winters are harsh in your area, spring is the better option. To plant a crabapple, dig a hole twice the size of the container it comes in; don't enrich the soil you use to backfill the hole unless it's almost pure sand, in which case, add compost or composted manure. You want the roots to grow into the surrounding soil for good anchorage, not to stay in a carefully prepared, rich planting pocket. And remember: more trees are killed by being planted too deeply than by any other cause. Look for a change in colour on the bark (belowground bark will be darker) that indicates how deeply the tree was planted at the nursery—don't assume the level in the container was correct—and adjust the planting depth to match. Firm the soil to remove air pockets, leaving a slight depression to direct water down to the root zone. Like regular apples, crabapples can suffer from several diseases, though they're seldom much

↓ *M.* 'Makamik'

Native Crabs

The sweet wild crab (*M. coronaria*, Zone 4) grows from southern Ontario down to Missouri, forming dense thickets that are late to come into bloom but, when they do, burst into a froth of white. Its common name is a misnomer: the green, slow-ripening fruit is never sweet, and even birds turn up their beaks until the apples are softened by frost. Selection from this species gave us early hybrids such as 'Charlottae', a double-flowered form with good bronze fall colour that was discovered in 1902 and is still available. Like other double-flowered cultivars, it usually sets less fruit than single-flowered types.

The West Coast is home to the Oregon crab (*M. fusca*, Zone 7). It's native from the Aleutian Islands in Alaska, through British Columbia and into northern California. Pink or white flowers in spring give way to pale green, pleasantly scented, somewhat dry fruit that's good for making jellies. But its crowning glory is its orange and scarlet foliage in fall.

← *M.* 'Rousseau', Rosybloom Series

of a problem. In my 27 years as curator of the Dominion Arboretum in Ottawa, there was rarely a serious outbreak among the dozens of crabs growing there. However, disease resistance depends on which cultivar you choose. For best results, plant disease-resistant varieties and keep an eye out for the following problems.

Cedar-apple rust – The fungus causes yellow spots on leaves but needs junipers or cedars nearby to complete its life cycle. Inspect conifers in early spring and prune off any orange galls. Try not to plant crabs near junipers.

Apple scab – A fungus that causes dark spots on leaves and corky patches on fruit, but the birds will still eat them. Apple scab overwinters in bark crevices and on fallen leaves. Good sanitation and spraying with lime sulfur in late winter help control it. Severe attacks can weaken the tree over a few years and eventually kill it.

Fire blight – This bacteria, true to its name, makes a branch look like it's been burned with a blow torch. It can spread rapidly, so remove infected wood as soon as you see symptoms; prune back to where there's no brown discolouration on the exposed end of the cutting. Be sure to disinfect pruning tools between cuts with a 50/50 bleach-water solution or undiluted rubbing alcohol to avoid reinfecting the wound.

Mildew – Another fungus, it covers the leaves with a white coat; it's likely to occur in humid regions. Repeated attacks can defoliate and weaken the tree.

↑ *M.* 'Sutzgam' Sugar Tyme

Many crabapples brought here by settlers were crossed with native varieties for improved characteristics, but some are disease-prone and are still readily available. 'Maybride' is a Canadian introduction with good disease resistance.

↓ *M.* 'Maybride'

Recommended varieties

Many crab varieties that were popular in the past and are still available are highly susceptible to certain diseases. Here are some you should steer clear of: 'Almey', 'Hopa', 'Klem's Improved Bechtel', 'Makamik', 'Radiant', 'Royalty', 'Snowcloud' and *Malus ionesis* 'Plena'.

Another group of lovely crabapple cultivars have been around for some time but are somewhat disease-prone and should be planted with caution. They include: 'American Beauty', 'Indian Magic', 'Kelsey', 'Profusion', 'Red Jade', 'Red Splendor', 'Royal Beauty' and 'White Angel'. 'Maybride' is a Canadian introduction with good disease resistance, but it may be a bit difficult to find.

The columnar Siberian crab (*M. baccata* 'Columnaris', Zone 2b) is a tall, slender tree, growing up to 9 metres tall and only 1.5 metres wide. Its white spring flowers are followed by small yellow or red fruit, easy for birds to eat. Any fruit they miss in fall persists on trees over winter and are quickly devoured in spring.

The dark pink buds on the Japanese flowering crab (*M. floribunda*, Zone 5b) open a pale pink and turn almost white as they age. The tree has a spreading habit, growing about 6 metres tall and 4.5 metres wide and is fairly disease-resistant. The two-toned red-and-yellow, pea-size fruit drop in early winter—if the birds don't get to them first.

The diminutive, disease-resistant Sargent's crab (*M. sargentii*, Zone 5) grows a mere 2 metres high and will eventually spread to 3 metres, making it a good choice for a small garden. Its newly introduced cultivar 'Tina' is reputed to be even smaller, growing only about two-thirds the size. The flowers open white from bright red buds; small, shiny red fruit follow.

New cultivars of crabapples are continually being added to the list of what's available. The following varieties are especially desirable, both decorative and disease-resistant. Keep in mind that dropping fruit can be bothersome by a patio or driveway, so site trees accordingly. "Persistent" means the fruit stays on the branches well past leaf drop, or at least until the birds get to it. A number of crabapples such as the ones that follow have both cultivar and trademark names; they may be listed by one or both in nurseries.

Columnar forms

- 'Hargozam' Harvest Gold grows to 9 by 4 metres; it has pink flowers and 2-centimetre yellow fruit that lasts until midwinter, Zone 5

Weeping forms

- 'Mazam' Madonna grows to 6 by 3 metres, has double, white flowers and 1.5-centimetre yellow fruit, Zone 4
- 'Molazam' Molten Lava reaches 4.5 by 6 metres, with white flowers and persistent, 1-centimetre red fruit; yellow fall foliage, Zone 4
- 'Weepcanzam' Weeping Candied Apple grows to 4.5 by 4 metres, with pink flowers and 1.5-centimetre persistent red fruit; leaves are red tinged, Zone 5b

Oval to rounded forms

- 'Adams' reaches 7.5 by 7 metres with pink flowers and persistent, 1.5-centimetre red fruit has red flesh, Zone 4
- 'Centzam' Centurion grows to 7.5 by 7 metres; flowers are rose red and the 1.5-centimetre glossy red fruit lasts until midwinter, Zone 5
- 'Indian Summer' reaches 6 by 5.5 metres with rose-pink flowers and persistent, 1.5-centimetre red fruit; foliage is red in fall, Zone 5
- 'Prairifire' reaches 6 by 6 metres and has dark pink flowers; the 1.5-centimetre dark red fruit is persistent; bark is attractive, Zone 4
- 'Sutgzam' Sugar Tyme grows to 4.5 by 4 metres with white flowers; 1.5-centimetre red fruit is persistent, Zone 4

Spreading forms

- 'Dolgo' grows to 9 by 10 metres, with white flowers and 3-centimetre purple fruit that drops quickly but is good for jelly, Zone 2b
- 'Robinson' grows to 7.5 by 7 metres with pink flowers and 2-centimetre dark red fruit, Zone 4
- 'Thunderchild' reaches 6 by 6 metres and has pink flowers and persistent, 1.5-centimetre dark red fruit; the green foliage turns red-purple in summer, Zone 2b

favouritetrees&shrubs

The Magnolia

Hardiness

Zones 4 to 7, depending on variety

Growing conditions

Full sun; rich, slightly acidic soil

Features

White, pink to purple or yellow saucer- or tulip-shaped blooms; shiny, leathery leaves

Size

5 to 24 metres tall, depending on variety

Hardy plants that give the spring garden an exotic touch BY TREVOR COLE

Magnolias—their very name conjures up images of Southern belles in hoop skirts, languidly sipping mint juleps in the shade. And yet these trees and shrubs are not as exotic as they seem. Many varieties can be grown in Canada, some even in Zone 4.

The most popular types, such as saucer and star magnolia cultivars, are justly prized for their showy, fragrant flowers that open in early spring (at about the same time as forsythia and early narcissus) before their leaves emerge. Though a late frost can nip their flowers in the bud, in a good year their blooms will last for two to three weeks before dropping. The period of bloom can be extended even further by planting May-blooming magnolia varieties, such as lily magnolia (*Magnolia liliiflora*) or the spectacular yellow-flowered 'Elizabeth' or 'Yellow Bird'.

While magnolias are best loved for their dazzling, exotic, winter-blues-chasing spring flowers, they have something to offer throughout the seasons. Their large, shiny green, leathery leaves look fresh all summer and turn an attractive chestnut brown in autumn. In winter, the handsome, smooth, grey bark—similar to that of a beech tree—comes into its own, while the big, velvety flower buds are not only comely, but are good indicators of the following spring's potential blooms as well.

Large magnolias, such as the kobus variety (*M. kobus*, Zone 5), make good specimen or accent plants grown in a lawn, but they're equally effective at the back of a border, especially when backed by an evergreen hedge that shows off their flowers to perfection. Smaller varieties, such as the star magnolias (*M. stellata* cvs.), can be integrated in a mixed or shrub border. They work well with summer-flowering shrubs, including beautybush (*Kolkwitzia amabilis*) and various spireas, and offer a pleasing contrast in texture and form to imposing perennials such as ornamental grasses.

Growing

Plant magnolias in full sun or dappled shade in rich, slightly acidic, moisture-retentive loam. Like most plants, they tolerate less-than-ideal conditions if they're sated otherwise; many magnolias grow successfully in alkaline soil with a pH of 7.5 at the Dominion Arboretum in Ottawa (Zone 5), most likely because of its deep and moisture-retentive soil. The magnolias wouldn't thrive as well if planted in a shallow, alkaline soil that rapidly dries

← Yellow magnolia 'Elizabeth'

↑ Lily magnolia (*M. liliiflora*)

out. However, select the site with care, as established magnolias do not transplant easily.

All have shallow root systems, so the surrounding soil shouldn't be cultivated too much; underplant with perennials or groundcovers rather than annuals. Magnolias should be bought as balled-and-burlapped or container-grown plants: they have a fleshy root system that breaks easily if you try to plant them bare-root and, unless they're in active growth, the damaged roots will rot rather than heal. It's also preferable to buy small plants since they suffer less root damage.

In most of Canada, spring planting is best, although fall is feasible in regions that have milder winters, such as coastal British Columbia or southern Ontario. Prepare a hole at least twice the size of the root ball so roots can stretch out; site the plant no deeper than it was in its original container. Refill the hole with the original soil, water well and apply a 5-centimetre layer of

Meet "The Girls"

↑ 'Betty'

↑ 'Ricki'

↑ 'Jane'

Variety	Colour outside/inside	Flower size	No. of petals
'Ann'	red-purple/pale purple	10 cm	8
'Betty'	red-purple/white	20 cm	19
'Judy'	red-purple/cream	8 cm	10
'Randy'	red-purple/white	12 cm	11
'Ricki'	red-purple/red-purple	15 cm	15
'Susan'	red-purple/pale purple	12 cm	6
'Jane'	red-purple/white	10 cm	10
'Pinkie'	pale purple/white	18 cm	9 to 12

In the mid-1950s, staff at the U.S. National Arboretum in Washington, D.C., carried out a magnolia-breeding program to extend the blooming season, developing slightly later varieties whose flowers would be resistant to late frost damage. Eight named varieties, affectionately known as "the girls," were released in 1965. They need a more acidic soil than the star and saucer magnolias. Both flower size and number of petals vary from year to year, and may depend on prevalent conditions the previous summer while buds were formed. Hardy to Zone 5b, the girls form upright shrubs that grow to 4.5 metres tall. Many also have blooms that open sporadically during the summer. They're listed here in order of flowering sequence.

mulch to help retain moisture. Be prepared to water during any prolonged periods of drought during the first year. This is critical to a magnolia's survival (water if leaves feel limp to the touch).

Once established, magnolias may need occasional pruning to keep them in bounds. This should be done in early summer after flowering. Remove damaged and crossed branches, shoots growing toward the centre of the plant and, once the magnolia grows larger, any lower branches that have become an obstruction.

In the wild, magnolias grow in woodlands where they benefit from decomposing leaves. To compensate for this in the garden, feed them with a granular, slow-release fertilizer, such as a 10-10-10 formulation, in early spring. Apply around the plant's drip line, using 250 to 500 grams of fertilizer per 2.5 centimetres of trunk diameter, measured at chest height. For a multi-stemmed tree, add up the diameters of the various stems to determine the amount of fertilizer you need. However, don't fertilize at all for the first couple of years; you want the plant to develop a spreading root system.

While magnolias grown in the Deep South are subject to several fungal problems, the ones grown in Canada are relatively disease-free. Common pests such as slugs and aphids may cause some damage, but it's seldom serious, except on young plants.

Late-spring frost sometimes damages magnolia blossoms, but under the right conditions they hold their bloom two or three weeks. Extend the season by planting a late-blooming variety, such as the lily magnolia, with a saucer or star magnolia.

↑↓ Saucer magnolia (*M.* x *soulangeana*)

Yellow Magnolias

↑ *M.* 'Yellow Bird'

Magnolias with ivory or yellow flowers are growing in popularity and becoming more widely available in Canadian garden centres. Yellow magnolias are likely the result of crossing the native cucumber tree—which has small, insignificant, yellow flowers—with either the Yulan or the saucer magnolia. Hardiness depends on their parentage, but they're worth trying if you're looking for something different.

One superior variety is 'Elizabeth', introduced by Brooklyn Botanic Garden. A small, conical tree that grows to 6 metres tall, it has deliciously fragrant, pale yellow flowers. Although generally listed in catalogues as hardy to Zone 6b, these plants flourish in gardens in Ottawa's Zone 5 climate and flowered well in the spring of 2003, after a winter that was hard on many magnolia buds.

Other notable ivory and yellow magnolias include 'Gold Star', 'Butterflies', 'Golden Endeavor' and 'Yellow Bird', which have all survived and bloomed in Ottawa gardens. And, if you feel like experimenting, 'Sundance', 'Yellow Fever' and 'Yellow Lantern' are worth looking for as well.

Recommended varieties

The star magnolia (*M. stellata*, Zone 5) is likely the most widely grown. This slow-growing shrub may eventually reach 5 metres tall and about 3 metres wide, with dense branches and 10-centimetre-wide, white flowers. 'Waterlily' has pink buds with 14 petals each that open white, while 'King Rose' and 'Pink Star' both produce blooms with 22 pink-tinged petals. The most popular variety is 'Royal Star', with pink buds and fragrant white flowers that have up to 30 petals. It's also the hardiest and is worth trying in sheltered Zone 4 gardens.

The flowers of the saucer magnolia (*M.* x *soulangeana*, Zone 5) average nine petals and are much wider and larger—up to 25 centimetres across—than those of the star magnolia; inner petals overlap and form an almost closed chalice, while outer petals spread slightly to make a saucer. They're generally pale purple outside and white inside, but this varies. Like its blooms, the shrub is large—it can reach a height of 10 metres in good conditions. Growth is upright when the shrub is young but spreads as it matures. The saucer magnolia is a hybrid of *M. liliiflora* and *M. denudata*, and originated in the garden of Étienne Soulange-Bodin in 1820 in Fromont, France. He had been a cavalry officer in Napoleon's army and, following the defeat at Waterloo and sickened by the war, he turned to his garden for solace. As he wrote in an 1819 edition of *Gardener's Magazine*: "It had doubtless been better for both parties to have stayed at home and planted their cabbages." Other hybridizers have repeated this magnolia cross since then and there are now many varieties with flowers of varying colour and size.

Another group of popular magnolias is *M.* x *loebneri*, introduced in the early 1900s in

↑ *M. kobus*

The kobus magnolia doesn't bloom while it's young, but when the flowers eventually appear they are white and fragrant. Cucumber magnolia is named for its green, non-edible fruits, which turn pink at maturity. It's native to the area around Lake Erie and is considered endangered.

← Star magnolia (*M. stellata*) ↑ *M.* x *loebneri* 'Leonard Messel'

Germany. Two later selections from this cross are especially well known: 'Leonard Messel', the blooms of which have 12 petals flushed with pink on the outside and whitish pink with a central purplish line on the inside, and 'Merrill', which is exceptionally free-flowering, with 15-petalled, white blooms. Both are hardy to Zone 5. 'Ballerina' has pale pink blooms with up to 30 petals. It's slightly hardier than the other two but may not be as readily available.

Three other species magnolias are solid choices for Canadian gardens.

The Yulan (*M. denudata*, Zone 5b) is a large, rounded shrub or small tree that grows 9 metres tall and has fragrant, white, cup-shaped flowers 15 centimetres across. It tends to bloom very early; if planted in an exposed location, its nine-petalled flowers may be damaged by a late frost.

Cucumber magnolia (*M. acuminata*)→

Kobus (Zone 5) becomes a large shrub up to 12 metres tall with fragrant, white flowers. This species doesn't bloom while young—a plant in my garden started from seed about 20 years ago has only just started to flower.

Bull bay, also known as southern magnolia (*M. grandiflora*, Zone 7), is evergreen and flowers in late spring with occasional blooms throughout summer and fall. This large tree reaches 24 metres tall and spreads 15 metres across. Its dark green foliage often has rust-coloured fuzz on the underside. 'Little Gem' is better suited to average-size gardens—it grows only 6 metres tall and 3 metres across.

favouritetrees&shrubs

It's a colour, a scent, a season, and one of our best-loved spring plants

BY PATRICK LIMA

The Lilac

↑ *S. vulgaris* 'Champlain'

Hardiness

Zones 2 to 3

Growing conditions

Minimum half-day of sun, neutral to sweet soil pH

Features

Intense scent; white to cream, pink to red and purple single and double flowers

Size

1.5 to 4 metres, depending on variety

Lilacs are among the most familiar of shrubs, but the observation "familiarity breeds contempt" does not hold true for them. Only a jaded gardener or a dyed-in-the-wool plant snob would disdain a lilac in full bloom. A far more natural response is to walk right up to it, bury your nose in the flowers and inhale deeply—then stand back and gaze at the pyramids of blossoms swaying against the sky.

A sentimental favourite, the lilac has come to represent more than a garden shrub. It's a season: lilac time, late-May and early-June days of gentle warmth—a prelude to summer. It's a colour: a floral hue like primrose, violet, rose, lavender or gentian. And perhaps most evocatively, it's a scent: a waft of sweetness, described as a blend of almonds, spices, musk and nostalgia, that carries you back in memory to a farm, or a second-storey room where scented blossoms peer over the windowsill.

Lilacs are not native to Canada, although you might think otherwise. How else to explain their presence among hawthorns and sumachs along country roadsides with no habitation in sight, or lilac thickets growing in the middle of

Hybrid lilacs are sometimes referred to as "French lilacs," a reminder that many varieties were bred in France. This isn't true today—many new ones are hybridized in Canada.

S. vulgaris 'Krasavitsa Moskvy' ↑

↑ *S. vulgaris* 'Frank Peterson'

↑ *S. pubescens* ssp. *microphylla* 'Superba'

↑ Unnamed garden variety

↑ *S. hyacinthiflora* 'Mary Short'

Lilacs range from species types to single and double French hybrids, early-blooming hyacinthifloras and late-blooming Preston lilacs. The Prestons, botanically known as *S.* x *prestonia*, were developed in Canada by Isabella Preston and have long, loose panicles of flowers with an exotic, spicy scent.

meadows? Hardy, carefree and easily "slipped," lilacs have been part of almost every homestead, farm and small-town garden from pioneer days onward. The old house may have fallen into decay, but the lilacs endure, suckering and seeding to form thriving colonies near the original sites. In our area in southern Ontario, they join wild apple trees in an exuberant May flower festival.

Masses of tall white lilacs, holdovers from an earlier farm, are a prominent feature in our Zone 4 garden. Left largely unpruned, the decades-old shrubs shade a border of primulas, and then curve around to encompass a quiet corner of ornamental grasses, hostas and white-flowered perennials. For the work they do, few plants match them for low maintenance.

To my eye, lilacs are their most glorious in an unrestrained mass—a dense weave of branches and high-piled flowers. Allowed to spread, one bush will form a thicket in about six seasons. An unpruned lilac hedge at the edge of a large property forms a beautiful (and impenetrable) barrier—and a most effective windscreen. Nothing could be cheaper or easier to make if you have access to offshoots from older bushes. Dig up rooted suckers and plant them about 1.8 metres apart in a zigzag, double line. Young slips will shoot up quickly if the ground is turned over and cleared of competing growth, but they take off even if planted in holes dug in the grass.

On a small property, a lilac is well suited to a sunny corner where it has room to creep forward; it may also be integrated into a foundation planting. We have both common lilacs and hybrids at the back of wide perennial borders.

Growing

Lilacs are not overly fussy about soil or site, but avoid soggy, acidic or shady spots. They like sun for at least half a day, well-drained earth and a neutral-to-sweet pH. I have never fertilized a lilac—they hardly need the encouragement. Suckering can be a nuisance. The remedy is to remove suckers as close to the main root as possible—pull them up toward the centre of the bush, and dig down a bit so you can get closer to their source. (Cutting suckers at ground level only encourages more to form.) A lilac grown on its own rootstock (rather than grafted) sends up fewer suckers.

The trick to shaping a lilac is to do a little pruning every year, rather than letting it get overgrown. Since lilacs bloom on old wood, it's best to prune in early summer, after the flowers fade. This allows next

S. vulgaris 'Charles Joly' ↑

↑ *S.* x *chinensis*

↑ *S. vulgaris* 'Clarence D. Van Zandt'

↑ *S. vulgaris* 'President Carnot'

year's buds to form. Remove crossed, broken or damaged branches at ground level. Every year or two, cut away some suckers at the base of the plant and prune back branches bending over walkways or otherwise out of place. Major renovation, recommended every three or four years, involves sawing out a few of the thickest older branches (again at ground level), leaving room for new shoots to grow into future main branches. Maintaining an open framework—and better air circulation—helps prevent powdery mildew, an unsightly fungus that forms in wet or humid summers. For most lilacs—the common white seems to be an exception—flowering is improved if the current year's seed heads are snipped off. This annual June pruning is easier said than done. A stepladder, steady balance, long-handled pruners and an extended reach all help.

Recommended varieties

Native to the mountains of Eastern Europe, the common lilac (*Syringa vulgaris*) was introduced into English gardens in the mid-1500s. Known variously as the "lelach tree," "laylock" and "lily oak"—all from the Persian word "*lilag*"—it was also called the blue pipe tree because its pithy stalks are easily hollowed for making smoking pipes.

Lilac Companions

A time-honoured site for a lilac is in a mixed shrub border with hardy bushes such as mock orange, spirea, forsythia or honeysuckle. A bed of spring bulbs and woodland flowers—primulas, lungworts, bloodroot—works well on the shady side of such plantings. For companion colour on the sunny side of lilacs, consider late tulips, early alliums, creeping phlox, perennial candytuft, fleabane, doronicum, catmint or other late-May perennials.

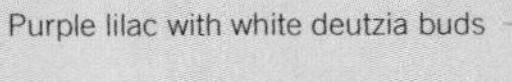

Purple lilac with white deutzia buds →

In the 1840s, a double-flowered lilac seedling appeared by chance in a Belgium nursery and became the impetus for decades of breeding. The most significant early contribution was by the French firm of Victor Lemoine, which introduced 214 cultivars between 1876 and 1955. Hybridists sought to enlarge both individual flowers and the pyramidal panicles of flowers. New colours appeared; the traditional mauve was deepened to purple and wine, and lightened to pink and white. Double flowers were also prized.

A Canadian garden ought to have a lilac—call it an homage to our pioneer past—and it may well be a hybrid of the common lilac. These are sometimes referred to as "French lilacs," a reminder that a lot of past hybridizing was done in France. (The term is not accurate today, though; many hybrids are bred in Canada.) There are literally hundreds of lilac hybrids, and the choice may be as simple as colour preference or availability. Introduced in 1890 and still around, 'Mme. Lemoine' has creamy buds that open to large, double white flowers. Dark reddish purple, double and heavily scented, 'Charles Joly' has endured since 1896; 'Ludwig Spaeth', 1883, is a similar shade, but single-flowered. The purple petals of 'Sensation', introduced in 1938, are edged with cream for an unusual effect. Raised in 1922 and compact in growth, 'Katherine Havemeyer' displays double lavender-blue flowers, and 'Edward J. Gardner', 1950, is a fine pink. In 1949, an unusual pale yellow lilac, *S. vulgaris* 'Primrose', was introduced from the Netherlands. The deep purple 'Agincourt Beauty', 1973, is a newer, Canadian introduction, with exceptionally large panicles of blooms.

Because of their showy flowers and breadth of colours, lilac hybrids will probably always command attention and admiration, but a number of species lilacs merit space in the garden, too—for their wild grace and carefree growth. From Korea comes *S. oblata* var. *dilatata*, a 4-metre scented shrub similar to the common lilac, but blooming a week or two earlier than *vulgaris*. The Persian lilac (*S.* x *persica*) bears slender panicles of light lavender flowers in May; left to its own devices, it eventually reaches 3 metres tall and 4 metres across. Its fine fragrance has led to the name "blue Persian jasmine." Like other lilacs, this shrub came to Canada with early French and British colonists as a reminder of gardens left behind.

Where space is limited, consider the dwarf *S. meyeri*, which grows to a height and width of about 1.6 metres, has small leaves, a neat habit and mounding form. In a good year, it covers itself in flowers from top to bottom. 'Palibin' is a cultivar with fragrant, mauve blooms. At a larger 2.5 metres, *S. patula* 'Miss Kim' is a compact, round shrub with dark green foliage right to the ground, setting off small but abundant clusters of light lavender, fragrant flowers. Hardy to Zone 3, these shrubs are well suited for foundation plantings and informal hedges; they bloom after the common lilac.

↓ *S.* x *prestonia* 'Sholokhov

Lilacs aren't fussy plants, but they like some sun and well-drained soil with neutral or slightly sweet pH. Prune them right after the flowers fade to avoid cutting off the buds for next year's blooms.

Canada's Lilac Queen

In May of 1920, a young woman named Isabella Preston was hired as a day labourer by the Ottawa Experimental Farm. Her work was noted, and later, when "trained and promising men could not be found" for the position of assistant, she was given that post—sort of. Although the job description remained the same, the title was changed to Specialist in Ornamental Horticulture, with a drop in pay from $2,400 to $1,400 per year. This was in a day when a female plant propagator might have been listed on the payroll as a librarian—there is, after all, a suggestion of sex in the title.

↑ *S. vulgaris* 'Sholokhov'

A self-taught hybridist with a passion for lilies, Preston worked on roses, Siberian irises, crabapples and lilacs. By the 1940s she was referred to by colleagues as "the dean of hybridists," the federal government's leading horticultural expert.

Exchanging pollen between flowers of two Chinese lilac species, *S. villosa* and *S. reflexa*, Preston developed a group of late-blooming shrubs that bear her name, *Syringa* x *prestoniae*. A Preston lilac is an eye-opener for those who know only the common lilac and its hybrids. Instead of typical heart-shaped leaves, it bears elongated, pointed, deeply veined, darker green foliage; out of bloom, you might not guess it's a lilac. Leaning to the rosy side of the spectrum, panicles of flowers are longer, looser and airier, with an exotic, spicy scent. But the biggest surprise is the timing: Preston lilacs start to bloom a week or two after common lilacs finish, putting them in season with peonies and early roses. In our garden, a massive Preston lilac neighbours prickly bushes of the light apricot-yellow rugosa rose 'Agnes', another of Preston's creations. At ground level, silvery mauve globes of ornamental onions (*Allium cristophii*) hover over lavender spires of catmint. Cultivars of Preston lilacs include 'Miss Canada', with red buds that open to pink flowers; the pink 'Coral' and pale lilac 'Donald Wyman'.

Hardy to Zone 2, Preston lilacs grow quickly in almost any soil to grand proportions—up to 4 metres high and wide. Happily, they do not send out suckers, and may be pruned (more or less) to fit your space—even shaped into a less expansive, treelike form with three to five trunks, and few lower branches. Blooming when quite small, these fast-growing shrubs are resistant to powdery mildew and, like most lilacs, are not much prone to insect damage. They make good windbreaks. As befits a Canadian introduction, Preston lilacs are slightly hardier than common or French lilacs (Zone 2a versus Zone 2b).

Hydrangeas

These beautiful, low-maintenance plants are a boon in any garden BY JANET DAVIS

↑ Climbing hydrangea (*H. petiolaris*)

If versatility is a virtue, then the wonderfully diverse family of flowering hydrangeas is just about as good as it gets. One branch of the family, a shrubby vine that uses aerial rootlets to cling tenaciously to walls or scramble sideways along a fence, is very different from others that excel at lighting up shade-dappled woodlands. Still others, blowsy stars of sunny, late-summer gardens, lend a lush, romantic feeling to the dog days of late July, August and September with their blue, mauve, pink or white flowers.

Not all hydrangeas are right for all gardens, of course. Although a few can survive harsh Zone 2b winters, others prefer the cool summers and mild winters in Zone 7 on the West Coast. But all are relatively disease-resistant and, provided soil is not too alkaline and a few basic pruning needs are met, they're very easy to care for.

Recommended varieties

The following hydrangeas are five of the best choices for Canadian gardens.

Bigleaf or florist's hydrangea (*H.* x *macrophylla*)

The name "hydrangea" derives from the Latin for "water jar," referring to the shrub's cup-shaped seed vessels. The description is especially fitting for the old-fashioned, bigleaf

↓ Smooth hydrangea (*H. arborescens*)

Hardiness

Zones 2b to 7, depending on variety

Growing conditions

Sun to light shade; humus-rich moist soil

Features

Blue, mauve, pink or creamy white to greenish flowers, late summer

Size

Shrubs from 90 to 180 centimetres; climbers to 7.5 metres

Bigleaf hydrangea (*H.* x *macrophylla* 'Blue Bonnet') →

The name “hydrangea” comes from the Latin word for “water jar” and refers to the shrub’s cup-shaped seedpods. It seems fitting for the bigleaf hydrangea, which requires copious amounts of water.

↑ Oakleaf hydrangea (*H. quercifolia*) in fall foliage

↑ Peegee hydrangea (*H. paniculata* 'Grandiflora')

hydrangea because it requires copious amounts of water. Popular both in the garden and as an Easter-season flowering houseplant, this hydrangea is the result of complex hybridizing of *H. maritima*, a seaside species, and one or more Japanese woodland hydrangeas. It was brought to Europe by Carl Thunberg, who discovered it in Japan in the 1770s. Bigleaf hydrangea comes in two forms: hortensia (spherical heads of sterile flowers) and lacecap (flat clusters of fertile flowers surrounded by a ring of sterile flowers). Because one of its parents is a seaside species, bigleaf hydrangea is very salt-tolerant and thrives in cool seaside gardens.

Shrubs grow from 90 to 180 centimetres tall, depending on the cultivar and the climate—a milder climate means taller specimens. They enjoy sun or light shade and humus-rich, moist soil, preferably with a summer mulch to keep their roots cool. In acidic soil, the blue cultivars are more vividly blue; soil on the alkaline side favours the pink cultivars. Tinkering with the pH by adding aluminum sulfate or iron sulfate to acidify the soil eventually turns blue-flowered cultivars pinkish mauve; adding lime or a high-phosphorus fertilizer to raise soil alkalinity turns pink cultivars blue. Rejuvenate bigleaf hydrangea when stems become thick and woody: remove three to five of the oldest stems at ground level in late winter while the shrub is still dormant.

Bigleaf hydrangeas, especially the lacecaps, are generally bud-hardy only in Zone 7 or warmer. In Zone 6b, the roots may overwinter, but the top growth often dies back to the ground—self-defeating, since most *H.* x *macrophylla* cultivars bloom on buds made the previous year. The exception is 'All Summer Beauty', a hortensia that flowers on new growth. The hardiest hortensia is 'Nikko Blue', while the hardiest lacecap is said to be 'Blue Billow'; these may make it through winter in protected sites in Zone 6. For West Coast gardeners, reliable hortensias include the old favourite, blue 'Seafoam', and compact 'Altona', which has large blossoms ranging from dark pink to blue-purple.

Hydrangeas grow as shrubs or climbers, although all varieties don't survive harsh Canadian winters. The hardiest is smooth hydrangea, which overwinters as far north as Zone 2b. Peegee survives to Zone 3b.

↑ Peegee hydrangea 'Ruby'

Climbing hydrangea (*H. petiolaris*)
The shrubby vine is slow to establish—it seems to crawl by mere centimetres for the first few years—but it eventually clambers more than 7.5 metres up a strong wall with gusto, sending out woody stems covered with lustrous, dark green leaves. In late June and early July, climbing hydrangea is literally smothered with large, flat, slightly fragrant, creamy white blossoms. It's also attractive in winter with its peeling bark and long-lasting flower bracts.

↓ Lacecap hydrangea (*H.* x *macrophylla*)

Climbing hydrangea is often recommended as a good vine for shade, but in fact it blooms poorly in a north-facing site, making its best flowering show in moist soil in full sun. In his book *Gardening with Trees and Shrubs*, Ottawa-area plantsman Trevor Cole says if you're in Zone 5b, the limit of its cold hardiness, you should plant it on an east-facing wall. South walls heat up too much in winter, which can prove fatal to the shrub. In milder winter areas, it can be planted facing south or west.

Pruning isn't required unless you want to keep the vine compact or create a flatter profile. If so, prune it back immediately after flowering.

Japanese hydrangea vine (*Schizophragma hydrangeoides*) looks similar to climbing hydrangea and is sometimes confused with it. Although related, it has only one petal-like sepal on the outer sterile flowers, giving it a more fragile appearance than climbing hydrangea, which has four sepals.

Smooth hydrangea (*H. arborescens*)
Native to the eastern U.S., where it was discovered in 1736, smooth hydrangea and its various cultivars are now a mainstay in many shade gardens. The species grows from 90 to 150 centimetres tall, with dark green leaves and upright stalks topped with rounded flowers that start off ghostly green, gradually turning creamy white, then brown. It's an open, sprawling, yet graceful shrub that lights up the feel shadows of deciduous woods in Florida, Louisiana, Mississippi and Georgia.

To make smooth hydrangea feel at home in your garden, give it moist, humus-rich, slightly acidic soil. If the July flowers are deadheaded, a second, smaller crop is possible in late summer. Although this is a woodland plant that looks lovely with ferns, hostas and dark green yews, it does well in a sunny spot as long as the soil is kept moist. The hardiest of all hydrangeas, it overwinters as far north as Zone 2b. Like peegee hydrangea, smooth hydrangea blooms on new growth, so cut the shrub back hard, almost to the ground, in early spring.

Cultivars of smooth hydrangea, like 'Grandiflora', have much bigger, pom-pom flowers than the species. When well fertilized, the flowers of 'Annabelle' can grow to melon size. While spectacular, they tend to look somewhat vulgar and overpowering in a mixed shrub border or perennial bed where they're expected to share the stage with others. Let 'Annabelle' be a prima donna alongside shrubs with neutral green foliage, or pair it with a variegated-leaf shrub like

↑ Bigleaf hydrangea cultivar (*H.* x *macrophylla*)

silver-edged dogwood (*Cornus alba* 'Elegantissima'), a summer perennial with spiky white flowers such as black snakeroot (*Cimicifuga racemosa*), or with Culver's root (*Veronicastrum virginicum*).

Peegee hydrangea (*H. paniculata* 'Grandiflora'). Native to Japan, Russia and China, peegee hydrangea is a reliable, old-fashioned shrub or small tree for the late summer garden. Its common name comes from the first initials of its species and cultivar names.

Hardy to Zone 3b, peegee hydrangea needs sufficient sun and moist soil to put on a good flowering show, but appreciates light shade in the hottest part of the afternoon. The showy, cone-shaped white flowers form on growth made in the current season, so pruning is done in early

Drying Hydrangea Blossoms

The rich colours and voluptuous shapes of hydrangea blooms make them popular with dried-flower arrangers, but buying a bouquet at a craft store or florist can be pricey. Luckily, it's easy to dry your own.

The blooms of bigleaf hydrangea (*H. x macrophylla*) are arguably the showiest when dried; hortensia types dry better than lacecaps. You can also dry peegee hydrangea and *H. arborescens* 'Annabelle' blossoms.

Pick blossoms near the end of the flowering season. Make sure they're dry to the touch and slightly leathery in feel; if not, they'll rot rather than dry evenly. Remove all leaves and any withered or brown florets. Place in a tall vase in 3 to 5 centimetres of water. Leave for four or five days, or until they have absorbed all the water, and then hang upside down in a dry, warm, dark place. Keep dried blossoms out of direct light to prevent fading.

spring—this is one shrub that needs the gardener's intervention, not just for flowering but for vegetative growth, too. Unpruned plants languish and sprawl and eventually stop flowering altogether. Prune back to just above the second or third strong bud on last year's wood to promote vigorous new growth and strong flowers.

Although the lightly scented 'Grandiflora' cultivar bears mostly sterile flowers on a shrub that matures at around 2.7 metres, there are enough fertile flowers mixed in to attract lots of bees. As the flowers age in September and October, they take on delicious hues of rose and green before turning parchment brown, often staying on the shrub until spring.

Several new *H. paniculata* cultivars have been introduced recently. 'Tardiva' is fall-flowering with loose, pointed blossoms; 'Pink Diamond' is compact at 120 centimetres, with large flower panicles in June and July that turn deep pink with a red reverse in September; 'Praecox' has a mix of sterile and fertile flowers that give it the appearance of a white lacecap; and 'White Moth' has long-lasting, rounded flowerheads composed of sterile flowers. A new introduction, 'Grandiflora Unique', has flowers even bigger than its parents'—not necessarily an improvement since peegee's flamboyant blossoms make it hard enough to integrate into a garden design, except as a specimen plant or focal point in an all-green border.

Like all hydrangeas, the peegee makes a lovely addition to a lush, romantic summer bouquet.

Oakleaf hydrangea (*H. quercifolia*). Oakleaf hydrangea is a beautiful shrub with much to recommend it. Its leaves are leathery, dark green and shaped like those of white oak (hence the name), and turn a rich burgundy-red in October. White flower panicles bear showy sepals, which often turn pink as they age, and small fertile blossoms appear in June and July.

Hardy to Zone 5b, oakleaf hydrangea grows 180 centimetres tall and slightly wider. Native to Florida, Georgia and Mississippi, shrubs rarely reach their potential height except, perhaps, in mild gardens on the West Coast. Although there are many named cultivars that grow much taller, to 3.5 metres, with spectacular long flower panicles, they tend to be tenderer than the species.

Oakleaf hydrangea needs moist, humusy, acidic soil in full sun or part shade. Like bigleaf hydrangea, it flowers on old wood, so pruning should be done immediately after flowering. A woodland-edge plant, oakleaf hydrangea is lovely in a shrub border with other acid-loving shrubs such as blue holly (*Ilex* x *meserveae*), Oregon grape holly (*Mahonia aquifolium*), redvein enkianthus (*Enkianthus campanulatus*), downy serviceberry (*Amelanchier canadensis*), azaleas and rhododendrons.

↑ Oakleaf hydrangea (*H. quercifolia*)

↑ Peegee hydrangea (*H. paniculata* 'Annabelle') in foreground with hortensia hydrangea (*H.* x *macrophylla* 'Nikko Blue')

↑ Weeping Nootka false cypress (*Chamaecyparis nootkatensis* 'Pendula')

OTHER PLANTS THAT WEEP

Grasses

Fountain grasses; hakonechloa; feather grass

Roses

Father Hugo's rose

Perennials

Campanula 'Elizabeth'; solomon's seal

Bulbs

Shooting star; *Fritillaria meleagris; Allium cernum; Nectarscodium siculum; Lilium specious* 'Rubrum'

favouritetrees&shrubs

Weeping Trees *and* Shrubs

They can arch, nod or cascade—weeping plants add character to a garden

BY FRANK KERSHAW

As a gardener I've always had a soft spot for weeping plants. Maybe it stems from my childhood, when I hid under a weeping willow during games of hide and seek. Whatever the connection, I'm happy to see weeping plants gaining popularity in home gardens.

In the past, weeping plants were often used in cemeteries and formal gardens to help create a sombre, respectful mood. But now they have a much livelier function, adding interest and animation to the landscape as living sculptures, foliage "draperies" on a wall, cascading leaves to mimic a nearby waterfall, or tunnels and domes of greenery to contrast with other more common plant shapes. And many weeping trees have a narrower profile than other trees, making them a good choice for small gardens.

The range of choice and hardiness of weeping plants is broad, and it's not uncommon to find several selections on nursery aisles with enticing descriptions like "pendulous," "arching," "nodding" and "cascading."

Many weeping trees are cultivars or specialty grafts of old garden standbys such as birch, beech, larch and crabapple. Grafts of specially trained slow-growing conifers, which have to be tended for a number of years before they reach nursery shelves, are often more expensive than other trees. But they're worth the extra money—even if they don't appear to be initially. When one of my friends bought a cutleaf weeping caragana (*Caragana arborescens* 'Walker') a few years ago, he was disappointed because it had only a few branches. However, in three years it became a wide, hanging mop with character and presence.

Choosing the right shape

A weeping plant's form—mophead or dome-shaped, cascading, draping, narrow and drooping, or pendulous—often determines how it's used. English gardeners have long used mophead or mushroom-shaped weeping forms of caragana (*C. arborescens* 'Pendula'), mulberries (*Morus alba* 'Pendula') and cherries (*Prunus* x *subhirtella* 'Pendula') as living sculptures in parterre beds, borders, planters and grassy terraces. Weepers with domelike shapes, such as Camperdown elms (*Ulmus glabra* 'Camperdownii'), weeping cherries, golden chain tree (*Laburnum watereri* 'Vossi') or weeping mulberry are sometimes planted in parallel rows to form dramatic tunnels of foliage to link areas or to draw the eye through to a vista beyond. Planted on a grassy terrace with a backdrop of rolling hills, these same plants mimic their surroundings with their rounded silhouettes.

Flowing, cascading weepers work well in Japanese-style gardens and small water gardens. Japanese maples (*Acer palmatum* 'Dissectum'), threadleaf cypress (*Chamaecyparis pisifera* 'Filifera') and Sargent's weeping hemlocks (*Tsuga canadensis* 'Sargentii') help create a relaxing mood, soften boulders and shade koi pools. Weeping Norway spruce (*Picea abies* 'Pendula') and weeping white pine (*Pinus strobus* 'Pendula') also soften hard surfaces, and draw the eye down to their reflections in garden pools.

Weepers with long branches, such as the spectacular blue atlas cedar (*Cedrus atlantica* 'Glauca Pendula') and weeping larch (*Larix decidua* 'Pendula') make effective curtains on poles, arbours or garden walls. Achieve the same effect by letting weeping forsythia (*Forsythia suspensa*) spill over a wall. In winter, its leafless branches look like dangling ropes. Weepers with long branches

Cascading or fountain forms are good companions for pyramidal weepers, such as Nootka false cypress and deodar cedar. Large weeping trees make a significant statement in an open space, especially combined with the contrasting shape of an angular, neatly clipped hedge.

Weeping Higan cherry (*Prunus* x *subhirtella* 'Pendula') ↓

↑ Weeping Norway spruce (*Picea abies* 'Pendula')

In the past, weeping forms were often used in cemeteries or formal gardens to create a sombre, respectful mood. Today they're considered living sculptures.

can also act as a groundcover when allowed to grow down a slope.

Weeping plants with an upright, narrow, drooping shape, such as the spike-like purple fountain beech (*Fagus sylvatica* 'Purple Fountain') and drooping Serbian spruce (*Picea omorika* 'Pendula') with its slender, twisted branches, are frequently used in small spaces such as courtyards, side yards and shallow front yards. Nurseries also train ground-hugging plants into narrow, weeping forms on bamboo poles; once the plants reach a predetermined height on the pole, they're allowed to cascade to one side, much like a shepherd's crook. Blue rug juniper (*Juniperus horizontalis* 'Wiltonii'), 'Blue Chip' juniper (*J. horizontalis*) and various cotoneasters are examples of pole-trained plants.

Pendulous plants with soft, wispy foliage, notably weeping caragana, weeping larch and various ornamental grasses animate the garden with the slightest breeze.

Some weeping trees grow tall and wide, such as the golden weeping willow (*Salix alba* var. 'Tristis') and weeping beech (*F. sylvatica pendula*); they give large, open areas and pond edges a more human scale. Other large weeping trees include weeping Nootka false cypress (*Chamaecyparis nootkatensis* 'Pendula') and cutleaf weeping birch (*Betula pendula* 'Gracilis'); both start off with narrow, upright shapes, but sometimes surprise gardeners when they reach more than 15 metres and spread to 10 metres. Give them ample space.

Sometimes a plant's weeping characteristic is obvious at all stages of growth—weeping Nootka false cypress and purple fountain, for example. Other weepers, such as shingle oak (*Quercus imbricaria*) and eastern hemlock (*Tsuga canadensis*), take on a more pendulous outline as they age, but it's well worth the wait.

For other plants, the weeping characteristic may be seasonal—spruce trees laden with snow; the scented flowers of purple wisteria (*W. sinensis*) drooping over a bower in spring; a golden chain tree (*Laburnum* x *watereri* 'Vossii') weighed down in summer with yellow flowers.

More Than Trees Weep

When people think of weeping plants, they usually think of trees, but there are hundreds of shrubs, vines, perennials and annuals that provide effects similar to weeping trees, on a smaller scale. By including a few of these in perennial or mixed borders you provide a contrasting form and a less stiff, more relaxed look. They add a graceful, elegant look, and have the added benefit of providing shade for smaller plants below them.

Arching, weeping shrubs and perennials include fountain grasses (*Pennisetum* spp.), Father Hugo rose (*Rosa hugonis*), bridalwreath spirea (*Spiraea x vanhouttei*) and Solomon's seal (*Polygonatum* spp.). Plants such as *Allium cernuum*, with its clusters of white to magenta flowers hanging like lanterns, the equally showy shooting star (*Dodecatheon meadia*) or the dainty, checkered fritillary (*Fritillaria meleagris*) have a graceful, nodding look, too.

Recommended varieties

The weeping trees listed below are proven performers with dramatic forms. They're widely available at most nurseries.

CONIFERS

Weeping Norway spruce (*Picea abies* 'Pendula') is a distinctive, pole-trained, low-growing graft approximately 3 metres wide and 1 metre tall. Untrained, it becomes a cascading mat. Used in rockeries to spill over rocks, as a groundcover in conifer beds and as an accent around pools. Its dense, dark green foliage is attractive year-round. It requires full sun, good drainage, moderately fertile soil and is hardy from Zones 4 to 9.

Sargent's weeping hemlock (*Tsuga canadensis* 'Pendula') is a slow-growing conifer approximately 3 metres wide and up to 2 metres tall. Overlapping branches give it a dense, fountainlike appearance. Use it as an accent around waterfalls, where its form mimics flowing water, or in shady rockeries and foundation plantings. It prefers moist, humus-rich soils and is hardy from Zones 5 to 8.

Weeping white pine (*Pinus strobus* 'Pendula') is a graceful plant with long branches that sweep the ground with their blue-green needles. It spreads to a width of up to 2 metres, grows to 1.5 metres, and it can be pole-trained for greater height. It's a useful accent for a rockery, entrance or walkway. It requires full sun and good drainage and is hardy from Zones 4 to 9.

'Tolleson's Blue Weeping' juniper (*Juniperus scopulorum* 'Tolleson's Blue Weeping') is an elegant, treelike form that grows to 5 metres with stringy, cascading grey-blue branches. Use it as an accent for courtyards, patios, raised beds and entrances. A hardy graft, it prefers full sun and well-drained soil; it's hardy from Zones 5 to 9.

Happy Combinations

There's an art to combining weeping plants with other plants in your landscape, or with other weepers. Here are some suggestions that will help show them off to best advantage.

- Limit the number and types of weepers in close proximity; otherwise they can be visually annoying. Use them as accents or to contrast with other plant shapes.
- Position tall, weeping plants so they reach down to shorter plants below; this gives a pleasing, unified look. Try spiky plants such as yuccas, iris and Japanese bloodgrass (*Imperata cylindrica* 'Red Baron') under umbrella-shaped weepers such as weeping Higan cherry, 'Red Jade' crab-apple and weeping mulberry. Or combine tussock- or mound-shaped plants such as mugho pine (*Pinus mugo pumilio*), 'Little Giant' globe cedar (*Thuja occidentalis*), and globe blue spruce (*Picea pungens* 'Glauca Globosa') with taller grafted weepers such as weeping caragana or weeping cherries.
- Cascade or fountain forms such as weeping Norway spruce and weeping hemlock are good companions for pyramidal weepers such as weeping Nootka false cypress and deodar cedar (*Cedrus deodara*).
- Arching and fountain-shaped plants such as fountain butterfly bush (*Buddleia alternifolia*), European bleeding heart (*Dicentra spectablis*) and variegated Japanese sedge (*Hackonechloa macra* 'Aureola') work well with mid-size dome and cascade weepers, particularly over walls or rocks.
- The vertical lines of mid-size weeping trees set up pleasing tensions with low, spreading groundcovers. Pachysandra and hostas are frequently used as underplantings beneath the weeping forms of mulberry, cherry and birch.
- Identical weeping plants used in groups can be striking: a group of four or five weeping Nootka false cypress planted close together, for example, look like they've joined hands across the landscape. A row of weeping mulberry with branches to the ground can be eye-popping. Just remember these groupings need lots of room, as well as unobstructed sightlines, for maximum effect.

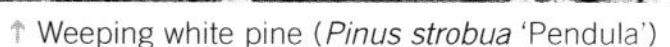

↑ Weeping white pine (*Pinus strobua* 'Pendula')

↑ Weeping birch (*Betula pendula* 'Youngii')

↑ Golden chain tree (*Laburnum* x *watereri* 'Vossii')

A group of identical weeping plants such as the imposing Nootka cypress can be striking. Placed close together, they look as though they've joined hands. But a single specimen can be a focal point in a garden.

Weeping threadleaf cedar (*Thuja occidentalis* 'Filiformis') is a grafted form of the native white cedar, with pendulous branches that hang to the ground; it grows 2.5 metres tall and 1.5 metres wide. A showy accent for pools and patios, it needs full sun and good drainage and is hardy from Zones 4 to 9.

Weeping Nootka false cypress (*Chamaecyparis nootkatensis* 'Pendula') is a popular conifer with outstretched branches and drooping bluish green cedarlike foliage, it can easily grow to 13 metres in southern Ontario, and much taller on the West Coast, with a branch spread of 4 metres. It is often used around pools and as a front-yard accent with other conifers. A group planting forms a wonderful curtain backdrop for a perennial border. Full sun to light shade and cool, moist soil is best; it's hardy from Zones 5 to 9.

Weeping blue atlas cedar (*Cedrus atlantica* 'Glauca Pendula') is an unusual accent plant that can be trained on poles like an espalier to various heights and forms; untrained, it spreads like a groundcover. In its most common form, it's about 4 metres tall, with extending arms up to 7 metres that display weeping curtains of ice-blue foliage. Full sun and good drainage with some wind protection are assets. It's a popular choice for gardens in Vancouver and Victoria, where it may be trained over a wall, on a garden structure or as a front-yard accent and is hardy from Zones 7 to 9.

Weeping European larch (*Larix decidua* 'Pendula') is upright, with thin, wispy, pendulous branches trained on poles to various heights (4 to 5 metres is common). With age,

Pruning and Staking

Weeping plants require maintenance that keeps their distinctive character—pruning to maintain shape and desired form is the most common requirement. Without regular pruning, plants such as weeping mulberry and weeping pussy willow (*Salix caprea* 'Pendula') develop multiple mophead crowns and a messy tangle of living and dead branch tops. Prune in the spring by cutting branches back to a more uniform umbrella shape and removing leggy branches that destroy the shape. Others such as weeping caragana, weeping larch and weeping cherries can be tip-pruned to stop their branches from touching and running across the ground. Also, thin a few branches to keep the tree's profile loose and flowing.

Many weepers are grafted forms on non-weeping parent rootstock, which may offer improved hardiness or disease resistance. On these, prune sprouts when they appear below the graft union; otherwise they'll grow straight up, destroying the desired form.

Cascading Japanese maples such as the cultivars of *Acer palmatum* 'Dissectum' may also require pruning because old growth is often brittle and susceptible to snow and ice breakage.

Weepers trained on bamboo poles, such as weeping larch and blue atlas cedar, need annual pruning to maintain the curtain effect, otherwise they may get too rangy and lose the shape you're trying to achieve. Stake them so they face into the wind; having the wind behind them pulls them away from their supporting pole. Shelter from a nearby wall or a belt of conifers also helps prevent wind damage and keeps them from being dislodged from their support poles.

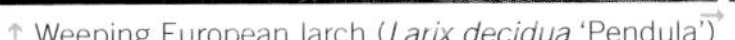

↑ Weeping European larch (*Larix decidua* 'Pendula')

↑ Weeping Nootka cypress (*C. nootkatensis* 'Pendula')

↑ Crabapple (*Malus* 'Red Jade')

its domelike top may be up to 3 metres wide. Clusters of soft, bright green tufted needles turn gold in autumn before falling off, leaving behind stringy branches. Commonly used as an accent on patios, in foundation beds and in raised beds, it's staked and pruned as a mophead standard, or left unstaked for cascading groundcover. A grafted plant, it prefers full sun, light shade and medium to dry soils and is hardy from Zones 3 to 9.

DECIDUOUS

Weeping pea shrub (*Caragana arborescens* 'Pendula') is an old standby usually grafted at a height of 1.5 to 2 metres. Plants have stiff, hanging branches covered with dainty yellow pea-shaped flowers in spring, and soft, bright green oval leaves. It's frequently used as a front-yard accent, in foundation beds, parterre beds and courtyard areas, and likes full sun and good drainage; it's hardy from Zones 2 to 9.

Weeping forsythia (*F. suspensa*) is a rangy shrub that can grow to 2 metres tall, with arching branches that spread up to 3 to 4 metres; it can also be used as a good groundcover for embankments or to drape over walls, rocks or planters. It's particularly showy in spring, with bright yellow flowers. Likes full sun to light shade and good drainage and is hardy from Zones 6 to 9.

Camperdown elm (*Ulmus glabra* 'Camperdownii') is a flat-topped tree usually grafted at 4 to 5 metres, it can achieve heights and widths of up to 6 metres. It's a spectacular specimen tree with a perfect umbrella shape, and long, tendril-like branches hanging to the ground. The dark green foliage turns yellow in the fall. A good accent plant where there's sufficient space. Lovely on a terrace silhouetted against the sky. It likes full sun and good drainage and is hardy from Zones 5 to 8.

Weeping Higan cherry (*Prunus* x *subhirtella* 'Pendula') is a popular spring-flowering cherry with pale pink flowers. Since it's frequently grafted at 180 centimetres on robust rootstock, the large diameter of the trunk may look somewhat out of scale with the size of the crown and its stringy branches. An accent often used as a front-yard specimen or courtyard planting in a formal bed or on the edge of a woodland. It does best in full sun and fertile soil and is hardy from Zones 6 to 9.

Young's weeping birch (*Betula pendula* 'Youngii') is an attractive, slow-growing small birch, up to 5 metres tall and almost as broad at maturity. Often used for entrance plantings, side lots or around garden pools. The dark green foliage turns bronze-yellow in the fall. It likes full sun and moist, fertile soil and is hardy from Zones 3 to 7.

'Red Jade' crabapple (*Malus* 'Red Jade') is a graceful, fountain-shaped plant commonly pole-trained to 3 metres tall and equally broad. Untrained, it's a low, cascading plant. It has attractive pink buds in spring, followed by white single flowers on coppery stems, and glossy green leaves. It likes full sun to light shade, with good drainage and neutral soil. Good for a woodland edge, in a raised bed or as a backyard accent, it is hardy from Zones 5 to 9.

'Purple Fountain' beech (*F. sylvatica* 'Purple Fountain'). An upright form of weeping beech with a pencil-like outline and striking purple foliage through the summer that turns bronze in the fall. It grows up to 7 metres tall and about 2 metres wide. A good selection for tight spots, or as an accent in a front or side-yard entrance, it likes full sun, rich soil and good drainage; it's hardy from Zones 6 to 9.

favouritetrees&shrubs

Fragrant Shrubs

Make your spring garden smell as good as it looks

BY JANET DAVIS

↑ Golden currant (*Ribes aureum*)

↓ Azalea (*Rhododendron luteum*)

Shrubs adorned with attractive blossoms are always a welcome sight in the spring garden after a long, cold winter. But why settle for shrubs that merely look beautiful when you can have some that smell fabulous as well?

Fragrance in the plant world is a serious business. Plants release aromatic oils or alcohols (indol, geraniol or citral, for example) to attract the right insect, bee, moth or butterfly to pollinate their flowers and ensure reproduction—plants aren't wafting perfume on a spring breeze merely to please the gardener. But taking advantage of nature's survival tactics by landscaping with scented plants can turn any garden into a more romantic place.

When choosing fragrant shrubs, shop with your nose: visit botanical gardens, parks or nurseries when the lilacs or roses are in bloom and note your favourites. When siting them in your garden, look for a warm, protected spot enclosed by hedges, walls or fences to keep out wind and trap fragrance. And be sure to place fragrant shrubs near a path, window or sitting area, where their perfume can be appreciated.

Recommended varieties

Azalea (*Rhododendron* spp.)

Old-fashioned Ghent hybrids, bred in Belgium before 1880, smell of clove and honeysuckle, and include double lemon-yellow 'Narcissiflora' and 'Daviesi', white with yellow splotches. Hardy to Zone 6b, they reach 180 centimetres in height where winters are mild, but stay shorter in colder regions. One of the parents of 'Narcissiflora' is the tall, clove-scented, yellow *R. luteum*, hardy to Zone 6a. It makes a lovely hedge underplanted with bluebells or purple violas.

Of the ultra-hardy (some survive to –43°C) Minnesota-bred Northern Lights Series, most of which grow to 120 to 180 centimetres tall, 'Golden Lights' (Zone 3) is the most highly perfumed. 'Pink Lights' (Zone 2) and 'Spicy Lights' (Zone 3) are also fragrant, the last said to evoke the scent of peaches or apricots. But 'Orchid Lights', developed from our native *rhodora*, has a skunky odour.

Deciduous azaleas need sun to set next-year's flower buds; an east-facing site in morning sun is perfect. They prefer slightly acidic, moist soil and a cooling mulch in summer.

↓ Carolina allspice (*Calycanthus floridus*)

OTHER FRAGRANT SPRING PLANTS

Bulbs

Iris danfordiae and *I. histroides*; hyacinths; *leucojum*; 'Ballerina' tulip, 'Thalia' and 'Poeticus Recurvus' narcissus, among others

Perennials

Dianthus; peonies; lily-of-the-valley; sweet violets

The fragrance of spring shrubs awakens a gardener's senses. Be sure to plant them where you can enjoy them—by an entrance or sitting area, or under a window.

Carolina allspice (*Calycanthus floridus*)

Sometimes this is called strawberry-bush because of the scent of its spidery reddish brown June flowers. The fragrance (also likened to plum preserves, ripe apples and green tea) carries better on warm days and is said to vary from plant to plant, so it's important to buy this one in bloom. Even the stems and leaves have an aromatic scent when crushed—although of camphor or bayberry, not strawberries. It's hardy to Zone 5, likes rich, moist soil in sun or light shade, and grows in a rounded shape to 180 centimetres. It's not particularly showy, so use it as a background plant.

Golden currant *(Ribes aureum)*

Hardy to Zone 2, it flowers in late April or early May with masses of small yellow blossoms with red centres. It's more readily available, but not as strongly scented, as its cousin the buffalo or clove currant (*R. odoratum*) of western Canada. Golden currant grows 180 to 240 centimetres tall and doesn't require rich soil. Plant in full sun, where it will be less prone to mildew, and its lobed leaves will turn red in fall. It's rather lanky when mature, but when kept sheared it makes a sweet-scented informal hedge. Prune back to keep the hedge compact as soon as the blossoms fade so the plants have time to form next-year's buds. (The *Ribes* genus are alternate hosts of a fungus called white pine blister-rust, so don't plant near white pines.)

Daphne (*Daphne* spp.)

Perhaps this is the most fragrant family of shrubs. Their scent, which reminds some of rubrum lilies, carries freely outdoors and just a few cut blossoms fill a room with perfume.

Daphne x *burkwoodii* cultivars 'Somerset' and the variegated 'Carol Mackie' grow to about 180 centimetres and are hardy to Zone 5. Both are a sight to behold in late May, smothered with masses of pale pink flowers. Sadly, *D.* x *burkwoodii* has a penchant for dying unexpectedly. Plant it in moisture-retentive but perfectly drained soil of average fertility. Since it dislikes summer heat as much as winter wind, plant in a lightly shaded protected site and add a good layer of mulch.

Lower growing at 30 centimetres, rose daphne, or garland flower (*Daphne cneorum*), is an evergreen that prefers deep, sandy or rocky, alkaline soil in sun or light shade. Its fragrant pink (or white) blossoms appear in mid-spring and, if deadheaded, again in fall. Rose daphne, hardy to Zone 2b, also has a reputation for dying suddenly.

D. mezereum, or February daphne, is one of the first shrubs to flower (though usually in April); its magenta flowers are redolent of lilac and viburnum. It prefers poor, sandy soil in full sun, grows to just over a metre and is hardy to Zone 4.

Magnolia (*Magnolia* spp.)

Certain magnolias emit a light scent which, though not intense, is often likened to tropical fruit—lemon, pineapple, papaya. One is *M.* x *loebneri* 'Merrill', a star-flowered magnolia that blooms in April or May with large, waxy, spidery white blossoms. It grows about 6 metres tall and needs full sun and moderately rich soil, but should be sited in a protected spot to prevent early frost damage to the flower buds; it's hardy to Zone 5. Shorter and more sprawling, *M. sieboldii* gives off a light fruity scent from large cup-shaped white flowers with prominent raspberry-red stamens; it's hardy to Zone 6b.

↓ Magnolia (*M. seiboldii*)

Lilac (*Syringa* spp.)

Although we think of lilacs as fragrant shrubs, many are unscented, so sniff before you buy. All lilacs prefer slightly alkaline soil of average fertility and full sun.

Common lilac (S. vulgaris), with its distinctive lilac perfume and familiar mauve flower panicles, is widely available, as are its offspring, the French hybrids. Superlative fragrance is found in these double-flowered lilacs: purple 'Charles Joly', white 'Madame Lemoine', magenta 'Paul Thirion', lavender 'Katherine Havemeyer' and mauve-pink 'Belle de Nancy'. Common lilac and its French hybrids are hardy to Zone 2b; left unpruned, they grow at least 2.7 to 3.5 metres tall.

Royal Botanical Gardens in Burlington, Ontario, flags *S. oblata* var. *dilatata* for its perfume. Its pale mauve flower panicles are more delicate than common lilac and (unlike most of the lilac clan) it displays good wine-red autumn leaf colour. It grows to 180 centimetres and is hardy to at least Zone 6b.

↑ Mock orange (*Philadelphus* spp.)

Mock orange (*Philadelphus* spp.)

Although hybridizing has knocked some of the scent out of mock oranges, a few can be relied upon for heady fragrance, redolent of oranges, jasmine and gardenia, from late May through late June, depending on the cultivar.

Intensely perfumed, single-blossomed *P. coronarius* grows to 3 metres and is hardy to Zone 3. Two fragrant semi-double mock oranges are *P.* x *virginalis*, hardy to Zone 3b, and 'Bouquet Blanc', hardy to Zone 4. *P. coronarius* 'Aureus', though not as strongly perfumed, has gold foliage that shines like a beacon when planted in a sunny garden. It grows 240 centimetres tall and is hardy to Zone 3.

'Galahad', 150 centimetres tall, is a compact Manitoba-bred mock orange with highly fragrant single blossoms that is hardy to Zone 3. 'Buckley's Quill' is compact at 120 centimetres, with lightly scented double flowers and quill-shaped petals and is hardy to Zone 4.

↑ Father Hugo's rose (*R. hugonis*)

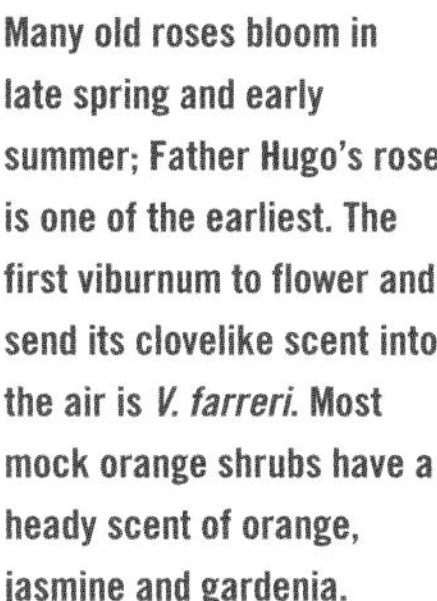

Many old roses bloom in late spring and early summer; Father Hugo's rose is one of the earliest. The first viburnum to flower and send its clovelike scent into the air is *V. farreri*. Most mock orange shrubs have a heady scent of orange, jasmine and gardenia.

↑ Viburnum (*Viburnum* x *burkwoodii*)

Rose (*Rosa* spp.)

Many antique roses (known prior to 1867) such as the damasks, albas, centifolias, bourbons and gallicas, display the typical perfume that indicates the presence of geraniol, the alcohol component in a rose's essential oil. The disadvantage is that most bloom once, in late spring and early summer. Depending on the other chemicals present, a rose can have undertones of fruit, honey or spice. In Turkey and Bulgaria, fields of spice-scented damask roses (*R. damascena*) are devoted to the production of rose attar, used in perfume.

Father Hugo's rose (*R. hugonis*) is an early-blooming Chinese species whose arching branches are covered with sweet-scented, single yellow blooms and ferny foliage that turns orange in fall. It grows to about 215 centimetres and is hardy to Zone 5b.

June-blooming roses of notable fragrance include *R. rugosa* (Zone 3), *R.* x alba 'Semi-Plena' (Zone 4); apple-scented *R. eglanteria* (Zone 5), the apothecary rose (*R. gallica officinalis*) (Zone 5) and Rosa Mundi (*R. gallica versicolor*), a crimson-and-white rose said to be named for King Henry II's mistress, Fair Rosamond (Zone 5).

Viburnum (*Viburnum* spp.)

The spring-flowering viburnums are among the most fragrant of all shrubs, with a clovelike spiciness. First to flower, in late winter or early spring, is *V. farreri* (syn. *V. fragrans*). Reddish buds open to almond-clove-scented, pale pink blooms on a rounded shrub that reaches about 275 centimetres. It needs a protected spot to shelter buds from late frosts and is hardy to Zone 6b.

Burkwood viburnum (*V.* x *burkwoodii*) has shiny leaves and smallish white flower clusters in May. Spread and height reach 180 centimetres and hardiness is to Zone 5b.

Fragrant snowball viburnum (*V* x *carlcephalum*) reaches about 240 centimetres and has the largest flowers of the fragrant spring viburnums, but its foliage is coarser and its growth habit is awkward. Its perfume tends to be heavier than its cousins and it's hardy to Zone 6.

Koreanspice viburnum (*V. carlesii*) is considered by many to be the most fragrant viburnum. A neat, sphere-shaped shrub, it reaches about 150 centimetres and its leaves turn red-purple in autumn; it's hardy to Zone 5b.

Witch hazel (*Hamamelis* spp.)

Except for native Eastern witch hazel (*H. virginiana*), which blooms in autumn, witch hazels are valued for flowering in late winter or very early spring, often under snow. Their perfume is variously described as dusky, pungent or incenselike. Most have yellow fall leaf colour, grow between 4.5 and 6 metres tall and are hardy to Zone 6b. They prefer moist soil.

Chinese witch hazel (*H. mollis*) is the most fragrant, with large, spidery, jonquil-scented golden flowers. Especially lovely is pale yellow *H. mollis* 'Pallida'. *H.* x *intermedia* includes colourful winter-blooming cultivars such as bright yellow 'Arnold Promise', which has fragrance not as intense as Chinese witch hazel.

↓ Chinese witch hazel (*H. mollis*)

index

Page numbers in **bold type** indicate photographs.

D

E

F

G

index